PERFIDY

by
Ben Hecht

MILAH PRESS
Jerusalem New London

Edition   15 14 13 12 11 10 9 8 7

Gefen Publishing House, Ltd   Gefen Books
6 Hatzvi St.   600 Broadway
Jerusalem 94386, Israel   Lynbrook, NY 11563, USA
972-2-538-0247   516-593-1234
orders@gefenpublishing.com   orders@gefenpublishing.com

www.israelbooks.com

Printed in Israel   *Send for our free catalogue*

Library of Congress Cataloging-in-Publication Data
Hecht, Ben / Perfidy
See Cataloging In Publication Card
ISBN 0-964-6886-38

97-070694
CIP

To Samuel Tamir—

"A man stood up in Israel."

INTRODUCTION TO THE NEW EDITION

What has come to be known as the "Kastner Affair" was one of the most painful chapters in the history of the state of Israel. The American fascination with the recent O.J. Simpson trials pales in comparison to the degree to which the Israeli public and government were preoccupied with the progress of this nine-month trial in 1954-55. In the wake of the verdict of the trial, the Israeli government fell.

For the conspiracy-minded, the Kastner Affair has everything. The trial results were appealed, but before the appeal could be heard, Kastner was murdered. Some blamed right-wing fanatics and others believed that Israeli intelligence had Kastner killed for fear of what he might reveal about contacts between the Nazis and the Israeli government during the time of the Holocaust.

Despite the sensational nature of the Kastner Affair, it is little known today. It's painful revelations, many feel, are best forgotten. A definitive history of the episode has yet to be written.[1] Here are the basic facts:

In a pamphlet published in August, 1952, Malchiel Greenwald, an Israeli citizen who had come to Palestine from Hungary in 1938, accused Rudolf Kastner, at the time the press spokesman for the Ministry of Commerce and Industry in Israel, of testifying on behalf of SS Lieutenant General Kurt Becher and thus saving him from punishment for his war crimes. Greenwald further accused Kastner of collaborating with the Nazis and contributing to the death of over 400,000 Hungarian Jews during WWII when Kastner served as a major leader of the Jewish Agency Rescue Committee in Hungary.

Kastner was an intimate of high Labor government officials, and the government had to decide whether to defend Kastner or fire him. In 1953, The government of Israel brought charges against Malchiel Greenwald for slandering Rudolf Kastner. The trial lasted from January until the end of September, 1954. After deliberating another nine months, Judge Benjamin Halevi found Greenwald innocent,

---

[1] Research in progress by this writer

explicitly accusing Kastner of collaboration and aiding in the defense of Nazi General Kurt Becher:

> The Nazi's patronage of Kastner, and their agreement to let him save six hundred prominent Jews, were part of the plan to exterminate the Jews. Kastner was given a chance to add a few more to that number. The bait attracted him. The opportunity of rescuing prominent people appealed to him greatly. He considered the rescue of the most important Jews as a great personal success and a success for Zionism. It was a success that would also justify his conduct - his political negotiation with Nazis and the Nazi patronage of his committee. When Kastner received this present from the Nazis, Kastner sold his soul to the German Satan.....[2]

On the charge that Kastner was instrumental in saving Nazi Becher from punishment, Judge Halevi ruled:

> It is clear that the positive recommendation by Kastner, not only in his own name but also in the name of the Jewish Agency and the Jewish World Congress was of decisive importance for Becher. Kastner did not exaggerate when he said that Becher was released by the Allies because of his personal intervention. The lies in the affidavit of Kastner and the contradictions and various pretexts, which were proven to be lies, were sufficient to annul the value of his statements and to prove that there was no good faith in his testimony in favor of this German war criminal. Kastner's affidavit in favor of Becher was a willfully false affidavit given in favor of a war criminal to save him from trial and punishment in Nuremberg.[3]

The verdict was a major blow to the ruling Labor coalition. Kastner's name, which had been part of the Mapai list to be submitted to the electorate the following month, was removed.

Just as the government initially had to decide whether to fire Kastner or file charges against his accuser, they now faced a similar dilemma - to appeal the verdict or not. Respected political journalist of Haaretz *newspaper, Moshe Keren, was very critical of Judge Halevi's verdict, yet wrote:*

> Kastner must be brought to trial as a Nazi collaborator. And at this trial Kastner should defend himself as a private citizen, and not be defended by the Israeli government.[4]

---

[2] See p. 180, this book

[3] Ibid., pp. 182-183.

[4] Ibid., p. 184 and also Segev, Tom *The Seventh Million* (New York, Hill and Wang, 1993), pp. 286-287.

ii

On p. 185 of this book, Ben Hecht tells us:

After writing seven installments on the Kastner case, Dr. Keren flew to Germany. His intention was to interview Kurt Becher. A few days after his arrival in Germany, journalist Keren was found dead in a German hotel. The diagnosis was "heart attack."

Two opposition parties filed no-confidence motions against the government. Prime Minister Sharett demanded the government appeal, but faced a revolt within his own cabinet. Not only did the General Zionists, who had three ministers in the ruling coalition, oppose appealing the verdict, but they announced they would abstain instead of voting confidence in the government. One General Zionist said: "There is an impression that the government is continuing to protect Kastner," and contended the impression was based on fact.[5]

Ben-Gurion, who had been in temporary retirement, recommended that Sharett let the government fall and form a new one without the rebellious General Zionists. Sharett resigned and Ben-Gurion resumed leadership of the coalition. In the elections a month later, Mapai remained the largest party in the coalition, but lost five seats. Menachem Begin's Herut party increased their strength from eight to fifteen seats. This was the beginning of a steady rise in Herut's strength in every election until Begin became Prime Minister in 1977.[6]

The government appealed. The Supreme Court upheld the exoneration of Greenwald on the charge that he slandered Kastner by saying his testimony was key in obtaining Becher's freedom; on a split verdict, they reversed the lower court's exoneration of Greenwald on the second charge; the appeals court ruled that Kastner had not collaborated with the Nazis and thus Greenwald had slandered him.

Consider these two opposing opinions by the divided Supreme Court. They illustrate two very different understandings of the evidence that was presented to the appeals court. Did Kastner's death, prior to the time the appeal was heard, affect the judges?:

---

[5] Segev, op. cit., p. 289.

[6] Ibid., p. 293.

iii

Judge Moshe Silberg:	Judge Shimon Agranat:
We can sum up with these three facts: A. "That the Nazis didn't want to have a great revolt - 'Second Warsaw' - nor small revolts, and their passion was to have the extermination machine working smoothly without resistance. This fact was known to Kastner from the best source - from Eichmann himself.... B. That the most efficient means to paralyze the resistance wheel or the escape of a victim is to conceal from him the plot of the coming murder.... C. That he, Kastner, in order to carry out the rescue plan for the few prominents, fulfilled knowingly and without good faith the said desire of the Nazis, thus expediting the work of exterminating the masses...."	"I sum up my final conclusions as to the conduct of Dr. Kastner during the extermination of the people in the country as follows: A. During this period Kastner was motivated by the sole motive of rescuing all Hungarian Jews.... B. This motivation coincided with the moral duty of rescue by virtue of this task as manager of rescue in Budapest. C. Influenced by this motive, he exercised a system of financial or economical negotiations with the Nazis. D. This system can withstand the test of reasonableness..... F. Therefore, one cannot find moral defects in that behavior; one cannot find any causation between it and the expediting of the deportation and the extermination and one cannot consider it amounting to the degree of collaboration with the Nazis."

The Supreme Court upheld the District Court ruling that Kastner had, after the war, saved a Nazi war criminal from punishment. Judge Silberg wrote:

Greenwald has proven beyond any reasonable doubt this grave charge.... I shall not touch here upon all the many contradictions - endless in number - in which Kastner contradicts himself in connection with this affidavit. It is enough for us that a Jewish man, an ex-Zionist leader, dared to recommend [mercy], almost in the name of the whole Jewish people, for one of the major sharks of the German war criminals before the authorities who detained him, and to cause, alone or together with others, the release and evasion of punishment of this great criminal.[7]

As I have written elsewhere, the final arbiter of the disagreements among historians is the reader of history. This book is must reading for anyone seeking insight into this remarkable historical period.

David Morrison

---

[7] See pp. 276-277, this book.

PREFACE

In my own time, governments have taken the place of people.
They have also taken the place of God. Governments speak for
people, dream for them, and determine, absurdly, their lives
and deaths.

This new worship of government is one of the subjects in this
book. It is a worship I lack. I have no reverence for the all-
powerful and bewildered face of Government. I see it as a less-
ening of the human being, and a final looting of his birthright—
the survival of his young. I see it as an ogre with despair in its
eyes.

I have written chiefly of one government in this book—that
of the new Jewish State of Israel. I wrote of it, partly, because
I am a Jew. I come of a long, never-broken line of Jews. My ancestors were booted out of a score of lands, and libeled and be-
deviled since the time of Ahab and Jezebel.

Yet they did well by the world during these centuries. They
kept an unfalteringly human light burning amid upheavals that
toppled old kingdoms and gave birth to new ones.

The kingdoms were alien ones to my ancestors. In the soul of
the Jew, in his tabernacle and kitchen, there was only one Kingdom—that of God. There was only one set of laws—the exercise
of humanity.

What happened to this fine heritage when the Jews finally
fashioned a government of their own in Israel; what happened
to Jews when they became Jewish politicians, what happened to
a piety, a sense of honor, and a brotherly love that 2,500 years

of anti-Semitism were unable to disturb in the Jewish soul? My answers are in this book.

Such a book was not easy for me to write. For the heart of a Jew must be filled with astonishment as well as outrage when it speaks out with Prospero in *The Tempest:*

"I pray thee, mark me—that a brother should be so perfidious!"

"THE ACCUSED"

On a December morning of 1953, Malchiel Greenwald, age seventy-two, a neatly trimmed goatee, a tilted fedora, a bright muffler with mittens to match, a seedy overcoat, holes in his shoes, a cigar stub threatening to ignite the tip of his nose, and a walking stick swinging briskly—this jaunty old Jew is looking for a lawyer—in Jerusalem. His daughter, Rina, a blonde out of the Psalms, walks beside him.

As is his daily habit, Malchiel has had a satisfactory conference with God in his synagogue. Whatever else you can say about Israel, it is a satisfactory thing to be able to stand in practically the same place in which your forefathers stood twenty-five hundred years ago and offer God unchanged hallelujahs.

But now for a lawyer—an inexpensive one who will take the case for other considerations than money. After all, how many lawyers get the opportunity to defend a man who has been sued for criminal libel by the government of Israel itself!

Yes, Prime Minister Moshe Sharett, Mapai leader David Ben-Gurion, Attorney General Chaim Cohen, and all the other renowned chieftains of the State of Israel have summoned Malchiel Greenwald to the bar of judgement. There were even a few lines about it in a newspaper, on an inside page. Granted, a few lines do not make a man famous, but he is no longer a nobody.

"How much further?" Greenwald asks.

"Three minutes," says daughter Rina.

"Maybe I can offer him my stamp collection," says Greenwald.

"He is not the kind of a man who collects stamps," says Rina.

The goatee points forward. Lawyer, lawyer—find me a lawyer who is not afraid and who also, God grant, cares almost nothing about money.

Thus on this chill December day, Malchiel Greenwald walks into the history of Israel.

WHAT GREENWALD? WHAT HISTORY?

I shall tell you in my own way. For though I write a history I am not an historian; that is, if an historian is a man full of facts and with an objective attitude. Facts I have, but I am not objective. I put this down so that if my book disturbs any reader, particularly a Jewish reader, too much, he can solace himself with the thought—how can you believe a writer who confesses he is not objective? So you see how sentimental I am about Jews. I think of solacing them even when I have set out to condemn much that they hold dear.

Malchiel Greenwald is one of the three heroes whom I shall do my best to celebrate in my history. There are other heroes and heroines who will emerge to beam on the reader, but these three will be my central ones. My history deals with the astonishing revelations of the Kastner trial that smote Israel with shame and disillusion for four years beginning in this December 1953; and shook a Prime Minister, Moshe Sharett, out of his Jerusalem swivel chair.

Among the astonishments of these events is that a man like Malchiel Greenwald started them. In Israel you expect a Samson to tumble the pillars of the false temple, not an elderly stamp collector without muscles. A simple man, pious, hard-working. Granted, a busybody, but a busybody with an unauthoritative face. The home orator who makes his family sigh, "Malchiel, Malchiel—how many times are you going to say that?" But there is also this about Greenwald. He is not only a stamp collector, he has another hobby. He likes to write.

And there is another fact. Long before the British picked out the Lion as a symbol of how brave they were, there was the Lion of Judea, who still crouches in Jewish hearts. Not all of them. Courage is a special thing in any people. I do not mean the courage to die. The Jews have had good training in that, better than most. But the courage to protest, to stand up against the fearful odds of authority—there's a rarer quality, and a more mysterious one. The mystery here is how did it come to roost

2

in seventy-two-year old Greenwald? How did Voltaire and Tom Paine leak into his Talmudic soul, and the sword of Spartacus find lodging under his tallith?

Malchiel Greenwald hails from Hungary, where he married, sired a son and a daughter, and, until his fifties, worked there and in Vienna as a part-time journalist who had frequently to stoop to unliterary labors.

This was a time, after World War I, when geniuses, as often as not Jewish, filled the cafés of Budapest and Vienna, and showered Europe with tunes, bon mots and witty dramas. But there were also Jews who were not geniuses—among them, Greenwald.

I will not lie about my hero. Even in his heyday he lacked style and the proper connections.

Nevertheless, he kept on writing, rushing his copy to the editor in person, and watching it usually flutter into the waste basket. But disasters are more likely to create journalists than stop them. Greenwald persisted. And he had a certain following. Fifty-two close relatives bought newspapers every day to see if the name Malchiel Greenwald was signed to something.

Then one day an event occurred. A pack of citizens, Christian ones, came running into a Vienna street and started killing Jews. They used big cudgels and long knives, and they shouted the battle cry of the renaissance that had come to Europe—"Death to all Jews."

Greenwald happened to be in the street with his young daughter, Rina. Run, he said to her and she made fleetly for a synagogue, two patriots after her. Greenwald had less speed in his legs. As a result, every one of his teeth were knocked out of his mouth; his tongue was slashed, his legs and arms were broken, and he was cracked over the head with cudgels until he fell unconscious to the ground. This was a lucky thing. For, believing he was dead, the patriots lost interest in him and gave their attention to Jews who were still standing, or leaning.

When he was able to walk again and use his tongue once more, Greenwald decided to migrate with his family to Palestine. At that time (early in 1938) you could still go to Palestine without being shot or drowned by the British Protectorate Policy—or was it Protective Policy? Whatever it was, you can be sure it had a soothing name.

"KNOW YOU THE FAR LAND WHERE THE LEMON TREES BLOOM?"

Come to Jerusalem with his head of false teeth, his wife, son, daughter, and stamp collection, Malchiel Greenwald bought a small hotel with his life's earnings. A few hundred pounds down, no more. Hotel Austria, not far from where Solomon once reigned. It could accommodate twenty-five guests a night if you put three or four in one room. Rate, 25 piasters a head ($1.00).

For a few years Greenwald helped his sturdy wife make beds, sweep floors, fill kerosene stoves, and journalism was a dream on a shelf.

Then other chores came to hand. The big killing of Jews started in Europe. The British stepped in, first with a quota cutting down immigration to Palestine, then with a new policy called the White Paper. What it amounted to was that the Palestine ports were now closed and the doomed Jews had to outwit not only their German killers but the British authorities guarding the shores of Empire.

Greenwald busied himself in the tricky business of illegal immigration to the Holy Land. He had helped his two brothers to organize illegal immigrant runs to Palestine.

Greenwald's activities subsided, however, when his fifty-two relatives were shipped off to Auschwitz and put to death in the German ovens.

In the meantime a sort of war had been going on in Palestine. An underground army of young Jews had come into existence. In 1937 this army startled everybody by announcing it was going to drive the British forces out of Palestine and set up an independent State of Israel. The name of this first army of Jewish fighters for freedom was the Irgun Zvai Leumi, Hebrew words meaning Organization, Military, National. Its insignia was the map of an Israel on both sides of the Jordan, over which was a hand holding a rifle and the Hebrew words, "Only Thus."

The most startled were the Jewish leaders of Palestine. The idea of a war of liberation to win an independent Israel had

4

never been in any of their heads. Weizmann, Ben-Gurion, Sharett, Greenbaum, Dov Joseph and all the Jewish factotums in Palestine had limited their dream of Zion to a British-Jewish suburb.

The Irgun seemed an old story to the British—Fuzzy Wuzzy all over again—a few hundred "terrorists" against the might and right of Empire. The British took the usual measures: death or life imprisonment to any Jew caught carrying arms. Not too difficult to handle. Particularly, since the British had all the fiery leaders of the Jewish Agency on their side. Not to mention all the potent and esteemed Semites of the United States and everywhere else.

Led by Weizmann, the chieftains of Jewry pledged allegiance to the British war on the young Hebrews fighting for freedom. Later they were to offer more than lip service to their British masters. They proved their loyalty daily by helping the British to capture, torture, hang, and imprison hundreds of young Jews fighting under the first independent Hebrew flag since Bar-Kochba.

Malchiel Greenwald's young son Itzhak joined the Irgun and was killed fighting in the Battle of Mount Zion. Greenwald put away the Irgun medal his brave son had won and changed the sign of his Hotel Austria. The new sign read, "Mount Zion Hotel."

Greenwald's daughter, Rina, was also in the war that the small Irgun army was fighting against the British and the Jewish Agency Policy. During the day she was respectably employed as a nurse in a Hadassah Hospital. But at night she worked among the wounded of the Irgun.

It finally all ended with the British decamping and the Arabs taking to cover, and the State of Israel being established, and all the Jews of the world (or nearly all) blowing grateful kisses and offering massive donations to the great heroes of Israel—Ben-Gurion, Weizmann, Sharett, Greenbaum, etc.

And Malchiel Greenwald, confronted by this topsy-turvy denouement of lambkins crowned as lions, grew a goatee, bought a walking stick, and decided to become a journalist again.

But who would hire a seventy-two-year-old man unable to write Hebrew? Nevertheless, Greenwald became a journalist—by himself. Every week or so he composed an article, had it

5

translated into Hebrew, and had it mimeographed into a three-page pamphlet. The pamphlet carried a chronic headline, "Letters to My Friends in the Mizrachi." This is the name of a religious party of Israel. Journalist Greenwald spent his last nickels mailing out one thousand copies of each issue. The pamphlet was free. All the reward Greenwald asked for his hard work was that somebody read it.

Fifty pamphlets—and nothing happens. Supper eaten, dishes washed, Greenwald hurries to his chief news source, in quest of hotter items. His "beat" is the Café Vienna, opposite his hotel. It is practically the only café in Jerusalem that stays open after supper.

Here journalist Greenwald consumes a great deal of tea as he table hops among the town's gossips. They all know Malchiel Greenwald, and have a tolerant smile for him. They say, "Thank you, much obliged," when he hands them his latest pamphlet. And they leave it behind on the table, unread, when they go home.

What is it Malchiel Greenwald writes in his pamphlets? Nothing anyone hasn't heard a hundred times before better written and better printed. It takes a strong pair of eyes to distinguish the smeared lettering in Greenwald's mimeographed gazette. It needs an equally sharp vision to pick out Malchiel Greenwald, himself, from the hundreds of ancient nobodies, full of hair-raising pasts, who chatter, pray and scribble in the new Jerusalem.

Then comes Pamphlet number 51. Another letter to his pious "Friends of the Mizrachi." The same length, three pages of smeared type. But this time the pamphlet is a success. It produces a case of criminal libel—the State of Israel versus Malchiel Greenwald.

And I am up to my hero again as he walks with his daughter beside him, looking for a lawyer who is not afraid.

I am impressed by Malchiel Greenwald, and I would not be too surprised to hear from some Jerusalem rabbi that God, as much as daughter Rina, guided him on this walk. Not because of what he dared to write in his pamphlet about an esteemed government official named Rudolf Kastner. But for another reason.

Malchiel Greenwald, whose teeth were all knocked out of his mouth, whose tongue was slit, whose arms and legs were broken and whose head bashed in, who was left for dead in a street of murdered Jews; whose fifty-two close relatives were all incinerated by the Germans, whose son died fighting on Mount Zion —now at seventy-two this Malchiel Greenwald walks under a tilted fedora, briskly swinging a cane, unafraid of any authority but the truth in his own heart. That such a man exists impresses me.

HOME IS THE WANDERER

The headlines have gotten us used to the State of Israel as if it were an old story. Headlines can get us used to everything, including the patriotic necessity for putting an end to the world in order to save it from something or other.

Nevertheless, my eyes remain widened. "The State of Israel versus Malchiel Greenwald." Fifty years ago a Jewish nation called Israel was as eerie a prospect as a colony of Martians laying down sidewalks on our planet.

Since the Greenwald-Kastner trial will uncover the roots of the new nation, I pause to make an interlude about Israel. About Israel and Jews in general.

They are not one and the same; in fact, they are bewilderingly different. I mean the Jews of the world and the Jewish leaders of Israel. But a sort of courtship goes on between them, a half-sincere courtship, because both parties are married to somebody else. Yet they woo each other, the Jews, Israel; and Israel, the Jews.

First, about Israel. Who made this unexpected land that owns a fine army today, roaring cities, burgeoning farm lands, strong youths and beautiful girls, a machine for splitting the atom, and at least five thousand gabbling politicians; that waves a flag of world power? Who concocted this land, midget in size, but undisputed champion of its neck of the woods?

Was it the seventeen million Jews of the world holed up in a

7

hundred nations? The answer is no. Hardly two per cent of them were involved, and not many more were aware that anything was going on.

It was a handful that created Eretz-Israel, just as a handful of Irgun and Lehi fighters won its independence from the British. The creators were mostly European Jews—pick-and-shovel dreamers, gun-toting visionaries who beheld Jewish cities where there were only Arab, Turkish and English sands.

They were Jews of all kinds—dumb ones, smart ones, rich, poor, some pale with learning, some muscled like gladiators. They came out of Polish tailor shops and Polish social soirées, out of Russian synagogues and counting houses, out of Ukrainian farms, German universities, Hungarian salons, out of Europe's back roads and boulevards. No more than a trickle, but what a trickle! Who would have suspected that international Jewry was full of Davy Crocketts and Daniel Boones, with talliths in their saddle bags? Or that so many statesmen, philosophers and "Hatikva" singers could come tumbling out of the Jewish cornucopia almost overnight? But tumble and come they did, and whatever the print on their visas said, they came seemingly out of the Old Testament. Where else were there Jews with Jewish anthems in their eyes!

The rebirth of the Jews as a nation began in Jerusalem. For hundreds of years there had been a sparse Jewish population in the old city of Jerusalem, and in ancient Tiberias, Safad, and other cities left over from the past. After ages of inertia, these sons and daughters of Abraham began saying goodbye to Jerusalem's ghetto walls, and moving into the land to till and plant. An urge was in them. Who or what put it there, I don't know. It may have been God renewing His interest in His once favorite children, and bidding them to make the land of David bloom again with Jewish orange trees. Whoever told them, this is what they did. They established small colonies on the desert edges. They were a hardy, tenacious people. And they plunged into a love affair with the land of their fathers.

There were several waves of "aliya" (literal translation, "ascension"), first in the eighties and nineties of the last century, of Jews fleeing persecution in Rumania and Russia. Baron Edmund de Rothschild helped settle a swarm of Jews, mainly from Rumania. These also started colonies and sang around new Hebrew camp fires.

At the opening of the century came the first large flocks of the original "Zionists," most of them from Russia. They brought with them intellectual ferment. Many of them were Tolstoyan socialists, and all of them were full of dreams of a new Zion. Out of these bands of settlers came the future ruling clique of Israel.

In the beginning most of these adventurers to Palestine had forthwith to learn to ride horses better than the Arabs, which was difficult; and to shoot straighter, which was easy. And to become lumberjacks, well diggers, plow hands, cowboys, scouts, sentinels. And to sleep without roofs, battle malaria, suffer thirst, hunger, sunstroke and harassments equal to the Seven Plagues; and remain, the while, full of joy and hope. This, too, was easy, for they were half daft with old dreams.

In the thirties came a great surge of Jews out of Poland. These were chiefly workmen and their families, more tools in their kits than dreams; house builders and plow hands. They came to Zion as its people, and remained its people.

The advent of Hitler in 1933 brought a massive wave of immigrants from Germany. Hitler's oratory had uprooted them from their long-beloved German cities and villages. They brought with them the German talent for music, philosophy, and truth-telling, the German pedantry and respect for the law—all the things that the new Third Reich had decided to jettison. There were also among them people of financial talent.

The next wave was the "illegal" immigration, beginning in 1937. Defying the quota and later the White Paper, in ships of every size, tens of thousands from Central Europe and the Balkans came flocking to Palestine. Most of them were young Jews.

The last wave was the million from everywhere, including the concentration camps, who hied them to Israel when it became an independent state. The dam was broken. Israelis poured in.

And what bright leaders hopped around the world playing Pied Piper for this dream and passing the hat for the new land of Zion. The first of these was the Hungarian literary light, Theodor Herzl. Into his worldly, witty head came full-blown the plan for a Jewish nation.

9

He created this nation in the pages of a book. The book done, he wrote in his diary that the Land of the Jews would become a reality in fifty years. And off he went to buttonhole kings and queens, prime ministers and plutocrats, asking for a bit of territory that might become a homeland for the Jews.

"My dear Herzl, not a bad idea," said Prime Minister Gladstone of England, "Why don't you try Egypt?"

"We've been there," said Herzl.

The dour Gladstone, warmed by Herzl's wit, became an ally.

Max Nordau, a practising psychiatrist and famed author, whose works were translated into many languages, was among Herzl's first converts. It befell this way. One of Herzl's elegant friends, a fellow champion fencer, was concerned over his lapse into the parochial fogs of Jewish affairs. He explained Herzl's plan for a Jewish nation to Nordau and asked, "Will you talk him out of it, Doctor?"

Nordau, an atheist who wrote in German and held himself apart from Jewish life, agreed.

Herzl came, talked, and conquered. Thereafter, Max Nordau's eloquence spread the Herzl dream through Europe.

There were also the brilliant Dr. Aaron Aaronson and his lovely sister, Sarah. They lived in a Palestine still under Turkish rule. Dr. Aaronson was a brilliant scientist, and as witty and attractive as Herzl. He fished for Jewish homeland converts in the salons and government offices of Europe.

Sarah was one of the great beauties of her day. Around her in Palestine swarmed the first handful of Jewish homeland patriots. World War I was on. Aaron and his sister organized an underground to work behind Turkish lines for the British, and for the Jewish homeland Britain would gratefully set up in Palestine after winning the war and ousting the Turks.

From the night-black shores of Palestine, Sarah and her followers signaled information to the British. Sarah was caught. The Turkish police tried to torture the names of her Jewish followers out of her. Sarah pretended to faint under the torture. The ruse worked. Released for a moment, Sarah shot herself and died, with the names of her disciples locked in her skull.

Vladimir Jabotinsky, the soldier-novelist, was another drum beater for the coming land of the Jews. I shall write more of him later. Here only that in the 1930's he raised his voice in the ghetto towns of Poland, Hungary, and Rumania, warning of the annihilation tomorrow held for the Jews of Europe, and urging them to trek by the millions to Palestine while they could still get in.

Another Zionist Pied Piper was Louis Brandeis, to become Supreme Court Justice in Washington. Brandeis was one of the few American Jews of stature who looked beyond assimilation as a future for Jewry. I interviewed him in my young reporter days in Chicago. He was attending a World Zionist Congress. I remember a few of the things he told me, also that he told them with gusto and irony. "Jews? They keep disappearing from the world. Disaster re-invents them. There are better mothers than disaster. A native land is the best of all mothers. We American Jews have a native land we love. But it is even better to have a native land who loves us."

There were scores of these dream salesmen, all men and women of purity of mission. They were out to change the identity of the Jews from a people of the Torah, to a people of Zion, a nation. There was much outcry from the orthodox at this seeming demotion. During the centuries in which other peoples had taken turns riding in armadas of power, the Jews had remained forever bobbing along on a raft of a book, their Torah. They were reluctant to leave the raft, to exchange the only greatness they had known—the words of God—for some dubious political status.

The dream of a new land of Israel had flickered in the Jews for the nineteen centuries of their search for unmenacing places to live. They sighed the phrase, "Land of Israel," during this long time, and felt refreshed. And certain that God would return them to their original habitat and make them a great nation again.

I have sometimes wondered, while reading their histories, how the Jews could believe themselves the Favored of God despite the calamities that endlessly fell on them. But it is not a Jewish quirk, alone. Christianity is based on the belief that the crucifixion of Jesus proved Him the beloved Son of God. By a similar logic the Jews have remained convinced that the crucifixion of their kind was proof that they were very dear to God.

11

A small account of the dream and birth of Israel. Next, about the Jews of the world outside it—I have a briefer summary than they usually receive from their generalizers. But I have written of Jews before and have learned how to be precise about them. Also how to love them without lying about them; how to smile at their brick-bats, and how to remain dreamily on their side while they are denying me burial in holy ground. These things have happened to me. Enough now, that if I have any enemies they are mainly Jewish ones. And, as I used to sign all my letters to my mother, "I remain, your loving son."

During the creating of Palestine by the Herzl Zionists, the Jews of the world heard rumors. Their basic reaction was that something absurd and a little sad was going on in Jerusalem. And possibly a little dangerous. This reaction was only natural, for there had been no good tidings for Jews out of Jerusalem since the crucifying of one of their young rabbis—by the Romans. The Jewish hell born of that misreported incident had never cooled off.

Hearing dimly of a new Zion being hatched in that same territory, and of the trickle of settlers heading for the new Zion, the Jews of the world stuck to their troubles at hand. They remained steadfastly in all the cities of the world where they were not too wanted or too esteemed. They were content to accept the inferiority or unpopularity of Jewishness, rather than to go wrestling with deserts.

I say this with no derogatory overtone. You can't blame Jews for fancying themselves part of the human family, despite its inhuman protests now and then. Protest, pogrom, ostracism, disdain—the Jews accepted these gentile tricks and manners with an indifference that was a gift of time.

I understand these Jewish world squatters, for I was born one of them, and remain one. I was for the first forty-five years of my life as unaware of Jewishness as I am now of space problems. Happily preoccupied elsewhere, I stayed out of synagogues, lodge meetings, and the philanthropy get-togethers dear to Jews.

But even in that time of pleasant Jewish anesthesia, I noticed some Jewish matters. I noted that there were Jews around me fleeing from their Jewishness as a man trying to run away from his shadow. And there were Jews pooling their Jewishness into ghetto oases. And Jews rising above their Jewishness with the aid of ego, talent and wealth. Or so these believers in levitation thought. I noted also a small change over into Christianity going on—Abraham's elite tiptoeing out of Jewishness as out of a sick room.

And there were Jews like myself, immune to the critical attitudes of our neighbors, for we had attitudes twice as critical. For us anti-Semitism was a target, if we were lucky enough to catch sight of it, and never a menace. This, of course, was in the United States, where anti-Semitism is considered officially a neurosis. Although Americans suffering from it more often get sent to Congress than to a hospital.

If I write truthfully of American anti-Semitism, I must put down that I have found it, on the whole, either pleasing or stimulating. It is pleasing to be disliked by obvious fools, and it is stimulating to knock such dunderheads off their perches, even if nowhere else than in one's own soul.

Actually, anti-Semitism is among the lesser hatreds I have noted in the United States. Hating Jews has remained a furtive American pastime with a sickly sound to it, and no responsible leaders of Church and State have given it sanction.

God forgive me if I am too optimistic. I was a foreign correspondent in Berlin for the *Chicago Daily News* in 1919, 1920. Any German in that time, sad and bleak though it was, would have sworn passionately on the heads of his children that mass murder could never become a German political ideal.

One has to think of such things when making pronouncements.

There was never any doubt about the status of Jew-hatred in Europe. In nearly all its countries, anti-Semitism was esteemed as a patriotic necessity or a religious must. There were a few minor areas of tolerance—Scandinavia, Holland and Italy, after it stopped producing saints.

Nevertheless, European Jewry continued to thrive on the world's displeasure as if it were a Christmas plum pudding. And it remained, as a whole, indifferent to the Covered Wagon Days in Palestine, endorsed by the Balfour Declaration in 1917—"Let us give the Jews a homeland," and by the pact of 1925—"Let Britain prepare a homeland for the Jews in Palestine."

Here is the point of my interlude. How different it is now!

13

With all the Jews of the world who were unaware of Eretz-Israel, who made no personal sacrifices for it, and who denounced the fighters for its freedom—patting themselves on the back for the State of Israel. Their baby!

I have heard them in London, Paris, Rome, North Africa. I hear them constantly in New York, Chicago, Hollywood and wherever else I run into Jews. And not religious or "organization" Jews, but assimilated American ones who usually go to Temple only in a coffin. They boast of having been to Israel as they used to boast of having basked on the Riviera. Their eyes gleam. They used to feel this way when a Jew became a World's Ring champion or when Einstein's name appeared in the newspapers.

It is a new high in diplomatic representation. Although the State of Israel is a strip of land hardly big enough for a railroad line, it has some eleven million ambassadors-at-large. This is, roughly, the number of Jews the Germans left on the planet, counting the dark ones of Africa. And all as ignorant of what is going on—or went on—in Israel as if it were a foothold on the moon. But still, ambassadors.

Here is a problem. Is it better to let illusion thrive than (try to) expose it? Plato wrote that the only sound way to ensure people's happiness was to let them sup on sweet lies rather than bitter truth.

It is not entirely bad advice. But it is like a medicine that permits the patient to die without too much pain.

I vote otherwise. I end my interlude with the hope that a fraction of the myriad ambassadors may get a clearer line on their duties after attending the case of "The Government of Israel versus Malchiel Greenwald."

THE GLORY THAT WAS BRITAIN

If it were only wicked people who kept hounding Jews from century to century, it would be an easier history to understand. You could say then, the Jews have a little too much virtue in

14

them, which seems to be a constant irritant for baser folk. But the Jews have not too much virtue and their enemies include the elite of Christendom—its finest kings, its noblest humanitarians and philosophers, and even its holiest saints.

Now we come to one of the most honorable of its enemies, Great Britain. Not only honorable, but the gallant defender of civilization, 1939–1945; nevertheless, an enemy of the Jews. This is what makes a Jewish historian seem hard to please. He has to scowl when all other historians look happy.

Luckily, I write no history of the Jews, just the bit of it that is relevant and material to the trial of Malchiel Greenwald.

The Greenwalds arrived in Palestine. Here they felt was an end to their Jewish unpopularity. For in 1923 Britain accepted the mandate from the League of Nations,[1] countersigned by the non-member United States, to convert Palestine into a homeland for the Jews.

This magnanimous project was the result of World War I, which was fought by our side to rid the world of militarism, power politics, and human injustice, generally. Our side won. A homeland for Hebrews was one of the proofs of virtue's victory. Another such proof was World Disarmament, which also got happily under way in the 1920's.

The English, in their best Galahad manner, accepted the job of fixing up the new Promised Land for the Jews. But after a breather, they secretly proceeded to do just the opposite—began to turn it into a British-Arab dominion. There was no anti-Semitism involved. It was practical Empire building. Fifty million Arab allies and their inexhaustible oil wells were a brighter prospect than a handful of Jews with nothing but gratitude to offer the Crown. To achieve this altered project it was necessary to keep the Jews from overrunning Palestine.

After nearly two decades, the British finally put their Colonial cards on the table and stopped pretending they were the fairy-godmother for the Jewish "homeland." In 1939, Great Britain issued the famous White Paper on the Palestine situation.[2]

This royal document contained two major points. One, Jews were almost completely barred from buying any more land in Palestine. Two, the White Paper proclaimed a last limited immigration for Palestine and then ordered its ports closed as soon as this last handful had passed the Customs. The "Protectorate Policy" then warned any Jews who might try to evade extermination at Nazi hands by sneaking into the Holy Land that they would be treated as enemies of the Crown.

A clever phrase, White Paper. Wrap evil in righteous words and who will examine the package? Statecraft is as simple as that, and so are the multitudes who buy its wrappings. All they ask is assurance from the proper authorities that black is white.

There was debate in the British Parliament whether this right-about-face of barring the Jews from their new homeland was the proper thing to do. The pro-White Paper statesmen had luck on their side. The famous Jews most involved in the new Homeland business were too full of loyalty for England to do anything about being swindled out of Palestine. There was also the lucky fact that World War I was over, and any pro-Jewish public opinion in the United States was no longer of any importance.

Among the strongest argufyers against the White Paper was Winston Churchill. Minus government post of any sort at the time, but bright with vision, Churchill denounced the White Paper as a shameful document; a crime, indeed, against the menaced Jews of Europe.[3]

The debate was brief. In a short time, despite the press and public, the government of England proceeded under the White Paper to keep the Jews out of Palestine.

And the statesman actively in charge of this anti-Jewish policy was Winston Churchill, become now Prime Minister. I make no criticism of this. What a man feels as a human being and what he feels as a politician are bound to be different.

The English, themselves, are much inclined toward decency. But that never helps. Authority knows how to take decency out of play. There is no devilish deed that cannot be shined up into a patriotic necessity by the right propaganda. All that is needed is for people to believe in their duly elected leaders.

This they have always done. The talent for believing in authority is the backbone of every civilization. Even though our present civilization consists of nations red-faced with hate and threatening fiercely to destroy each other and the planet to boot, this belief does not waver.

Should our planet go up in smoke on some tomorrow, such a

16

finale will not lessen the status of authority. I feel sure the last hundred million earthlings to expire in the hydrogen blasts will do so with unshaken faith in the correctness of their leaders.

"JUST FOR A RIBBON TO PUT IN HIS COAT"

I must ignore Malchiel Greenwald for another few pages in favor of further matters, relevant and material to his trial. The first of these is his accuser, the Government of Israel.

To understand the malignant drama soon to erupt in a Jerusalem court room, it is necessary to know the character of the accuser as well as the accused. The character of Israel's bosses who are suing Greenwald is not the traditional Jewish character of the past. The piety and sorrow of the Dispersed Ones, the humorous and exotic brotherhood of the unwanted, have given way to a political mentality. The Jewish leaders in the 1930's had begun to feel their oats as the rulers of a new Zion.

Rulership produces a character of its own—the unbending Ego. This certainty-drunk figure has dominated history since the dawn of government. And he is no different as Jew than he was as Roman, Greek, Vandal, Norman, etc.

He knows what is best for the people—his continuation in power. He knows what is right—the ruses and shenanigans that keep him in power. And he knows what is wrong—anything that endangers his power.

It is these politicalized princes of Jerusalem of whom I shall write with a cold pencil. They will not think of Jews dying in Europe, but of government thriving in Palestine, and they thriving with it. And when their behavior becomes too wanton to seem human to me, the Jews of Palestine and of the world will still be looking on them with love and pride. For that is the way of people (Jewish and non-Jewish) toward authority. They are loyal to it even when it is not loyal to them. Just as they are loyal to God when He strikes them down. It is a human instinct —this loyalty to destroyers. But it is not the only human instinct. (I haven't got it.)

17

The British know every bit as much as I do about the character of rulership. They were aware in the 1920's that the Jewish rulers of Palestine were to be regarded not as Jews but as politicians. And they had taken the measure early of these great ones who had emerged in the Holy Land. They found them a bit gabbier than most Colonials, but they noted in them the proper bend-the-knee philosophy toward the source of their power, England. Naturally, they were not all to be trusted, but the top boys proved to be stout British loyalists. These were "Zionists" with a mania chiefly for prestige. Since no prestige was possible without a British ribbon on it, you could wager—come what might —on their loyalty to the Crown.

Thus for years before legally closing the ports of Palestine, the British had relied on two factors to further their secret plan for an Arab Palestine: the apathy of Jewry to pull up stakes for the Holy Land; and the eloquence of the official Zionist leaders, who were currently urging an "elite immigration" to Palestine and deploring any wholesale movement of the Jewish masses into Eretz-Israel.

The meaning of all this to the Jews of Europe was, "Stay home!"

The spokesman for the scuttling of the old Jewish dream of a homeland in Zion for the six million Jews of Europe was Dr. Chaim Weizmann. Born in the ghetto of Pinsk, Russia, Weizmann had migrated to London and become, magically, an Englishman. I say *magically* because that is the way ghetto Jews once felt, and possibly still do, when they passed from being lowly undesirables into being high-class social figures. They felt that a good-fairy wand had been waved over their heads.

In no time at all our undesirable Weizmann from the ghetto of Pinsk became a socially esteemed English Jew. Wherefore a reverence for everything English salaamed in his soul.

This understandable human fact of Jewish gratefulness is important to my story. It is, in fact, one of the basic issues in the trial of Greenwald, this gratitude to England versus concern for the lives of millions of Jews.

18

THE RELUCTANT MOSES

This was Chaim Weizmann, the new type of leader produced by modern Jewry, the Englishman with Jewish leanings. He is another character in Malchiel Greenwald's trial. His ghost is now the Government of Israel.

That Weizmann, first president of Israel, was a man of greatness is obvious. He was a winsome man of talent; persuasive, apparently modest and, to boot, as bull-headed as any Caesar. When he died he left an illusion in the world that he personally had created the new State of Israel.

The truth of Weizmann is that he was stirred by the Jewish dream of a New Zion, which somehow did not include the Jews of reality—of Petticoat Lane, Hester Street, the Warsaw Nalevki, and the ghetto of Pinsk.

In the 1930's, Dr. Weizmann made many eloquent speeches explaining the aims of his Zionism. He offered the world a picture of a Zionism toiling to turn Palestine into a Tiffany's window for glittering Jews, and not another ghetto for pushcart vendors and lowly tallith-wearers.

In August, 1937 Dr. Weizmann, as leader of World Zionism, addressed a Zionist convention in London. Hitler at the time was sowing their new mission into German souls, the extermination of the Jews of Europe. This new factor in "Jewish affairs" did not alter Weizmann's blueprint for a selective Jewish homeland; neither did it move him to urge the six million Jews of Europe to save themselves by coming to Palestine. Dr. Weizmann remained loyal to his "idealistic" concept of the Promised Land—that it was no place to crowd up with Jews.

Of the six million Jews who were in a few years to be exterminated by the Germans, Dr. Weizmann, addressing the 480 Zionist delegates, fifteen hundred visitors, two hundred press correspondents from all corners of the earth, and official foreign representatives from a score of nations, had this to say:

"I told the British Royal Commission that the hopes of Europe's

19

six million Jews were centered on emigration. I was asked, 'Can you bring six million Jews to Palestine?' I replied, 'No.' . . . The old ones will pass. They will bear their fate or they will not. They were dust, economic and moral dust in a cruel world. . . . Only a branch shall survive. . . . They had to accept it . . . If they feel and suffer they will find the way—*beachareth hajamin*—in the fullness of time . . . I pray that we may preserve our national unity, for it is all we have." [4]

In Jewish tradition the Hebrew phrase Weizmann used, "*beachareth hajamin*," meant that "When the Messiah comes, all the Dead will be revived."

At the close of Dr. Weizmann's speech, as reported in the *New Judea*, official gazette of the Zionist organization, "The assembly rose and sang the Jewish anthem, the 'Hatikvah,' the Song of Hope."

In 1939 at the outbreak of the war, Dr. Weizmann, the uncrowned king of Jewry, announced he was taking a recess from all Jewish activities. He was going to concentrate on the scientific war effort.

Here is another pen picture of this Jewish leader at the time of the beginning of the Jewish disaster, reported by one of his most talented admirers, the American playwright S. N. Behrman. The piece appears in a book called *Chaim Weizmann— the Builder of Zion*, published by the Hebrew University of Jerusalem.

The dramatist reports:

Somebody has turned on a radio. 22nd of June, 1941. The radio brought the news. Germany has launched an offensive on Russia. The Germans have already marched through the border. I watched Weizmann. His eyes were dark.

"This is the second time," he said.

He recalled that when the First World War broke out, two years after the death of his father, his mother still lived in Pinsk and had to escape from the fear of German invasion.

And now they come again—the Germans. What will be the fate of all these people? I saw in his eyes the tragic vision of what has really happened to them. There was a silence in the room. "Yes," he said, "For our people there, for millions

20

of them, a horrible and monstrous fate is waiting." But after
a moment his eyes lighted, his body leaned forward. "At the
end—and this is the most important thing—this war is bound
to bring about a blessing to England," he added.[5]

Dr. Weizmann's Anglophilism never wavered to his death.[6]
There were those who noted that Weizmann's speech to the
World Zionist Congress proclaiming the Jews as the "dust of
Europe" was virtually a plan to abandon them in their danger.
Jabotinsky noted this, and barnstormed the ghettos of Europe
telling his people that they were sitting on a powder keg, and
urging them to flee before they were wiped out.

He and his Irgun comrades were attacked by official Zionism
as dangerous trouble makers.

I do not cry villainy at the Zionists, not now. But there is a
puzzle here. The British wanted no more Jews in Palestine. The
Zionists wanted "only the best Jews." [7] I do not know whether the
Zionists cooked up their selectivity policy to coincide with British
aims in Palestine, or whether the British took advantage of the
Zionist Jew-snobbery to slap their ban on the Holy Land. Very
likely both factors were mutually involved.

The Weizmann-Zionist credo that implemented the British
aims in Palestine was possibly more a sin of bounderism than
betrayal. It was the work not so much of conscious hypocrites
as of the split personality of the assimilated Jew.

One more item about the Weizmann-Zionist accomplishment.
In addition to being a half-conscious ruse to help the British,
it was an ideological fraud. Granted there was charm in the
notion of a high-falutin' Palestine, behind the charm was the
voice of the con man. It was a shrewd spiel for money from
rich Jews—with no truth in it. There could never be any such
elegant land for Hebrews.

Genius and glitter are not a corsage you import. They are a
tree that grows with much difficulty out of the soil of a nation.

The millions of ghetto Jews of Europe were thrilled by this
Zionist snobbery that chose to ignore them. They stepped up
their contributions and doubled their prayers in the synagogues
for the creation of such a noble and superior land of Zion.

This is a normal response for the lowly with dreams. Just as

21

the poor skimp and save their pennies to send their children to a far-off university full of learning and glamour, so did Europe's Jews, prior to their extermination, finance the lucky ones of Palestine.

As for the rich, important Jews, they were as usual harder to get at. In those pre-Hitler days Jews were inclined to measure their importance by the fact that everybody had almost forgotten they were Jewish.

But such rich ones as had ears for the Zionist pitch dreamed along with Weizmann of a Buckingham Palace of a Holy Land. Who wants to be related to Chaim Yankel from the ghetto when he can re-claim kinship with Solomon in all his glory?

In 1939 the British realized that such Jewish oratory as Dr. Weizmann's was not enough to ensure an Arab Palestine. The Germans were promising to exterminate the Jews, and when this slaughter got going it would obviously take more than the fine speeches of Weizmann, et al, to keep the doomed ones from packing off to Palestine. Thus, the British White Paper.

THE LAWYER

The lawyer who may take the case, says Rina to her father, Malchiel Greenwald, is in that building across Jaffa Street. If her parent had consulted her in the first place, he would be out of trouble by this time. Rina is a divorcée with a child and a longing in her heart for her ex-husband. But she is always able to solve other people's troubles, even her father's.

Greenwald is impressed by the building, three stories high, fine Jerusalem stone, and rather new. It looks like a good building, says Greenwald, very promising. And the pair cross Jaffa Street to call on Attorney Shmuel Tamir, who is the most important of the three heroes in this history.

Unlike Greenwald, he is not a hero by accident. When the battle is joined it will not be a haphazard trouble-stirrer who mounts the barricades. It will be one of the boldest brains in

Jerusalem since the prophets of old walked its streets, bawling the hell out of the Jews.

Lawyer Tamir's main office is in Tel Aviv. The branch office in Jerusalem was opened only a week ago. Expansion was necessary to meet a booming law practice, a good part of which entailed the defense of people who were victims of government discrimination—Arabs included.

In 1953, Attorney Tamir, despite his youth, was one of Israel's brightest and most successful lawyers, and was already considered by the government as an important nuisance.

Attorney S. Tamir was born in Jerusalem as Shmuel Katznelson. He had led a rather full life in that city, including courtship, marriage, university education, and the blowing up of a number of buildings. These buildings were the armed headquarters of the British military forces under orders from the Crown to hang on to Palestine and turn it into an Arabian annex. The Irgun Zvai Leumi, which included Tamir, was opposed.

Shmuel Katznelson had joined the Irgun at the age of fifteen and been given the nickname Tamir, the Hebrew word for "tall and straight." Nicknames were necessary in the underground forces to keep identities hidden from the British. As did most of the Irgun youths, Shmuel later adopted his nickname as his family name.

The man who inspired and brought about the creation of the Irgun was the artist-soldier Vladimir Jabotinsky. Outside of Ireland, literary heroes are rare. Byron, Victor Hugo, Paine—Jabotinsky was of this elite.

He wrote novels, essays, poems, and battle hymns. He was also an exciting orator. His speeches had the effect of magic, and young people were ready to give their lives at his call. But Jabotinsky was no literary zealot or orator only. He organized the Zion Mule Corps that fought under British colours at Gallipoli. He created, also, the Jewish Legion, commanded by Col. John H. Patterson, that valiantly helped rout the Turks out of Palestine in 1917. Colonel Patterson remained a champion of the Irgun and one of its training officers.

Jabotinsky's right-hand man was the one-armed hero, Joseph Trumpeldor. Trumpeldor had helped him to recruit and organize the Zion Mule Corps for Gallipoli. Trumpeldor led the Jews in

23

that desperate battle. At his side in the fighting was his favorite sergeant and companion, Reuven Katznelson, father of Tamir.

Trumpeldor was an ex-officer in the Czar's army. This was an amazing place for a Jew—the Russian Officers' Corps that regarded Jews as our Confederate officers looked on the negroes in 1862.

But Trumpeldor was amazing. This one-armed Jew would have been welcomed as a leader in any corps of fighting men. His gaiety bloomed in danger. He went leaping and laughing into battles as if heading for a swim in the surf.

He died defending the settlement of Tel Hai from the Arabs in 1929.

The war over, Jabotinsky's first preoccupation was to ensure the self-defense of the Jewish community in Palestine. He organized a militia to guard Jewish settlers from the Arabs. He named it by the Hebrew word for self defense, Haganah.

In 1920, on the Passover, a fateful season for the Jews through the ages, the Arabs (with British leave) struck, in the first pogrom of the Holy Land, with all the ancient diversions of plunder, rape and murder. Jabotinsky fought, planned, flew battle cries in the air, and the Jews heard Maccabeus again—or, rather, some of them did.

The British looked with disfavor on this type of Jewish enterprise. They arrested Jabotinsky, tried and convicted him, and sentenced him to fifteen years in prison. A considerable uproar induced the British within the year to release Jabotinsky from his Acre prison cell and "commute" his sentence to exile from Palestine for life.

In 1936, an issue confronted the men of Palestine—whether to shoot back or not shoot back at the Arabs who, with British connivance, were raiding and terrorizing the Jewish settlements. All the various parties, clans, and sects of the new land voted for Havlagah—"self restraint"—all except one group. This group detached itself from the Haganah, pledged to passivism, and called itself the Irgun Zvai Leumi. The Irgun remained, almost to the end, an underground. The political followers of Jabotinsky who did not go underground became known as the Revisionists.

The Revisionist movement, led by Jabotinsky, apart from opposing the British-inspired Arabs and other British chicanery,

24

and arousing world public opinion for the cause of a Free Palestine, took one other daring decision of far-reaching consequences. This was to break the British blockade of Palestine.[8]

With the exiled Jabotinsky in this enterprise were two Homeric Jews, Abrasha Stavsky [9] and Joseph Katznelson (not to be confused with Ben-Gurion's *chaver*—Berl Katznelson). Joseph Katznelson was brother of Reuven. Abrasha and Joseph were as rough-and-tumble a pair of law breakers as ever disturbed the ports of the Mediterranean. They broke all the laws against Jews. As Jabotinsky's Chiefs of Illegal Immigration, they kidnapped thousands of Jews from under the Nazi noses and sent them bouncing off in ships to the Holy Land, ships that ducked the British fleet in fog and storm and dumped their contraband humans on the night-black shores of Palestine. They were the antidote to Ben-Gurion and his jittery Jewish Agency.

Tamir was their young disciple. At twenty-three he was acting Irgun Commander of Jerusalem, in charge of routing the British out of it.

OF TWO JEWISH TRIBES—THE TERRORISTS AND THE TERRIFIED

In 1944 the British were hammering away at a reeling Germany. It had been a long, hellish haul from Dunkirk to D-Day. From the start no people had ever defended the cause of humanity with stouter hearts than had the British. Nor had any leader ever spoken out with more resounding virtue and gallantry than Winston Churchill.

It is therefore with a sigh that I record the British activity in Palestine during these fine hours of triumph over the Nazis. They, the valorous British, busied themselves turning back the Jewish refugees arriving off the Palestine coast in their jammed, unseaworthy tubs. This blockade against Jews culminated in shooting down the human cargoes from Nazi-land.

The *Struma,* carrying 769 men, women and children fleeing from the German death mills, was kept from Palestine by the

British. As a result the unwanted *Struma* went down in the Mediterranean. Seven hundred and sixty-eight of the *Struma's* passengers were drowned, a score the Nazis might envy.[10]

At this time the Germans had already slaughtered almost five million Jews, with a minimum of protest from a busy world. And the Germans were preparing to murder the remaining million Jews in Europe. And here were the British vigorously repelling boat loads of men, women and children—pale, branded escapees from the German extermination camps.

Was the Jew so worthless that all nations felt free to bedevil and murder him? The answer was, yes—or silence. The German slaughter of Jews had in a way given the Jews a bad name: the name of defenseless, expendable creatures to be shoveled out of existence as human garbage.

Only the youths of the Irgun and the Lehi said no. The Lehi were the "Fighters For Freedom of Israel" known as the Stern Group.

The Irgun with its two thousand soldiers declared war on Great Britain. "There is no longer an armistice between the Jewish people and the British Administration in Eretz-Israel which hands our brothers over to Hitler. Our people are at war with this regime, war to the end. Build a protective wall around our fighting youths. Do not forsake them. They will not surrender until they have insured our people a homeland, freedom, honor, bread and justice. If you give them your aid you will see in our days the return to Zion and the restoration of Israel." [11]

A series of assaults by groups of Irgun Commandos against fortresses holding thousands of British troops filled the streets of Jerusalem, Tel Aviv and Haifa with smoke and blood. The assaults were remarkably successful. Under Menachem Begin's guidance the Irgun proceeded on a dual program, to open the ports of Palestine to the unslaughtered Jews of Europe, and to kick the British out of Palestine for good and all, and run up a Hebrew flag over the Holy Land.

A few words about the deserving Menachem Begin, before I go on. Begin was a man of strong heart; a Polish Jew come to Palestine from exile in Siberia; a lawyer by profession, a man of slight build. There was more than fearlessness in him. A passion for Jewish honor and freedom boiled in his words. The words came not only out of his heart but out of the great piles of tortured Jewish dead, out of the torn faces and fouled bodies of the millions.

The young Jewish battlers of the Irgun supped on his phrases. A Lion of Judea spoke to them. The agony of Jews burning in ovens became the valor of Jews with guns in their hands. No more sizzling battles were ever fought against towering odds than were fought by the Irgun against the British, to free Palestine and rescue the doomed Jews of Europe.

Lion-of-Judea-Begin conducted the war in the guise of a bearded rabbinical scholar—as pale and ineffectual a looking fellow as ever walked in Jerusalem. Under his pious disguise, he worked on military plans and eloquent calls to battle.

The British Military Intelligence Service and its talented allies of the Jewish Agency and the Haganah were unable to nab Begin. Neither torture nor hanging of his men produced a hint of his disguise or his whereabouts.

The Irgun that went to war was a handful, with some stolen guns hidden in a few basements. Their British opponents numbered more than one hundred thousand seasoned soldiers finely equipped with tanks, cannon, machine guns—and a gallows for good measure.

But the young Jews out to destroy the mighty British had an inner equipment of high military value. It was a power that neither tyrants nor progress has been able to remove from the human soul—the rage at its misuse.

The Irgun and Lehi fighters attacked the British government offices, including the Immigration Office, symbol of the closed gates. They assaulted and bombed the British Police Headquarters in Jerusalem, Tel Aviv, and Haifa. They raided one midnight the British radio station in the Arab town of Ramalla. They attacked police and military depots to "confiscate" arms for their war against Great Britain. They derailed British trains, blew up British armored cars, paralyzed the railroad movement of British troops in Palestine. They blew up oil installations in Haifa, and wrecked fifty British Lancaster bombers and fighters in the airports of Lod, Qastina, and Kfar-Sirkin. They put a stop to the whipping of Irgun soldiers by the retaliatory whipping of a number of British officers in the center of Tel Aviv. And they

27

drove the one hundred thousand British forces back into their camps and fortresses, where they holed up in a state of siege.

The Irgun's struggle for freedom and rescue was immediately denounced by most of the Jews of the United States, Great Britain, and other democratic havens, as a vicious outbreak of hooliganism, and a black eye for Jewry everywhere.

The worst critics, of course, were in Palestine. The Irgun's activities panicked the official Zionists and Jewish Agency nabobs. All the other high job holders of Jewry set up a clamor as if the world were coming to an end—their world of government. If the Irgun fight for an independent Eretz-Israel and for the rescue of Europe's unkilled Jews over-irritated the British, what would happen to their high posts as Britain's servitors?

These are not quite the phrases with which the Jewish factotums met the situation. They had resounding, "idealistic" phrases. Apparently they did not think of themselves at all, but of the future of Zionism. They were not hanging on through thick and thin to their own swivel chairs, mimeographs, flat-topped desks, lettered names and titles on their official doors. They were "saving Zionism." Since the Jews had not the "faintest chance of winning independence by a war of liberation," and since most of their finest leaders did not even believe in independence, the practical as well as idealistic thing to do was bend the knee to the British and smite the young Jewish fighters of the Irgun with all the power and wrath of vested authority.

BEN-GURION'S CURSE

Here is the very Voice of Authority out of Israel's annals. It is Ben-Gurion addressing the Histadrut Convention in Tel Aviv on November 22, 1944. The speech in its entirety was carried by the newspaper *Davar*, official organ of the Histadrut and of Ben-Gurion.

The speech is not to be found in the collected orations of Ben-Gurion. Whether this is a matter of shame or merely an oversight, I don't know. Here are a few excerpts of Ben-Gurion's oration:

"The time for action has arrived," spoke Ben-Gurion. "Words have no influence—they are blank bullets. We have decided to vomit them out of our midst. Let these words vomit them out of our midst, not empty phrases. The Terrorists are not influenced by phrases . . . The Gangs are now waiting what will. come out of this convention. The demand to vomit them out of our midst must be translated into a language of deeds by every one of us . . . We must suppress in our hearts every personal feeling—let them not preach piety to us. Let every boy and girl be taught by our Youth Organizations that if the Gangs come asking money of their fathers and mothers, he or she (the children) must immediately notify the proper authority. And if they don't know any other address, let them go to the [British] Police."

(Ben-Gurion plays plagiarist here. Children reporting to the police was an innovation of Stalin and Hitler.)

The speech continues:

"Since the British government and Police are intent on exterminating the terror, we are collaborating with them—to that extent . . . Without helping the British government and without its help we shall not uproot this contagious disease. I repudiate the kindness which was justified in other times. In our circumstances this is a twisted kindness, a kindness of fools . . . There is no neutrality between us and Terrorism. Either Terrorist Gangs or an organized Jewry—there is no escape from the alternative." [12]

Ben-Gurion backed up his fiery address by sending out special Haganah units to kidnap Irgunists. The Haganah forcibly extorted information from some of their Jewish captives and handed the others over directly to the British. Ben-Gurion's men also supplied the British with the names of hundreds on hundreds of other Irgun fighters, and tipped off the British to the secret hiding places of the Irgun's hard-won stores of weapons. The Haganah called these operations "The Season," meaning "open season," as for rabbits and grouse.

Irgun victims reported that the methods of Ben-Gurion's men were more sadistic than the techniques employed by the British in tormenting Jews.[13] Despite the anger among the Irgunists at their betrayal and brutal treatment, Commander Begin refused to allow retaliation. He ordered his dwindling troops to fight the British only.[14]

A year after his excoriation of terrorism, Ben-Gurion's Haganah forces joined the Irgun and Lehi "terrorists" in the battle for Jewish freedom. Working side by side, the three armies blew up military and police headquarters. And pounded the hell out of the British—in unison. This three-cornered honeymoon lasted for a few months only.

How did so Mad Hatter a thing happen as Ben-Gurion and his quaking satraps going to war against the British, after lying lamb-like at their feet for so long? It is this kind of thing that gives history such a lying sound, no matter who writes it.

The truth, minus all coloring matter, was this. It was not Ben-Gurion who ordered the armies to unite. The members of the Haganah, themselves, demanded action against the British. The Jewish Agency politicoes had to yield to their suddenly stormy members. Moshe Sneh, Commander of the Haganah, was put in charge of a Hebrew Resistance Movement. Moshe Sneh, a Jew of strong heart, took over his duties eagerly. In the Movement were the Haganah, Irgun and Lehi men. And, lo, all the young Jews of Israel stood together against their enemies.

The Haganah followed the Irgun in another anti-British action. They started a large scale transfer of Jews from the liberated concentration camps to Palestine. They were able to load fleets with Jews and start them for the closed ports of Palestine.

The British navy intercepted nearly all the illegal "Exodus" boats, and side-tracked their human cargoes to new concentration camps, chiefly in Cyprus.

A VISIT TO THE KING DAVID HOTEL

In its third month, the Hebrew Resistance Movement laid plans to blow up the chief British military headquarters in Jerusalem, situated in the King David Hotel. The Irgun suggested and plotted the action. Commander Sneh approved the plans and their execution.

The King David Hotel looked as impregnable as the Rock of Gibraltar. British tanks and crack troops guarded it behind high barricades. It was considered the "safest" place in Jerusalem. In addition to housing the British military staff and the highest British officials, it also had in safekeeping in the government offices the British dossiers on the Palmach, the striking force of the Haganah. It was these records that the Resistance Movement plotted to destroy.

A group of some ten Irgun men disguised themselves as the Sudanese who daily supplied milk to the British headquarters. They carried large milk cans on their shoulders, except that the cans were full of powerful explosives instead of milk. The explosives had a time-clock fuse.

The disguised Irgun men entered the King David Hotel without a hitch, and arrived in the basement kitchen. Instead of carrying their milk cans into the kitchen they placed them against the basement pillars.

British guards noted an oddity in the behavior of the milkmen as they started to leave. They were ordered to halt. A basement battle erupted. Several British soldiers were shot. Two of the Jews were wounded. The entire Irgun group escaped, however. One of their wounded died in the flight.

The British guards who had dispersed the "milkmen" were unaware of the explosives left behind against the pillars. As was customary in the destruction of public buildings where civilians might be present, the Irgun Command began telephoning warnings to the British headquarters in the King David Hotel. The calls informed the authorities that the building would be blown up in twenty minutes.

"This is the Irgun speaking," said call after call in English. "Your hotel is mined. It will be blown up and destroyed in twenty minutes (in eighteen minutes—in ten minutes). We warn you to evacuate the building."

One of the first warning calls was received by an aide of Chief Colonial Secretary for Palestine, Sir John Shaw. Informed of the warning, the Colonial Chief said, "I am here to *give* orders to the Jews, not to *receive* orders from them."

31

With this in mind, Mr. Shaw hurried to the front door of the hotel, placed guards on it and issued orders that nobody was to leave the British headquarters. A fine voice of Empire, Mr. Shaw's, but sounding off at a wrong time. A good number of military and government officials evaded the guards and slipped out of the building. But many did not.

At 12:30 P.M., precisely twenty minutes after the first warning, the King David Hotel blew apart. The wing containing the government offices and the Military High Command was demolished.

Ninety people were killed. Many were injured. The British records were destroyed.

At one o'clock, a Haganah spokesman for the Hebrew Resistance Movement announced a bit bombastically over the secret radio that the Underground had destroyed the British military and government Headquarters in Jerusalem, together with all its dossiers and documents.

Two hours later the fact that ninety had been killed and scores injured by the explosion first became known. Mr. Shaw, a survivor of the episode, spoke emotionally over the British radio, describing the dreadful business. His information was detailed, including even the fact that his pet dog had suffered death. He made no mention, however, of the Irgun warnings, or of his own refusal to "take orders from the Jews."

On hearing the full details of the victory, the Hebrew Resistance Movement collapsed in a twinkling. Jewish Agency and Haganah officials announced over the radio that they had had nothing to do with the explosion; repudiated it as a vile deed and declared their ally of two hours ago—the Irgun—an outfit that shamed the Jewry of Palestine. The honeymoon was over.

The British went into action. For the sake of the record, let it be noted that their action did not involve the reprisal killing or shooting of Jews in Jerusalem. Instead, the British arrested a thousand suspected terrorists. The Jewish Agency officials, from Sharett and Dov Joseph down, were also clapped into prison.

During these hours of violence and danger, the voice of Ben-Gurion was heard from afar. It was, alas, Leader Ben-Gurion's misfortune to be in Paris while all this planning, bombing and arresting was going on in Jerusalem. Leader Ben-Gurion spoke like a caged lion from his Champs Élysées suite:

"I am a prisoner of Paris."

Finally, shaking off his Paris bell boys and room clerks, Ben-Gurion returned to Palestine to repair the damage to the Jewish cause. He assured the outraged British that the Jewish Agency had had no hand in the "inhuman" King David Hotel blasting. That wretched deed had been the work of the Irgun terrorists whom he and his fellow honorable Jews had vowed to "vomit out of their midst."

The British knew the truth, but they also knew the value of repentance. They accepted the protestations of loyalty. As proof of this loyalty, Ben-Gurion, Sharett, Reuven Shiloach and other V.I.P.'s of Jewry resumed their basic work for the Crown—betraying the Irgunists and turning them over to the British for punishment.

This bit of history seems a little confusing despite the simplicity of its facts. Why didn't Menachim Begin announce the truth over his underground radio, and expose the hypocrisy of the Jewish Agency leaders? He didn't—and there's another side of Begin. Irgun High Commander though he was, fearless and dedicated to his task of ousting the British, Begin had an ancient Jewish schizophrenia in his soul—a Jewish revolutionist who respected Jewish Authority. He respected Ben-Gurion and his bellowing sidekicks who had vowed to crush him and his soldiers.

What happened to the Haganah Chieftain Sneh? He is today leader of Israel's Communist Party.

THE UNDAUNTED

The Irgun and Lehi fought on.

The main British bastion in Jerusalem was the Goldschmidt Fortress on King George Avenue, across the street from the Jewish Agency Headquarters building. Ramparts of sandbags and machine-gun nests protected the fortress.

At 3 P.M. on a Saturday, an Irgun truck disguised as a British lorry entered the military zone around the fortress. The Irgunists had never violated the Sabbath before. As a result, the defenders of the fortress always relaxed on the holy day of the Jews. There was no need to worry about Jewish "terrorists" when they were busy praying in their synagogues.

The Irgun had chosen Saturday for the same reason. There would be no one but themselves at large in the streets.

Five Irgun fighters were in the disguised lorry. They killed a challenging sentry. Three of the five jumped off the truck with a hundred kilos of explosives in their arms. The three ran to the fortress and tossed their bombs accurately into its windows.

At the same time, two civilians stepped out of a taxi that had followed the disguised lorry. One of the civilians carried a Bren gun. The other had an armload of hand grenades.

The Bren gun was in the hands of one of the Irgun's coolest and bravest young men, the incredible battler, Avshalom Haviv.

Haviv pumped Bren gun bullets accurately through the windows of the British fortress. Hundreds of British rifles cracked back.

Simultaneously, another few Irgunists rushed through the streets, soaking them with kerosene. The kerosene was lighted and a wall of flames rose around the fortress.

As the flames roared, a few more Irgun men came bounding out of the Jewish Agency building (unoccupied on the Sabbath). This group tossed smoke bombs on the fire-encircled barricades.

During the hullabaloo, a car carrying four British officers turned into the street. Avshalom Haviv saw them in time and killed the four officers. A few minutes later the Goldschmidt fortress and scores of officers were blown up.

The entire Irgun force that laid low the British fortress numbered fifteen men. All fifteen escaped, untouched.

The British declared Jerusalem in a state of siege, moved out of their battered fortress into another stronghold, the Schneller Fortress. Four days later the Irgun attacked this new bastion.

This time Yehoshua Goldschmidt, nicknamed Gall, carried a treasured Sten gun.

At 4 A.M., the Irgun attacked. Three British heavy-armored cars entered the battle area. Gall faced the three cannon-booming cars alone, and stood stubbornly pumping bullets into them.

Another lone Irgun soldier came to his side and started tossing grenades into them. The three heavy-armed cars turned and left the battle area.

A few minutes later, the Irgunists stormed the Schneller and blew it up with heavy explosives.

To offset the Jewish Agency's howls of denunciations of the Irgun fighters, there was the single statement by British General E. F. Davies, Military Commander of Jerusalem, "They struck like our best Commandos."

A year later, Gall, in command of the Jerusalem battle against the Arabs, captured the center of the city and was later killed in that battle.

Following the Schneller victory, the Irgun attacked the British prison in Acre, one of the oldest towns in Palestine. Thirty-four Irgun men took part.

A full British regiment was stationed in Acre. The Irgun fighters stormed the town, blew up the ancient fortress, and released forty-one important Irgun and Lehi prisoners.

But the Irgun lost some of their best; among them Avshalom Haviv, who was captured and hanged on the Acre gallows by the British.

At the time of the Acre battle, the Haganah troops were no longer in the picture of the Jewish revolt. It was Weizmann who guaranteed their obedience to the British, and Ben-Gurion had gone him one better by assuring the Anglo-American Commission of Inquiry that the Haganah did not even exist.[15]

The present-day government clique of Israel seems to be of two minds now about what happened at Acre. It has supplied the movie *Exodus* with a Haganah hero, a Commander who plans and executes the storming of Acre—a fortress Napoleon failed to breach. The Haganah fellow does it to save an old uncle who foolishly belonged to the Irgun.

Looking back more realistically on what really happened, Ben-Gurion saved the face of the inactive Haganah by turning the ancient fortress into a lunatic asylum, which it is today. Whoever travels to this shrine of Irgun valor will hear the whimperings and fantasies of the demented.

35

OF THE TWELVE WHO WERE HANGED

They were all young men of soul. They loom in Israel's new past like Jewish knights in shining armor. All died with hope and pride glowing in their last hour. Their names are: Eliyahu Beit-Zuri and Eliyahu Chakim, hanged together in Cairo; Yechiel Drezner, Eliezer Kashani, Moshe Elkachi, hanged in Acre; Meir Feinstein and Moshe Barazani, who cheated the hangman by blowing themselves up in their Jerusalem prison cell with a hand grenade; Jacob Weiss and Meir Nakar, hanged with Avshalom Haviv in Acre. None of them was older than twenty-five, except Gruner, who was thirty-five. All were soldiers hanged for fighting for their country. There were two more.

The first on the British gallows was an Irgun soldier, twenty-five-year-old Shlomo Ben-Yosef. He was captured after a battle with his rifle still in his hands; under English law, clear proof, this, of treason.

A few months later, waiting execution in Acre Prison, Shlomo sat smiling at his guards. The first man to die for Jewish freedom! A distinction that kept young Shlomo's eyes bright.

Still smiling, he went to the gallows. With the rope around his neck he sang the "Hatikvah," the anthem-to-be of the State of Israel.

Told of Shlomo Ben-Yosef singing in the British gallows, the exiled leader Jabotinsky said, "He is my teacher."

Another was Dov Gruner.

After fighting bravely in the British ranks in Africa, Dov Gruner joined the Irgun. He was wounded and captured by the British during an Irgun attack on a police station in quest of arms.

The British authorities offered Dov Gruner a chance to escape hanging by pleading to them for his pardon. Dov refused to plead.

Thousands of cables poured in from all over the world—"Don't hang Gruner."

Dov Gruner wore the red suit—the hanging attire of the doomed—for three months. A few nights before his hanging, Dov celebrated the Passover Seder in his red suit. Other Jewish prisoners sat around him. British guards stood nearby on duty. Aware that they had been standing for hours, Gruner invited the guards to join the ancient Jewish feast of freedom. The British guards sat down to another Last Supper.

On his last night, Dov Gruner wrote to his Commander, Menachem Begin.

"In a few hours I go to the gallows. In such a moment a man does not lie. I want you to know that I am not sorry for any deed I have done. And were I at the start again with a choice to make, I would choose again the same course that has brought me here." [16]

Professor Joseph Klausner, Israel's eminent historian, pronounced, "The State of Israel rests on the broken necks of the twelve who mounted the gallows."

After the State of Israel was established, Ben-Gurion avenged himself on all the Irgun and Lehi soldiers who had fought and died by denying pensions to their widows, orphans and parents. [17]

The Prime Minister B.-G. also avenged himself against the great dead leader, Vladimir Jabotinsky, by refusing to allow his bones to be buried in a free Eretz-Israel, as Jabotinsky had asked when dying in exile.

"We do not need the bones of dead Jews here," said the present wearer of the mantle of Zionism. [18]

THE ALTALENA

I add one more Irgun battle, also one more Ben-Gurion vengeance. This is the betrayal of the Irgun ship *Altalena* in June, 1948.

On May 15, Great Britain had bowed to the vote of the U.N. and resigned as the ruler of Palestine. Nevertheless, the Chaim Weizmann forces led by Moshe Sharett were fearful of declaring an independent State of Israel. Pressure by "the people of

Palestine" forced Ben-Gurion to step in. Afraid that the Irgun might be the one to proclaim independence, he announced the State of Israel against the wishes of Sharett. At the same time, patriot Ben-Gurion secretly assured the British that he would remain moderate, not penetrate into Arab territory, and destroy the Irgun.

The British, however, lingered on nervously in Palestine. They still worried that the hard-hitting Irgun would take the whole of Palestine, on both sides of the Jordan, and turn it into a strong Hebrew State rather than a small semi-English dependency.

Unable to imagine Ben-Gurion's plans for them, the Irgun men came joyfully out of their underground. They had participated in the liberation of the major cities of the land—Safad, Haifa, and (at the end of April) their finest victory had been their battle for the ancient port of Jaffa, adjoining Tel Aviv.

Ben-Gurion and Golda Meyerson, his chief political aide, demanded of the Irgun that it leave Jaffa alone. Jaffa must, they declared, remain Arab in accordance with the United Nations-British plan for the partitioning of Israel.[19]

Reassured by the hands-off strategy of the Jewish Agency, the Egyptian Army had prepared to land by ship in Jaffa, adjoining Tel Aviv, hit Tel Aviv from the rear, and put an end to the Jewish State during its gestation.

Menachem Begin ignored the Agency's cowardice and ordered his Commander of Operations, Gideon (Gidi), to take Jaffa. After three days of battle, the Irgun army of less than one thousand men and women stormed the city. Most of the seventy-five thousand Arabs had fled.

Item: Today's Israeli Government history books teach the children of the land that Jaffa was captured by the Jewish Agency Haganah.

Only Tel Aviv was saved by the Jaffa victory. At midnight of May 15th, 1948, the day Israel announced its independence, the armies of Egypt, Iraq, Lebanon, Syria, and Trans-Jordan invaded Palestine. Because of the liberation of Tel Aviv, the Jews were able to repel the first blow. Soon the retreats began. Daily, almost hourly, the five Arab nations closed in on the new and tiny state of the Jews. The Israel Army lost its big battle of Latrun to the Arab legions. Ben-Gurion explained the defeat by revealing that the combined Jewish forces had only thirteen hundred rifles.[20]

Now the betrayal begins. While the battle-worn Palmach and Irgun stand in the hills of Jerusalem holding off the Arabs with almost no arms or ammunition, Ben-Gurion assures the U.N. that his new government doesn't want Jerusalem, and cravenly agrees to "internationalize" the Old City.[21]

And riding to the rescue out of Marseilles is the Irgun ship *Altalena* (literary pseudonym of Jabotinsky). It carries five thousand rifles, one million rounds of ammunition, one thousand grenades, three hundred Bren guns, fifty cannon, four thousand aerial bombs, nine tanks and fifty anti-tank guns and quantities of medical equipment. Also 920 trained combat soldiers—volunteers. The arsenal had been financed by "The Hebrew Committee for National Liberation," established in New York by Irgun representatives Peter Bergson and Samuel Merlin. The recruiting and sailing of the vessel had been accomplished with the close cooperation of the French authorities.

The Weizmann-Ben-Gurion Government had given a precise and specific go-ahead to the *Altalena*. It had also promised to help unload the cargo that would ensure the safety of the new Israel and relieve the siege of Jerusalem.[22]

Dropping anchor off the shores of Palestine, the arms ship ran smack into Ben-Gurion's betrayal. Instead of being received by winches and cranes and friendly hands to help unload the desperately needed cargo, the *Altalena* faced an inconceivable reception—arranged by Ben-Gurion. Jewish soldiers on shore opened fire with rifles and cannon on the sitting duck of a rescue ship.

On board the *Altalena* were Begin, his aides, and Merlin. In the bow of the ship, looking at the land of Israel into which he had smuggled thousands of refugee Jews, stood the Homeric Abrasha Stavsky. He was returning after fourteen years to the haven to which he had piloted his thousands. He was shot facing his betrayers and died of his wounds.

Merlin was wounded. The *Altalena* was sunk. Twenty of its Hebrew fighters were killed, half of them in the water while trying to swim ashore, some on the shore in cold blood.

Afterwards, many wild stories and organized lies were circulated by the government to explain the miserable, foggy episode of the *Altalena*.

The facts were these. It had planned the whole scurvy business from the beginning. It would appease the British by selling out the Jerusalem fighters to the U.N., and it would explode an old rage at the Irgun even if it meant blowing up half the city of Tel Aviv. A single shell landing in the *Altalena* explosives would have accomplished this Neronian feat.

Ben-Gurion sank the cargo that could have brought total victory over the Arabs, but removed a possible political rival, the Irgun.

Flushed by this coup, Ben-Gurion made a ringing statement in the newly-established provisional parliament of Israel.

He said to the Jews and to all the world:

"Blessed be the cannon that blew up the ship. It should be enshrined in the Third Temple of the Jews." [23]

THE MISSING MEDALS

During one of his visits to New York in the late forties, Sir Winston Churchill spoke to Billy Rose in the home of Bernard Baruch. He said he had heard that Mr. Rose had been involved in some fashion in the Palestinian fracas. Billy Rose, who had worked with me in the Irgun propagandist committees captained by Peter Bergson and Samuel Merlin, stuck to his guns, but a bit modestly, before England's greatest man.

"Yes," said Billy Rose, "I became involved through my friend Ben Hecht in that Irgun business, without quite knowing what was going on," which was the truth.

Churchill answered:

"If you were interested in the establishment of an Israeli Nation, you were involved with the right people. It was the Irgun that made the English quit Palestine. They did it by raising so much hell that we had to put eighty thousand soldiers into Palestine to cope with the situation. The military costs were

40

too high for our economy. And it was the Irgun that ran them up." [24]

Thus Churchill, not Ben-Gurion.

The young Jews stood up to British bullets and Jewish imprecation and betrayals.

The Irgun and Lehi "terrorists" could fight and die for Jewish freedom, go to the gallows for it, and ensure its victory with their riddled bodies and broken necks. But the labels remained. All the quaking Jewish leaders kept the print fresh—hooligans, terrorists, murderers. The handful could win freedom for the Jews, but not a good press notice.

But tomorrow, when the present government regime of Israel crumbles, and its lies and rogueries have ceased to belittle the word *Jew*, the deeds I have recounted will emerge as a beginning worthy of any land, even the one which Judas Maccabeus and his heroes once fought to preserve.

Tamir was one of the handful.

During his activities as an Irgun "terrorist," Tamir remained outwardly a respectable Jew of the sort admired by the British authorities and the Jewish Agency. He was employed as a broadcaster on the British radio and as editor of a weekly gazette published by the British Government. This was a war-effort periodical written in Hebrew. The English were happy to employ so eloquent and keen-minded a young Jew.

Tamir also continued his studies at the Hebrew University and took up the study of law at the British Government Law School in Jerusalem.

Such things helped keep him *persona grata* with the English. A fine situation for a young man who was also chief of Irgun Intelligence in Jerusalem. There was also a family background to help provide cover. It was hard to imagine a son of well-to-do and cultured parents—the kind that Dr. Weizmann liked to have in his Tiffany window—running amok as a terrorist.

They did imagine it finally, with the aid of a Jewish Agency informer. Two British officers stuck guns in Tamir's belly and said, "You bastard—fooling us for three years!"

Luckily, Tamir was unarmed. The British had introduced a new law into Palestine: "If any Jew is found carrying a gun he

41

will be executed." There is this about the British, they take their laws seriously and literally. A law may be a scurvy one, but they usually administer it like gentlemen.

Tamir and his Commander, Avinoam, arrested with him, were put in solitary confinement and quizzed by the British for information. The British learned nothing.

Tamir was dispatched to the Gilgil Detention Camp in Kenya. Two hundred and sixty of Palestine's finest were behind its barbed wire—all Irgun and Lehi men; none of them Haganah.

After the Jewish Agency clique had become the proud custodians of the liberty for which others had fought, Tamir and Avinoam and their friends were released from durance by the British in July, 1948.

Come back to Palestine, now the State of Israel, S. Tamir bought himself a black gown and rented a law office in Tel Aviv. He had completed his studies for the bar while in the Kenya lock-up. What he saw going on in Israel made him lonely sometimes for his Kenya alma mater.

BRIEFING BEFORE BATTLE

A few more details before the trial.

If I have seemed to write a little sourly about one sort of Jew, the Nabobs of Palestine, it will be otherwise here. For Tamir is a type of Jew of whom nothing worse can be said than that he makes a dangerous enemy.

But first, how he looks on this December morning in 1953. He is thirty-one, sandy-haired, blue-eyed, a bony face, five feet ten, a trim waist line and good muscles. Put a Stetson on him and he would look like a Laredo broncho buster.

He grins boyishly, has a loud singing voice, swims, climbs mountains, hits a dance floor like a Cossack, believes firmly in Abraham, Moses, God, etc.; practices all the virtues, is a fine husband, a devoted father; and like most native Israelis, is up on the fine arts. A more polite-spoken and well-mannered fellow it would be difficult to invent.

Yet in this amiable Tamir there is danger, like a dynamite dump. It is the danger of a man who can look on authority and take its measure. This requires even a deeper courage than throwing hand grenades into British machine-gun nests. Men can die bravely who can only think timidly. And men·who are not afraid of the cannon's mouth will wilt before the mouth of authority. For in the subjugating of humans, attitudes are more powerful than armaments.

This is especially true about Jews. Their long jeopardy trained them to be a bit extra polite toward the authority of the hundred different nations who have been their reluctant hosts. They grew a talent for living and even thriving in the scabbards of their enemies.

But the Jew's conformity as a stowaway in gentile lands was a lesser thing than his conformity to Jewish psychology, his attachment to his own kind. To whom else could he turn? The world wanted neither him nor his love. As outcast he had the choice of losing or keeping faith in himself as a human equal. The choice he made continued to irritate and astonish his libelers. The worse the world treated him, the stronger grew his faith in Jews as fine people; and the deeper grew his belief in the honor, goodness and wisdom of his Jewish leaders. Thus driven to concentrating their love on each other (since nobody else wanted it), the Jews achieved a solidarity beyond the scope of nationalism or religion. They became married to each other. They might bicker and rant among themselves, but always as a family. It was as a family they survived, despite the scorn of their neighborhood.

In the old days, the leaders of the Jews were rabbis and sages sitting brightly on the invisible thrones of tradition. Most of this last crop of fine souls ended up in the German ovens.

Today a new crop of Jewish leaders presides in Israel; not rabbis and sages on ghostly thrones, but bona fide rulers who get their pictures in the newspapers, shaking hands with other bona fide rulers of the world.

And here the solidarity of the Jews elbows judgment out of the way. Never mind who these leaders were, what they did, what they are doing—they are the new leaders of the Jews. And there is hardly a Jew in the world who does not look on these

43

present chiefs of Israel with reverence and delight—as if Saul, David and Solomon were happily back in Jerusalem.

Thus for a Tamir to look on these new Jewish nobles and see their ignoble reality—and what is more to expose it, and leave it forever documented in the records of Israel's high courts—is a heavy spiritual task. It is a much easier thing for me to stand at his side and see with his eyes, and my own, too. For I was not born in Jerusalem or trained as a Jew.

My American mind is used to disillusion, to beholding demagogues and pudding heads in the seats of government—in fact, hardly anybody else. Then why—if there is so much skulduggery going on everywhere—why pick on the Jews and their harassed little State of Israel, so hard won after two thousand years of mass longing?

I shall answer this question often as I go along, starting here.

What Jewishness there is in me lines itself up with Tamir and with the prophets. I may be little worthy of them, but nevertheless I echo their cries—that sham and hypocrisy, betrayal and wicked dealings are doubly wrong when they wear the fine name *Jew*.

ENTER PAMPHLET 51

Tamir remembers Rina. A nurse in the Irgun. He was her Commander in Jerusalem. A fine, brave girl. And he has heard of Malchiel Greenwald, vaguely. Some trouble lately with the Government.

Tamir smiles. This is the way with many who come asking him to be their lawyer—the government of Israel is after them. There is small profit in such cases, since the government of Israel is seldom after any big shots. Usually little people, with not enough money to hire a taxi, let alone a lawyer.

Be seated, Malchiel Greenwald. A lawyer who is not afraid and who believes there are more important things in the world than money, is reading Pamphlet 51, for the authorship of which you have been charged by the government of Israel with "criminally libeling Dr. Rudolf Kastner, spokesman for the Trade and Industry Ministry of Israel," etc., etc., "with the intention to defame the aforesaid."

Here is what Tamir reads about "the aforesaid":

"I have waited a long time to expose this careerist whom I consider, because of his collaboration with the Nazis, an indirect murderer of my dear people."

Tamir smiles. The style is a bit abrupt even to an ex-Irgunist.

"Who," Pamphlet 51 continues, "is this spokesman for the Ministry of Trade and Industry; who is this big shot leader of Mapai; who is this boaster of great achievements in the rescue of Hungarian Jews; who is this fellow who has been put high on the list of candidates for Israel's parliament by the government party, Mapai?

"This character is Dr. Rudolf Kastner, political adventurer, driven on by a sickly megalomania."

Tamir becomes interested. He remembers the 800,000 Jews of Hungary shipped off in sealed trains to be gassed and burned by the Germans in Auschwitz, drowned in the Danube, and shot to death in Budapest.

Tamir reads on:

"For whom, on whose account, Dr. Kastner, did you go like a thief in the night to Nuremberg to become a witness for the defense of S.S. Colonel Kurt Becher, the murderer of Jews, the man who wallowed in the blood of our brothers in Hungary? Kurt Becher—Economic Administrator of the Gestapo!

"Why did you save him from the death penalty which he had so richly earned?

"You flew to Nuremberg to save a mass murderer of the Jews. What induced you to do that?

"What kind of gentleman's agreement was there between this murderer Becher and this man whom I accuse as a collaborator with the Nazis?"

Malchiel Greenwald watches proudly as Tamir turns to the last page and reads:

"And it is this same Kastner that Mapai has taken to its bosom and placed high on its list of officials.

45

"My God! Kastner's deeds in Budapest cost us the lives of hundreds of thousands of Jews!

"We demand an impartial public committee of investigation.

"Kastner must be removed from the politics and from the society of this land.

"We shall keep this on our agenda until the evil is ended." [25]

Selah. Malchiel Greenwald has spoken.

Tamir sits staring at the smeared type. There is no misreading its accusation, and its objective. In Israel there is only one crime that merits the death penalty—collaboration with the Nazis during their extermination of Europe's Jews.

Dr. Rudolf Kastner, head of the Jewish Agency Rescue Committee in Hungary, and now an Israeli big shot, editor of the nation's popular Hungarian newspaper—a Nazi collaborator!

MOURNING BECAME THE GREEKS

A matter occurs to me as Tamir broods. This death penalty for Nazi collaboration must seem a bit stiff to Americans, even Jewish ones. And carrying a grudge too long is not considered admirable. Particularly when everybody else has forgiven the Germans, including the Israeli Prime Minister, Ben-Gurion.

Chieftain Ben-Gurion's picture was in the newspapers lately (November 1960) beaming under his Winged Victory haircut, and shaking hands happily with Adenauer in New York. [26]

The Jewish Prime Minister is probably putting over a deal with the Germans. Something helpful for Israel's economy. He has already put over several neat ones, recently a large sale of Israel manufactured submachine guns to the German army.

The Jews have of necessity been good traders and bright salesmen, although they never before sold what the government clique have been selling to the Germans—their loyalty to their dead, their moral judgment of their enemies. If their ancestral

46

Jews had asked a price for these things, Jews would long ago have passed out of history. And Israel would never have come into it.

There is another overtone. Perhaps being a world figure now, Ben-Gurion has absorbed the Free World's attitude about the exterminated Jews. Six million dead Jews are not as important a political factor as sixty million live Germans, half of whom are excellent soldiers and can help us blow up Russia, should we have to. Russia and not inhumanity is the enemy today. No patriot can argue with that.

And as a Free-World leader, Ben-Gurion may feel there is another danger in carrying a grudge over the Nazi-Jewish business. It would be bad psychology for the Free World to keep up a righteous indignation over the murder of six million innocents. It would interfere with screwing its courage to the sticking point when it comes time to drop hydrogen bombs and exterminate hundreds of millions of other innocents.

We, the Free and Unfree Worlds, prepare ourselves for the great adventure of annihilation, like a suicide who must turn his eyes from all the lures of life before reaching for his bottle of pills. We must, like the suicide, concentrate on the ideologic lie that we are better off dead than the losers of an argument. Whoever believes otherwise, whoever speaks of humanity as being more important than the foggy rhetoric and high-blood-pressure angers of governments, is an enemy of the theme of the Future—to hell with man.

Atomic war is only possible on the theory that life is not sacred. Thus the slaughter of the six million Jews is a sort of pioneering gesture in our atom age; a triumph over our flesh to be remembered stoically in our stride forward as planet wreckers.

These are the attitudes of government, and of the multitudes who salaam to government; and who borrow their identity from the nation in which they were born. There are others who do not salaam or borrow, and who consider government as less than themselves, when it becomes the spokesman of unreason.

The ancient Greeks believed that unpunished crimes brought plagues to the people who harbored them. They sought out and punished the evildoers in order to purify human life. So I think now. So thought Tamir, grim over the slightly silly document in his hand—accusing a Jew in the case of the murdered Hungarian Jews.

Pestilence caused by cruel deeds is a myth. Not so—decency versus government. (Not yet.) Not so—truth versus those who would be its executioners. It is an ancient duel. Truth seldom triumphs, but it persists.

I speak for Tamir—and for myself. Chief of our un-Jewish anti-government attitudes is that we are Jews whose souls have been violated by the murder of our people. For us, honor does not lie in forgetfulness, nor does balm lie in the smile of the enemy. We do not look to hanging more Germans for their crimes. Vengeance is a tiresome echo of evils done. What we dream of is—Jews strong enough and honest enough to hate their killers . . . rather than Jews cooing diplomatically in German offices.

A LAWYER MOBILIZES

Author Greenwald chats about his problems. He tosses rumors about as if they were Torah-Gospel, and seems to Attorney Tamir as unfactual a litigant as ever consulted a lawyer. But there is a side to this old Jew that Tamir finds worthy of attention. He is straightforward and fearless.

Tamir asks has Mr. Greenwald any evidence to substantiate his charges against Dr. Kastner?

Greenwald, God love him, answers, Yes, indeed. He received an anonymous letter a few weeks ago full of the basic facts. Also, there was a certain discussion at the Café Vienna in which the same facts came out. Who engaged in this discussion?

"I am no good at remembering names," says Greenwald, "particularly of strangers. But I have a nose for news—from childhood on. You can take my word for it, I have written only the absolute truth about Rudolf Kastner—a *meshumed* of the first water."

Tamir frowns. Not a shred of evidence to back up the most defamatory attack ever made on an Israeli government official.

48

An anonymous letter and some café chatterers, also without names.

Why try to defend this gabby old scribbler who sounds and looks as unconvincing as a down-at-the-heels fortune teller? If Sholem Aleichem had invented a journalist from Yahupetz it would have been Malchiel Greenwald, goatee, walking stick, anonymous letter and all. Tamir makes a first decision. If he should be foolish enough to take the case he must keep Greenwald out of the witness box.

Tamir scowls at Pamphlet 51. Nonsense even to think of trying to defend such a case. A hundred to one shot. But so was the Irgun Zvai Leumi.

Despite his aversion to the whole thing, a thought comes to Tamir. It is the government that has sued Greenwald for libel. This could mean that Kastner, himself, refused to sue. And against such a walloping charge. Why?

A second thought arrives. Kastner, Greenwald are actually of minor importance in the case, should he be foolish enough to take it on. It is the Government of Israel that asks for battle— and the whole hierarchy of the new State.

Since his return from Kenya, Tamir's heart has glared at the craven past and arrogant present of Israel's rulers, at the nest of historic lies in which they roost.

There are many like Tamir at this time, sickened by their government and as powerless to act as if they were serfs under Ivan the Terrible. Most of the few who once battled it are tired of fighting. What holds them mum also is the tyranny of Jewish illusion. It is all over the world. Israel shares it. All Israel lives under the illusion that God's cherubim are hallelujahing over its government buildings. All except those like Tamir. Again a handful.

And what, according to this handful, are the crimes of this objectionable government? Does it steal, oppress the poor, take bribes, sit twiddling its thumbs instead of building up the nation? The answer is the same as can be made about all governments —no and yes. Not a loud no, not a thundering yes.

But this no and yes do not matter. The crimes are deeper than venality or swindle. They are the crimes of character, the same crimes against which the Prophets bellowed three thousand

49

years ago—in this same neighborhood. Egomania. Falseness of soul. A passion for hypocrisy. A cowardice that boasts of valor.

Overheated ambition that is cold to truth and honor. A leadership with a single goal—the continuation of its power. All Bossism is that. But there are moral limits to what Bosses may do to remain Bosses. The passion for Bossism in Israel's leaders seduced them into behavior too unsavory to believe without full documentation. I write in a room piled with documents.

These crimes involve, also, a hardness of heart difficult to imagine as a basic Jewish quality. But it is there in the leaders of Israel.

Itzchak Greenbaum, chief of the Rescue Committee of the Jewish Agency, announced in Tel Aviv in 1943, "When they asked me, couldn't you give money out of United Jewish Appeal funds for the rescue of Jews in Europe, I said, 'No!' And I say again, 'No!' In my opinion one should resist this wave which pushes the Zionist activities to secondary importance." [27]

Having thus turned their backs on the doomed Jews, the same leaders later utilized the extermination for raising millions on millions, and for collecting billions in reparations from the Germans.

But enough here. The play's the thing. The Kastner case will be the stage.

Tamir speaks:

"If I take the case, Mr. Greenwald, will you agree to one thing?"

"Anything," says Greenwald, magnanimously.

"Will you agree to let me handle it any way I see fit," says Tamir, "and not interfere with any direction I may take?"

Greenwald's answer, despite his Sholem Aleichem outlines, has a ring of valor in it. Tamir recognizes it as an oath of allegiance.

"I will be behind you in anything you do," says Greenwald. Rina, the Irgun nurse, nods.

Thus the case starts.

"HEAR YE, HEAR YE, HEAR YE!"

The court room is sixteen feet square. Twenty-five people can jam into its benches, no more. There is no jury box, no jury. There is only room for a judge. It has a high title—the Jerusalem District Court, but it is a teapot of a court room.

Tamir is ready. That is, he is in court at the appointed hour. He has no witnesses to call, no evidence to offer. It is a low watermark in his professional career. But he is there in his black lawyer's gown, looking sternly at the wall.

A freshly barbered Greenwald beams at him. A lawyer in a black gown, with a strong face, an ex-Irgun commander. Greenwald is almost sorry for the government.

The prosecutor enters. He is Amnon Tell, age fifty, narrow-faced, thin-bodied, short. A stickler for formality of speech, manner and dress. Except that he wears yellow socks. They flash now under his black gown.

Tell is one of the best "convicting" barristers in Attorney General Chaim Cohen's domain. With a hot temper. Sneers, invective, righteousness can pour out of this sliver of a man—enough for two prosecutors.

Tell smiles at Tamir. It is a government pre-victory smile.

The prosecutor chats amiably with Opposing Counsel Tamir. It is an easy case, he says. Normally, it would run two or three days. But with Tamir in it, it may run a full week. A sop of flattery for a doomed gladiator.

That the trial will run four years, knock Prosecutor Tell out of the box, and stand the government on its ear! Prosecutors are not equipped with crystal balls.

A tolling bell interrupts. It is the nearby Russian monastery summoning its monks to devotions. The court building is in the Russian compound of Jerusalem, a mile from the Wailing Wall and the tomb of Christ. A hundred other ancient scenic relics lie beyond its windows, great in the mind and shrunken in the eye.

51

Shlomo, the good-natured court clerk in khaki uniform stands up and announces,

"The Court!"

A door opens. Judge Benjamin Halevi, the third hero of this history, enters in black robe, a black yarmulka on his head. One of the handsomest men in Israel and one of its most respected figures. He was among the first Jewish judges appointed by the British during their Palestine adventures. Later the Ben-Gurion government appointed him President of the Jerusalem District Court—a lifetime job.[28]

Tamir has pleaded before this government paragon of a judge in the past. He knows his cool, unsmiling manner, and his disciplinarian quirks. Defense Counsel remembers gloomily Halevi's reputation as a judge full of trust for the government, with severe penalties for defendants plotting to harm it or violating its laws.

The judge places writing paper and pen before him. He is his own court stenographer. He will take down all the questions and answers himself.

This is not a judicial hobby. This is part of judicial practice. There is a lack of stenographers in Israel. Hebrew is a new language for court procedure. Shorthand experts have not yet been developed in large enough numbers.

Judge Halevi comes from Germany. He came to Palestine in the 1930's. Married, a father, a music lover (as what German-born *Weltanschauer* isn't), and every inch a servant of justice. A face without expression, a body without gestures. A closed door of a judge.

Halevi is the most unusual of my three heroes, for he is no more trained for heroics than for somersaulting. He is trained to believe in authority, one of whose leading mouthpieces he is. His spirit is as orderly as his mind. He is a man of twin faiths, one in God, the other in the State of Israel.

THE MAN FROM HELL

This is Dr. Rudolf Kastner, first witness for the prosecution. Journalist Greenwald's target, to be kept on his agenda "until the evil is ended."

Dr. Kastner's entrance produces the stir that ripples around important men. The Doctor is not one of the top greats of Israel, but he is aiming upward. He has the Foreign Office swivel chair in his sights.

The newspaper reporters on hand have only one attitude toward Dr. Kastner—respect. I shall borrow this attitude and look on Kastner only as he is known and admired on this opening day of trial.

A dark-haired, lean, clever-looking man in his forties, smiling through horn-rimmed glasses, and with the mannerisms of a personality. He tips slightly forward when he speaks, like a courtier. He presses his finger ends together in a little church steeple effect when he argues. A suave fellow and worldly as a Rolls Royce salesman. But politically solid. He can unloose clichés in five languages. And confuse a listener as if he were speaking no language at all. Obviously, a statesman to be reckoned with.

He comes from the Hungarian town of Kluj, three miles from the Rumanian border. In Kluj he was a journalist. Not a journalist like Malchiel Greenwald, but a sharp, important busybody.

But what can a journalist write about in Kluj to become important? To get a Herr Doktor tacked on to his name? In Hungary Herr Doktors are as prevalent as zither players. But still you have to do more than dress neatly and pomade your hair every morning. Young Kastner did the additional. He practiced law as a side line, hence the doctor title.

The aura around Kastner is his past. Informed people in Israel, which include journalists, know that Dr. Kastner stood fearless among the Nazi exterminators in Hungary and worked diligently to save Jews.

A calm, smiling Kastner enters the witness box. Eager to tell his story for the sake of Israel as well as himself. For if there was anything rotten about Dr. Kastner's activities in Hungary, the government of Israel would surely know of it. And what Jew in his right mind can imagine Israel's rulers condoning evil and taking an evildoer to its bosom! Thus he has a double responsibility in the witness box. An honorable Rudolf Kastner means an honorable government of Israel.

Dr. Kastner offers the contents of a bulging brief case as evidence for the clearing of his name. Documents, memos, cablegrams, affidavits, testimonials, press clippings, all souvenirs of his staunch work as head of the Jewish Agency's Rescue Committee in Hungary. All proof of his courage and efficiency under Satan's German nose. The exhibits are entered and labeled.

Judge Halevi takes notes of the proceedings.

Tamir listen, watches. The benevolent calm of Kastner, his halo of certainty, are almost enough to take the heart out of Opposing Counsel. For there is only one line of procedure open to Tamir—a direct assault on Kastner.

The only possible witness against Kastner must be Kastner, himself. Tamir has no other on tap.

Standing good-naturedly in the witness box, Dr. Kastner begins his story. Amnon Tell guides him with deferential questions.

The story begins in Kluj, 1941. It moves to Budapest. A man of courage works to save Jews from German and Hungarian murderers. A man of tireless stamina and sharp wits. A dedicated man who keeps his head in the Nazi hell. And continues to rescue doomed Jews. Quietly, with the aid of verifying documents and testimonials, Kastner unfolds his story. It is a story that saddens, awes. It brings tears to many who hear it.

Not to Tamir. He watches, listens. Not only to the words of Kastner but to the tones behind them. Not only to the tones, but to the expression of eyes, the movements of hands, head.

Tamir looks for the sign of a lie—the sign of one naked lie in this parade of courage and service. One such lie will be opening enough. (One breach in the wall and the way is open for grenades.)

But why should there be a lie in this moving tale of Jewish heroism and rescue?

What heroism?

The Jewish rescuer and his Jewish Agency aides are all alive, and where are the eight hundred thousand Jews of Hungary? What rescue?

THE SAMARITAN KASTNER

Dr. Rudolf Kastner's parade of virtues takes three days. It is lyrically reported in the press. What a Jewish hero, Kastner! What a fool, Tamir. This is the gist of the newspaper coverage. Never has there been such a triumph of virtuous authority over would-be smearers.

Despite their forty-year stranglehold on Israel, the Jewish Bosses still fret over characters like Tamir—"unscrupulous adventurers" who don't mind giving the government of Israel a bad name in the eyes of its people and the Jews of the world, with their tax-deductible donations. Defeating the worst of these detractors will serve the fable of government honor even more than slapping Greenwald into prison.

Kastner's testimony soon brings the Germans into Budapest. Warriors had captured cities before, cut off thousands of adult heads, slit open thousands of children. But these diversions always climaxed a battle lust.

The Germans brought no battle lust to Budapest. They entered calmly, almost like sightseers. They organized the slaughter of the last million Jews as if they were opening a meat packing business, rather than conducting a war.

Give them their due, they had fought well in their second zany attempt at world conquest. The warrior side of Germans was still worthy of the chant of their ancient bards. But it was not German courage that came to Budapest. It was the underside of the German soul that arrived.

This is the side that everybody agrees does not belong in the world—the inexplicable passion for murder; cool, thoughtful, destruction of human beings such as we sometimes see done in a horror movie by some solitary fiend holed up in the Carpathians,

Dracula's native heath. But it is not a lone German who has come to play torturer and murderer in Budapest. It is a nation of them.

Being assured by the Germans that they have reformed, the world has dropped the whole subject of what made Hans and Fritz commit the greatest mass horror in the pages of history. The only practical way yet discovered by the world for curing its ills is to forget about them. And hope for the best.

I think otherwise about the Germans. They have not reformed. They are resting.

Kastner comes to his account of the German killing business. He gives his testimony quietly and factually. Everyone who hears him knows what happened to the Jews. Yet his story holds amazement. Not because of the hills of Jewish corpses that fill it —the millions of mouth-open, skeletonized, naked cadavers in the death camps of Birkenau, Mauthausen, Dachau, Auschwitz; in the slaughter-pen towns of Lodz, Zamosi, Tarnow, Palmiry, Olkush; in the Polish meadows where thousands of naked mothers, carrying their naked babies, walked naked and shamed toward young Germans studying their pubic hair through machine gun sights; the blast after blast of bullets that splattered the meadow with thousands of infant brains and mother bellies; the myriad of dead girls hanging from street gibbets in Ustronic, Trunbunalski, Sornowuc as if a great puppet show had come to Poland—these six million gaunt dead ones are known in all their Jack-straw postures; oozing skulls, interlaced pipe-stem arms and legs, torn breasts, hunger-hollowed bellies, and faces like an alphabet of despair with their millions of white teeth that look still terrified of life; this great and ancient people of Jews turned into garbage; this rubble of Jews half-buried, hanging, burning—this part of the story is known. Its photographs are in the archives.

But this other part of the story is not known, at least not too well; only vaguely known—the Germans who did it. The spectacled German high officers in their long military overcoats and polished boots who gave the orders in Treblinka, Auschwitz, Dachau, Mauthausen; and stood by studying the efficiency of the killers and torturers—the juicy young-faced German soldiers. These superior Germans, proud, crackling-voiced, polysyllabic, who supervised the Jew-slaughter are dim figures that belong more to a bad dream than to a nation.

Kastner tells of these German top-notchers who handled the Jew-slaughter. What he says of them amazes Judge Halevi, and even Tamir. And me, a bit. The S.S. chieftains sat in fine offices, drank, smoked, played cards, listened to phonograph records, went horseback riding, made love to girls and often to each other—and there was no dark stare of memory in their eyes, no glint of rue. Kastner reports that there was no discernible twinge of remorse in them, as he brings each of the mass murderers into his narrative—Himmler, Becher, Eichmann, Krumey, Hoess, Klages, Von Wisliczeny. He relates their words and attitudes as they issued orders to German industrialists for bigger Jew-burning ovens, for new types of trains to carry the new kind of cattle going to Auschwitz—the Jews.

Kastner introduces the German hierarchy of killers to Israel—the idols of Germany only nine years ago; the efficient, hardworking exterminators; no hint of self-consciousness in them for having murdered two million children, their mothers, grandmothers, fathers, grandfathers, etc. To the contrary, they beam out of Kastner's story with a sense of German duty well done. They are full of triumph and self-congratulation.

There is another thing that shocks. These German leaders are not archaic evildoers out of medieval forests. They are contemporary. Their faces are still the faces of a nation. And nobody of any importance in the world has a bad word for them. They thrive, prosper and have a knowing wink for their recent Jew adventure. Standing before the world besplattered with Jewish blood like the pig-stickers I used to see in Chicago stockyards, these Germans know that apologia and repentance are both a bore and a waste of time. Nobody gives a damn how many Jews they killed, or how they killed them. Not even the Jews who survived. It is the Christian way to forgive—what Christians do.

If there is any blame going around, it is for Jews like myself who won't give up hating the Germans.

"In what way am I different as a hater or hate-monger than were Hitler and his exterminators?" I see a difference. The hate for a crime is different than the hate that produces the crime. The first makes civilization, the other wrecks it. If men cease to sit

57

in judgment on evil deeds it is not because they are tolerant, but because they are defeated.

I return to Dr. Kastner in the Jerusalem witness box. He tells Judge Halevi now of how he sat in the nicely furnished German headquarter offices. He looked into their eyes without fear. The blue eyes of the Master Race with its half-nose and its half-soul brought no quaver into the Jew, Kastner.

They, without remorse; he, without grief, discussed rescue deals. He offered them money, and a correct business attitude, and bargained for Jewish lives.

Dr. Kastner's story fills the press of Israel and preoccupies its kitchens, shops, cafés and synagogues. And during its telling, Rudolf Kastner becomes a hero, a symbol of Jewsh courage and honor. He becomes these things, it seems, to everybody in Israel except Tamir.

Tamir's eyes, ears and solar plexus remain intent on this noble rescuer of Jews. Tamir dislikes the man's voice, the smack of egomania in it, the smug political terminology that hangs seven veils on every fact.

But Tamir can catch no proof of or hear any evidence of a lie.

"AND STILL HE SPOKE AND STILL THE WONDER GREW—"

Dr. Kastner's goodness continues from the witness box. He was head of the Jewish Agency's Rescue Committee for the eight hundred thousand Jews of Hungary. Politely from Prosecutor Tell: Will Dr. Kastner inform the court how he became leader of this great work? Dr. Kastner does so, without any false modesty. It was a time of panic. The great bulk of Hungary's Jews were without organization. They belonged neither to Zionism nor the Jewish Agency. They belonged only to Hungary, its homes, streets, work shops, sports fields, cafés.

Who could speak for these assimilated Jews, these Jews without chairmen? Their only spokesmen were their goodness, their harmlessness and their talents. But these are spokesmen who can address only a fellow humanity. There was no such vis-à-vis in Budapest. Only Germans.

Thus the organized Jews took over the entire rescue work for the whole eight hundred thousand doomed.

But why should the Germans, after exterminating five million Jews, and come now to Budapest to arrange for the murder of another million Jewish men, women and children—why should these veteran executioners be interested in dealing with Jew rescuers? Why should these Germans who had no respect for Jewish humanity, have so much respect for Jewish officialdom?

These questions have come into Tamir's head.

Judge Halevi listens and makes his notes. He forgets his impassive manner. He looks with kindly eyes at this witness who worked unafraid in the Nazi hell.

Kastner testifies:

"Toward the end of April, 1944, the German military agents informed me that they had finally decided on the total deportation of Hungary's Jews . . . An agreement was made between Hungary and Slovakia for the transfer of deportation trains from Hungary to Auschwitz.

"I also received information from Auschwitz that they were preparing there to receive the Hungarian Jews . . .

"I was allowed by Colonel Krumey to go to Kluj and contact Major Von Wisliczeny. This was approximately the third of May, 1944.

"Von Wisliczeny told me that his partiality toward me had infuriated Eichmann, and therefore Eichmann had sent him to do the dirty work of concentrating the Jews in the ghettos. [Such preliminary concentration cut down on the work of shipping them off to Auschwitz.]

"Von Wisliczeny explained to me that Eichmann﹍gave him this assignment so that, as a killer of Jews, he would not be able to offer the Allies any alibi [after Germany lost the war].

"He did not give me all the details of the dirty work he had performed, but it was obvious that he would now be busy not in rescuing Jews [with Kastner] but in their extermination as one of the chief murderers.

"A few days later I visited Von Wisliczeny at his home in Budapest. He told me that it had finally been decided—total

59

deportation. He asked that we should do everything we could to comply with the demands of the new German Plan. Otherwise, he said, he could see no chance of helping Hungarian Jews."

In unofficial language—if you Jews want to please us, help us kill you off as quickly as possible.

On another topic Kastner testifies:

"Eichmann offered us the idea of sending somebody out of Hungary to arrange for materials in exchange for Jews. He mentioned trucks, 100 Jews for every truck."

Kastner wanted to go as emissary but Eichmann picked a lesser member of the Rescue Committee for the errand. Joel Brand went on the mission.

Kastner testifies:

"On May 20, 1944, I went with Mrs. Hanzi Brand [Joel's wife and Kastner's favored co-worker] to meet Eichmann. The deportation had started on an enormous scale and at a shocking pace. We demanded then that Eichmann stop the deportations, otherwise Brand's mission would fail. He answered negatively.

"It was the first time I had stood face to face with this monster. When I told him that a hundred human beings were jammed into a single train compartment under unbearable conditions, he answered, 'In the Karpato Ukraine, the Jews have innumerable little children. It will be possible there to jam even larger numbers into the compartments.' "

Kastner continues:

"It was agreed with Krumey that we submit a list of 600 Jews to be allowed to leave Hungary alive for the Free World —300 country people and 300 from Budapest. Eichmann approved the agreement.

"A few days later Eichmann told me he couldn't bring the 300 country Jews to Budapest [to send on to freedom] because he had promised the Hungarian government that not a single Jew would return alive to Hungary. He said he had had a rough time with the Hungarian minister. He was afraid now the minister [Andre] would suspect that the Germans had made a new pact with the Jews. And he said, 'I, of all people. No, I can't.'

"He ordered me out of his office. I went at once to his deputy, Krumey, and to the chief of the Gestapo, Klages. I informed both of them I would stop all my negotiations and notify Istanbul to this effect. I pressed Klages and Krumey to reason with Eichmann. They did, and Eichmann agreed to receive me again that same day.

"After threatening to send me to Auschwitz, Eichmann capitulated and agreed to bring from Kluj a group of two hundred families. This was on June 3, 1944.

"Eichmann talked to me constantly about Brand's failure to return, or to send back any word to him. At the beginning of June, Eichmann gave me an ultimatum. He said, 'If I don't get an answer from Brand in a few days, I'll let the mills of Auschwitz start grinding.' And had not Eichmann agreed to bring the group from Kluj, we would definitely have stopped negotiations. Later, after lengthy negotiations, I made a deal with Eichmann to increase the number in the group to 1,300 people.[29]

"After the Allied invasion of Europe and the beginning of the new Russian offensive, and also as a result of the intervention of international factors, Horthy instructed his government to stop the deportation. According to the documents, this happened on the 26th of June, 1944, and a day or two later rumors to that effect reached us.

"Though the deportations had stopped, we didn't feel secure. We therefore made an additional agreement with Eichmann in case the Germans managed to overcome Horthy's will."

Kastner relates his travels from Budapest to Switzerland, to Vienna, to Slovakia, to Berlin, to Hamburg. He is the companion always of S.S. Nazi leaders—chiefly of Becher. Says Kastner in the Jerusalem court:

"Heinrich Himmler came to Vienna to organize the military defense of the city. I was taken to the building where Himmler was conferring over the Vienna defense. Here I stood in the corridor with Becher and Krumey. When Himmler emerged, Becher approached him and pointed me out to him.

"After their talk, Becher told me Himmler had given him clear instructions not to harm the remaining Jews in any way. He told me also that Himmler wanted no more money from the Jews, and that all the money previously accepted from the Jews would be paid back to them. 'You must come with me to Berlin, Becher said to me, 'and hear all this from Himmler's own lips.'

61

"I went to Berlin with Becher but the meeting with Himmler failed to materialize.

"But the trip was not wasted because Becher and I decided to go to the Nazi concentration camps and take the necessary steps to bring about the plan on which we had agreed." [30]

In his direct testimony, Dr. Kastner's voice is firm, his words full of proud details. He is proud of what he did—of his great success "in saving vast numbers of Jews" from death; of the way he influenced the Nazi leaders to do his bidding. And all who hear feel a similar pride in the doings of their Jewish Agency hero. All but Tamir.

THE LIE

It is a matter of sound—the way a voice changes, becomes timorous or over-friendly; the way an apologetic note enters it and the soul of the speaker seems to add a frightened whisper to the bold and boastful words.

Tamir catches this change of voice in Kastner. It is like a tocsin sounding for the defense attorney. Here is the breach for which he has been waiting—the lie; the lie through which he can charge with his cross-examination grenades. Tamir looks casually at judge and press, and the twenty-five spectators jammed on the benches. No tocsin has sounded for them. They listen as before—to a hero. But defense counsel is not disturbed by this lack of response. He knows about tocsins—someone must always hear them first, usually the one who is waiting for them.

The witness is telling of his activities that season from August 1944 to May 1945. The war was still on. Nearly all the last million Jews had been disposed of in the Auschwitz ovens. From August on, Kastner was busy traveling. He traveled with S.S. Lieutenant General Kurt Becher, with Colonel Hermann Krumey, with other high S.S. officers. To Switzerland, Vienna, Bratislava, Berlin, Hamburg. He eats, drinks with them, takes walks with them, and seems on pleasant social terms with the exterminators.

Dr. Kastner tells little anecdotes of how he spent his time in the final months of the war, which saw the quickened killing of the last million. He tells of rescue efforts, of important Nazi contacts, of cables dispatched and received.

And while telling of these matters, a new quality enters Kastner's story. He boasts. He boasts of his Nazi companionships. The boastfulness is seemingly a natural part of his tale. It is not to be heard, except by a cocked ear. Everyone of his boasts is a dangerous admission. But boastfulness is stronger in him than any fear. This companionship with leading Nazis made him feel like a great man at the time. He wants everybody to see this greatness, to hear Himmler, Hoess, Eichmann, talking to him— on equal terms.

Yet while he boasts, an unboastful sound comes into his voice, the sound of apology.

And Tamir senses why and what for. He enters the truth of Kastner through the opened door of Kastner's fears. Attorney Tamir will find the facts later, but here, now, Kastner gives him the overall fact that Hero Kastner is frightened of being uncovered. The lie of shame, the lie of fear continue to sound out of Kastner. And Tamir, aware that Dr. Kastner, in an Israeli witness box, is apologizing for something, keeps a friendly look on his face. He does not want to alarm the witness.

Boasting and apologizing, Dr. Kastner goes on about the exhilarating time after August 1944, when he gallivanted through Germany and Nazi-occupied Europe as a companion of high S.S. officers.

The questions become clearer in Tamir's head. Why did the Nazis favor Kastner so much? Again—why should these mass killers of Jews be so considerate of the Jew, Kastner? Why did they allow him to be the only Jew in Budapest to live in a house unmarked as Jewish? Why was he exempted from wearing the yellow Star of David on his coat front? Why did they allow him the special privilege of having a telephone, after all the phones had been ripped out of Jewish houses to prevent communication? Why was he the only Jew in Budapest allowed to ride in an automobile and to own his own car? Why was he allowed to go alone and freely to Vienna, Bratislava and even Berlin? Why this unique favoritism? Why did the S.S. elite humor Kastner as if he were the representative of a great neutral power instead of powerless Jews without standing in German eyes as human beings? *Of what possible use could Jewish Agency Official Kastner have been to the exterminators of Jews?*

The answers grow in Tamir's head—answers grim and unbearable to the heart of a Jew. Rudolf Kastner was dear and valuable to the Nazis because he helped them slaughter Jews.

Kastner talks on, now about his postwar "achievements." And here, too, despite the boastful words there is a mysterious tone of confession. Witness Kastner gulps, wets his lips, smiles eagerly at everyone including Tamir as he continues:

"I went to Nuremberg from Switzerland at the beginning of 1947 at the invitation of General Taylor, chief Prosecutor for the International Court. I was the General's advisor in matters pertaining to Jewish extermination.

"I worked in Nuremberg until August, 1947. Then I returned to Switzerland in order to immigrate to Israel. I received a cable from General Taylor guaranteeing me my expenses and a fee if I would return to Nuremberg to assist him. I showed the cable to Ben-Gurion. He told me to go. After a conference with the top officials of the Political Department of the Jewish Agency, where we discussed how to exploit this trip for various political purposes, it was agreed that I join General Taylor. The Jewish Agency provided me with money for the trip.

"In answer to the defendant's accusation that I aided Becher after the war, *I will state that I gave no testimony in Nuremberg in favor of Becher.* I gave it neither to the International Court nor to any of its institutions or officials.

"Greenwald's statement in his pamphlet that I went to Nuremberg to save Becher is a total lie.

"The German court of de-Nazification of Becher invited me to give them testimony about Becher when I was in Nuremberg. I refused. I had no desire to appear before any Germans. I'd had enough of Germans during the war.

"I agreed, however, to give them a sworn affidavit, which I sent them. It is a total lie that I helped Kurt Becher escape punishment in Nuremberg. *I gave no testimony or affidavit in his favor.*"

Dr. Kastner's declaration of innocence thrills his hearers, including Judge Halevi and the newspaper men. Not so, Tamir.

He watches a liar and a knave—a sad slippery sort of knave whose Jewish eyes ask for absolution—leave the witness box.

But this is no moment of triumph for Attorney Tamir. He feels himself a brother of Hans Christian Andersen's little boy who cried out suddenly from the admiring throng, "The King has no clothes!"

The court room has seen no denuding. At the finish of Dr. Kastner's testimony all the newspaper reporters hurry to their typewriters to tap out the fine news to Israel that Dr. Rudolf Kastner is a hero clothed in purple.

I have no criticism of these or any other newspaper men. I was once one of them. I remember my own addleheadedness, blindness toward truth, deafness for its words. My sins were not purposeful. I did not draw my pay as a philosopher or seer. My duties were to report the obvious, to echo the loudest and most important voices. Since these were always the voices of virtue and authority, I was their nimble press agent.

Some cynicism accumulated in me as it does in all newspapermen who must report from hour to hour with a straight face and stern tongue the constant nonsense of politicians, lovers, reformers, judges, prophets. But as long as I drew a newspaperman's pay check, I stayed faithful to my boss, who was not a city editor, but society.

So with these Israeli journalists hurrying off with their tidings of government victory. And how criticize them when so honorable a man and penetrant a mind as Judge Halevi is on their side? Judge Halevi has heard nothing amiss in Kastner's three-day testimony. He has heard only a man of heroic mold successfully crush the libel against him.

As Kastner vacates the witness box, Judge Halevi puts a query to Attorney Tamir. Would counsel for the defense like to change his plea to "guilty" and trust the court to determine a proper sentence for his client?

There is no anger in Halevi's voice. He speaks as one who would like to spare a young lawyer the unpopular task of attacking so fine and invulnerable a figure as Dr. Kastner.

Tamir is silent for a few moments. Questions are busy as grasshoppers in his mind. Where Halevi heard honor and courage, Tamir caught the sound of incredible evil. It is an evil not only incredible, but one so deeply buried, so entombed in piety and power, that it will take tons of cross-examination to blast it into sight. It will take months of hunting for facts, digging into records all over the world, tracking the globe for witnesses. And all this without money on hand, and with all the forces of Israel—its renowned leaders, admiring press, and unlimited cash— against him.

Tamir turns to his client. He does as the judge suggested. He asks Greenwald if he wishes to change his plea to guilty. He tells him that it is likely the judge will not be too severe in his verdict, if the plea of guilty is made now. He hints to Green- wald that Judge Halevi may be less pleasantly disposed if his offer is rejected.

Defendant Greenwald has only one word for such a suggestion —"Never!"

The answer pleases Tamir. Defense Counsel answers the court, "Your Honor, we remain with our original plea, Not Guilty."

WEATHER REPORT—TEMPEST DUE

The cross-examination of Rudolf Kastner is rampant drama. I know of no indoor event in history that equals this agony of villainy unmasked.

The cross-examination by the ex-terrorist Tamir was a new type of "terrorism," which the forces of government were unable to malign out of existence. It was the terrorism of truth.

Day after day Tamir quizzed Kastner, a disdainful Kastner perched securely on his political height; a Kastner stirred to righteous anger; and finally a sweating Kastner, crushed and wordless. Tamir quizzed all these Kastners, sometimes coolly, sometimes softly, and sometimes with sledge-hammer logic. In the end he forced Rudolf Kastner, the man of many faces, to look at his one true face—the unlovely phizz of evil. Looking at it Kastner must cry out, "That is not I! I am someone else!" He must shout angrily and moan with disbelief; redouble his lies and deny the image with his last breath. For the image is not entirely true. He was not always a man of evil. Virtue and courage were once in him, and even a love of Jews.

But Rudolf Kastner's true face at which he cannot look remains hellishly visible for everyone to see. Not quite everyone. The great princes of Jerusalem have specially gifted eyes for seeing only honor in their own kind. Kastner was one of theirs.

DOSSIER ON A MASTER JEW-KILLER

Tamir beings his cross-examination on Kastner's relations with Kurt Becher.

As I write (May 1961), Becher's closest associate, Adolf Eichmann, is being tried in Israel as a mass murderer of Jews.

Kurt Becher, tall, handsome, a good horseman, a prosperous wheat broker, joined the Nazi party in 1934. He served as an S.S. Major in Poland, was a member of the Death Corps that worked around the clock killing Jews. He wore a death's head on his uniform cap, and his boot heels were weighted with steel plates so as to clank more fearsomely when he walked among the Jewish prisoners waiting for death. That was the time before German efficiency produced gas ovens and mass incinerators. The killing of the first few million Jews was a primitive business, requiring steady nerves. Before shooting down the Jewish women and children, it was sometimes necessary to fill their mouths with plaster of paris to prevent their screaming from disturbing their executioners.

Becher distinguished himself as a Jew slaughterer in Poland and Russia. He became an important liaison figure between Hitler and Heinrich Himmler.[31]

He was appointed by Himmler as Commissar of all German concentration camps and made Chief of the Economic Department of the S.S. Command in Hungary.[32] Together with Becher in the "Economic Department" was Adolf Eichmann.[33]

Economic Department was either a pompous or humorous German locution—I don't know which—for the Germans employed in removing the gold fillings from the millions of teeth of the dead Jews; in cutting off the hair of millions of Jewesses before killing them, and shipping these bales of hair to Germany's mattress factories; in converting the fat of dead Jews into bath soap, and in figuring out effective methods of torture to induce the Jews awaiting death to reveal where they had hidden their last possessions.[34]

Item: our American officers in West Berlin are still sleeping on mattresses stuffed with Jewish tresses, and still scrubbing themselves with high quality soap out of Auschwitz, Mauthausen and Dachau.

As Himmler's overall aide in the work of Jewish extermination, Becher was top man in Budapest from 1944 on, during Kastner's "rescuing" of Jews. It is time for the quotation marks.

In 1945, Hitler rewarded the elegant mannered and industrious Kurt Becher with the rank of Lieutenant General of the S.S. Waffen Command.[35]

As Emerson wrote, if you build a better mouse trap people (and honors) will come to your door. Becher's mouse traps in Auschwitz, Dachau, Mauthausen, Bergen-Belsen, brought him high German glory.[36]

THE LAWYER AND HIS AIDES

Tamir's first day of cross-examination is light. He tosses no grenades. He asks smiling questions. He touches on minor matters—such as Kastner's egoistic assertion that he was head of the Jewish Agency Rescue Committee in Budapest. Records show that a man named Komoy was its head. Tamir leads Kastner into admitting he elbowed Mr. Komoy out of the picture, allowed him to retain his title, but did all the work of leadership himself.

These casual questions are a reconnoiter before the breakthrough. Tamir wants to see how Kastner's mind works, how it fences, parries, and to take the measure of its quickness and sharpness on this first day.

In the brief wait for the trial, Tamir has lined up his small forces. The shapely Rina is out collaring witnesses. Another feminine aide sits in the packed court room—a lean girl with glowing eyes, Tamir's wife, Ruth.

She will help Tamir in many ways. Chiefly she will be his loyal troop that never leaves his side during the long, uphill pull. Every morning of the trial, after attending the needs of her three children, Ruth Tamir drives from Tel Aviv to Jerusalem—an hour and a half. Throughout the uproar against Attorney Tamir, by press and government, he finds in her eyes and words only the assurance that the battle is worthwhile.

Ruth Tamir is also the fastest mile-runner in Jerusalem, a mountain climber and a Bible teacher.

Tamir's headquarters during the trial is his parents home in the flossy sector of Jerusalem. Tamir's mother, Bat-Sheva Katznelson, one of the few women senators in the Knesset, makes room in her house also for Tamir's aides.

Tamir's father, white-haired, handsome, Reuven Katznelson, is himself one of the leading respectables of Jerusalem and one of the builders of Hadassah in Palestine, the hospital-health organization. He is away from home when the trial starts. After reading the reports in the press of the hero Kastner's three days of direct testimony, Tamir's father writes him a letter from Tiberias.

The letter reads, in part:

Dear Shmuel . . . this Kastner story is very strange. Go into it. What does it mean, 'they picked the prominent ones for rescue'? The masses were left behind. Uncle Joseph gave his life putting the masses of Jews on ships and smuggling them to Eretz-Israel. He didn't look for the prominent ones. He was unable to save all he wanted. And now you owe them the duty to speak for them in court, those who bécame the ashes of Europe . . . I feel you have embarked on one of the most important missions of your life. Don't give up.

Another aide on hand is Arie Marinsky of Tamir's office. He comes from China, fought in the Irgun, was kidnapped by the Haganah, but released. He fought with the Palmach against the Arabs. When the shooting stopped, he studied law.

Dan von Weisl is also in the defense lines. Von Weisl is a young man of impressive culture. He speaks fluent English,

French, German, and Hebrew. He sits translating Dr. Kastner's multitude of exhibits.

A third cohort is Dov Levin, once in Tamir's Irgun unit in Jerusalem and now his chief legal assistant. Levin is a barrister with a law library open in his head.

There is a fourth helper—Shraga Biran, tall, dark, good-looking, twenty-one years old, a law student in the Hebrew University. At the age of ten, Shraga saw the Germans take his parents and family to the killing place outside his home town in the Ukraine. He watched the slaughter of his kin. The ten-year-old Shraga managed to escape. The German bullets had missed him. After hiding for several days, he ran to the woods. A unit of fighting partisans took the boy into their ranks. After the war, Shraga made his way to Palestine.

At the start of the trial, Shraga Biran volunteered to help Tamir search for witnesses.

There will be other helpers. Never too many, never enough. Now, only these.[87]

THE UNMASKING OF KASTNER BEGINS

An amiable Dr. Kastner enters the witness box on the second day of cross-examination, obviously eager for more fencing. The newspapers recorded fully his witty answers of the first day; and Attorney Tamir's inept efforts to shake the heroic witness.

But Tamir is through with the thrusts and parries of the fencing preliminaries. He picks the Becher story for his first deadly attack for its shock potential. The Becher exposé will demote Kastner from hero to scoundrel. And set a pattern for Tamir's dissection of the "Rescue Work" of the Jewish Agency in Budapest.

An unsmiling Tamir begins his work of proving Hero Dr. Kastner a collaborator in the Nazi extermination of Jews.

The smallness of the court room places defense counsel within two feet of the witness box. He must ask his questions with his face close to Kastner's face—the way it is done in the movies when the inquisitor closes in on his quarry.

It starts:

> Tamir: Have you a copy of the sworn affidavit you gave the German inquirers into Becher's Nazi status?
>
> Kastner: I don't know. I may have. But I'm not sure.
>
> Tamir: You have brought into this court a briefcase bulging with documents, many of them of no importance at all. How is it you did not keep a document of such historical importance?
>
> Kastner: I don't have to keep every scrap of paper.
>
> Tamir: Was it a long or short affidavit?
>
> Kastner: I don't recall how many pages. But I think it was short.
>
> Tamir: Was it in favor of Becher or against him?

The witness pauses. He tries to look like a man searching for the exact truth. But the caution suddenly in his eyes reveals his actual problem. He is trying to figure out quickly how much Tamir can possibly know about the affidavit, about Becher, about everything. And he decides to answer adroitly—just in case.

> Kastner: (firmly) Neither in favor nor against. I tried only to tell the truth—not to help or damage.

The court listeners react. A gasp here and there. A first wondering look at Rudolf Kastner. A Jewish Agency leader who tried "not to damage" Kurt Becher of the Death Corps, of the Jew-slaughter pens!

Tamir continues in a friendly voice:

> Tamir: Am I correct in my assumption, Dr. Kastner, that your only aim in Nuremberg was to serve truth and justice?
>
> Kastner: That is true.
>
> Tamir: And it is also the truth that you had no reason, personal or Jewish, to do anything to help Becher?
>
> Kastner: That's true.
>
> Tamir: And you will also agree with me that the most you would do for this man Becher would be to tell the truth

about him without offering any personal opinion in his behalf?

Kastner: That is true.

Tamir: By the way, when was Becher released [by the International Court Authorities in Nuremberg]?

Kastner: December, 1947.

Tamir: And your testimony in Nuremberg was in no way decisive in securing his release?

Kastner: Not at all.

Tamir's friendliness drops from him abruptly, and his voice is savage with accusation.

Tamir: I tell you now that owing to your personal intervention, Kurt Becher was released from prison at Nuremberg.

Kastner: (yelling) That's a dirty lie!

Tamir: (quietly) May I have Exhibit 22, Your Honor?

Exhibit 22 was among the heap of documents introduced into trial by Dr. Kastner to help prove his innocence. It is the document that begins Kastner's downfall. That he and the government prosecutor should foolishly enter it as an exhibit is one of the many oddities of a righteous government and of Kastner's reliance on it. Poor Kastner.

A DOSTOEVSKY CHARACTER

"Poor Kastner," because he is full of demons he cannot control. Their *gilgul* voices will blurt out his love of Nazi chieftains, his pride in their friendship, his contempt for eight hundred thousand doomed Jews. And while these demons blurt these truths out of Dr. Kastner's mouth, the same mouth will continue to plead for his recognition as a man of holy virtue.

Exhibit 22 was a letter sent by Kastner to Jewish Agency official Eleazer Kaplan, July 26, 1948. Tamir holds it in his hand. It is a long letter full of facts and figures about the money deals between Kastner, Becher and Eichmann. In this letter Kastner

72

goes out of his way to explain in meticulous detail what became of the Jewish rescue money.

Toward the beginning of the letter, tucked away in a casual paragraph, are two vital sentences. Tamir had spotted the sentences when the pile of Kastner exhibit passed through his hands. He had shown no tell-tale reaction and said casually to the court, "No objection."

> Tamir: I read from your letter marked Exhibit 22—quote, "Kurt Becher was an ex-S.S. Colonel and served as a liaison officer between me and Himmler during our rescue work. He was released from prison in Nuremberg by the occupation forces of the Allies owing to my personal intervention." [38]

The court room is silent. The Kastner hosannah singers of the Israel press fidget a little.

> Tamir: Dr. Kastner, you wrote in this letter that Becher was released owing to your personal intervention.
>
> Kastner: Yes.
>
> Tamir: And you cried out a few minutes ago that when I said the same to you it was a dirty lie.
>
> Kastner: Yes.
>
> Tamir: Pick out which answer you prefer now.
>
> Kastner: I wish to emphasize what I said before—that it is a lie.
>
> Tamir: In your letter to the Ministers of Israel, did you write the truth?
>
> Kastner: (throbbingly) Only the truth!
>
> Tamir: And to this honorable court, do you tell the truth?
>
> Kastner: (throbbingly) Only the truth!
>
> Tamir: Will you try to explain yourself for the record, Dr. Kastner?

Tamir turns from the witness. For the moment Kastner's flushed face is evidence enough. Judge and journalists stare at the witness. How can a man call a statement a dirty lie, then admit the statement is true, and then call it a dirty lie again? Easily, if he believes that the sanctity of authority transcends truth and even sanity.

Kastner finally answers. His voice gathers steam as he tries valiantly to restore his virtue.

Kastner: I have no doubt in my mind that what I did in Nuremberg about Becher was favorable for him.

Dr. Kastner, a fine linguist, speaks the word "favorable" in English, hoping it will be less understood than if he spoke it in Hebrew, and that its meaning will sound vaguer.

Kastner: (continues in Hebrew) When I wrote to a minister of Treasury about Colonel Becher's offer to hand over certain Jewish money to the state of Israel, I wished to explain the reason for such an offer so that the minister would believe in its reality. For this reason, I phrased the letter somewhat boastfully, hoping to make it easier for Mr. Kaplan to realize that Becher's statement about the money was worth his attention. So if I'm guilty of an uncautious phrasing of a letter, I am willing to admit it.

Tamir: How did you have the nerve to say I was telling a dirty lie when I used your own words that Becher was released through your personal intervention?

Kastner: I have the right to answer you again—it is a lie.

Prosecutor Tell: I object, Your Honor. It is unethical for a lawyer to torture a witness.

Judge Halevi: It is unethical for a lawyer to interrupt a cross-examination when the opposing counsel has cornered your witness. Sit down.

Tamir: I tell you further, Dr. Kastner, that you not only saved Becher from the International court in Nuremberg, but that you gave a sworn affidavit to the de-Nazification court of the Germans, and also saved him from their punishment.

Kastner: No! That's untrue!

Tamir: Dr. Kastner, from the pile of exhibits, I see you have a tendency to collect things. Would you get us a copy of that sworn affidavit?

Kastner: Well, I don't think I have it.

Judge Halevi: Can't you manage to obtain a copy?

Kastner: I can. But it will take some time.

Prosecutor Tell: Your Honor, why is this a matter of any importance? Greenwald's libel doesn't mention any affidavit given to the German court.

Judge Halevi: It is important.

Tamir: Dr. Kastner, was there a recommendation for leniency to Becher in your affidavit?

Kastner: No, I don't think so.

Tamir: Dr. Kastner, will you agree with me that to intervene in favor of a high S.S. Nazi officer and bring about his release is a criminal act from our national point of view?

Kastner: My answer is positive. It is a crime from a national point of view.[39]

PINCH HITTER CHAIM COHEN—TO BAT

The Becher story spreads through Israel, and the land is darkened as if the wrath of God were in its sky. Tamir takes advantage of recesses demanded by the nerve-wracked government to dart about Europe, and return to Jerusalem with new evidence and new witnesses.

The government clique waits to see if an aroused populace will so far forget itself as to bounce them out of office. Such a prospect makes the management send Attorney General of Israel, Chaim Cohen, into the game.

The Attorney General of Israel, Chaim Cohen, takes over the case, not so much to send Malchiel Greenwald to jail, but to save the skin of the government. A mighty job, but Chaim Cohen is a mighty man. He is the government's legal Samson, renowned for his loyalty and righteousness. And he has run up an impressive score of government critics tossed into the clink.

I shall be careful of what I write about Chaim Cohen, for of all the cast of characters in the Kastner trial, he is the one I dislike most. I hope to avoid overstatement by sticking only to Chaim Cohen fact and quotation.

Chaim Cohen who takes over the Kastner case is a tall man with a glossy bald head and a theatric stride in the court room.

He comes from Frankfurt, Germany (in the 1930's), is married, has three children, and is a conversationalist of charm. He is also a savant of Rabbinical law, a "gifted orator," old style, an organizer and a pillar in the State of Israel. When Israel achieved independence he helped draft its laws. One of the laws which he tried to introduce into the Israel code was that even if a man confesses under torture, his testimony can be admissible as evidence.[40] Despite his able campaigning in behalf of this "torture-law," it was not adopted by Israel. However, he has had few such defeats.

Facing Judge Halevi, Chaim Cohen is an imposing-looking fellow in his late forties, a restless legal gladiator who can't sit down, who must keep pacing, his black gown billowing around him as if he were Elijah striding forth to debate with the abominable priests of Ahab and Jezebel. He licks his lips constantly and looks at people sideways.

Tamir resumes his cross-examination of Kastner.

Tamir: Did you go through the life story of Kurt Becher?
Kastner: Yes.
Tamir: Born 1909. Joined the S.S. in 1934.
Kastner: Yes.
Tamir: And in September 1939 was an officer in the S.S. police in Poland—and a bit later became a cavalry S.S. officer in Poland?
Kastner: Yes, I knew that.
Tamir: Do you know it was at that time the Germans began the torture and mass murder of the Jews in Poland?
Kastner: Yes, I know that.
Tamir: From June, 1941 to June, 1942, Becher is platoon commander on the Russian front.
Kastner: Yes.
Tamir: You know that the extermination of Jews took place in that area at that time?
Kastner: Yes.
Tamir: In March, 1942, Becher becomes a lieutenant colonel and is transferred to S.S. Headquarters in Berlin.
Kastner: Yes.
Tamir: On December 24, 1942, Becher received the Gold

76

Cross.

Kastner: Yes.

Tamir: January, 1944, he is made a colonel.

Kastner: Yes.

Tamir: In 1944 he is placed in charge of the Economic Department of the S.S. Command in Hungary.

Kastner: Yes.

Tamir: March, 1944, he is transferred to Hungary.

Kastner: Yes.

Tamir: In January, 1945, Becher becomes a lieutenant general.

Kastner: Yes.

Tamir: In the same year he is appointed Special Reichs commissar for Himmler and placed in charge of all concentration camps in German occupied territory.

Kastner: Yes.

Tamir: He is arrested immediately after the war and kept imprisoned for two years.

Kastner: Yes.

Tamir: He is released in December, 1947.

Kastner: Yes.

Tamir: On page 108 of your testimony before this court you stated, "When I was in Nuremberg I gave no testimony concerning Becher to the International Court or any of its officials." "No testimony or affidavit." Did you say that?

Kastner: Let me see. (He looks at record.) Yes, I did.

Tamir: I show you this affidavit. Is it your sworn affidavit?

Kastner: Yes.

Tamir: On page 241 of this court's record, you have said, "Every German was a robber when he had any chance to be one. And in this respect Kurt Becher was definitely no exception." Did you say that?

Kastner: Yes.

Tamir: On page 291 of this court record you agreed with me that to intercede in behalf of any high S.S. officer including Becher is a crime from our national point of view.

Kastner: Yes.

Tamir: I will read your sworn affidavit—"I, the undersigned, Dr. Rudolf Kastner, wish to make the following statement in addition to my affidavit submitted to the International Military Tribunal under document 2605 P.S. concerning former Lt. General Kurt Becher . . . There can be no doubt about it that Becher belongs to the very few S.S. leaders having the courage to oppose the program of annihilation of the Jews, and trying to rescue human lives . . . Having been in personal contact with Becher from June, 1944, to April, 1945, I should like to emphasize, on the basis of personal observations, that Kurt Becher did everything within the realm of possibilities to save innocent human beings from the blind fury of the Nazi leaders. . . .

"Therefore, even if the form and basis of our negotiations may be highly objectionable, I never doubted for one moment the good intentions of Kurt Becher. . . .

"In my opinion, when his case is judged by Allied or German authorities, Kurt Becher deserves the fullest possible consideration . . .

"I make this statement not only in my name but also in behalf of the Jewish Agency and the Jewish World Congress. Signed, Dr. Rudolf Kastner, Official Jewish Agency in Geneva. Former Chairman of Zionist Organization in Hungary, 1943–1945. Representative of Joint Distribution Committee in Budapest." [41]

Tamir comes to the end of this Mikado-like list of titles, and pauses. Judge Halevi has a question to ask. He has already heard things that have chilled his soul. Yet the "sworn affidavit" is a new shock. Judge Halevi still finds it hard to imagine a Jew making such an affidavit, and daring to lie about it in a high Israel Court.

Judge Halevi asks the red-faced Kastner, "Who gave you permission to offer this affidavit in the name of the Jewish Agency?"

Kastner: Dobkin and Barlas gave me permission to speak in the name of the Jewish Agency. And Mr. Perlzweig, chief of the political department of the World Jewish

Congress, and Mr. Riegener, European representative of the World Jewish Congress gave me permission.

(Dobkin is today one of the high chiefs of the Jewish Agency. Kastner's answer is a headache for Israel's politicoes. He has attempted to drag in the ruling clique as a co-collaborator with Nazi Becher.)

Halevi asks another question:

"Did they permit you to intervene for Becher and recommend leniency?"

> Kastner: From my talks with their officials, I understood I was permitted to make the statements I made.

Tamir resumes.

> Tamir: When you told this honorable court that you never gave any testimony or affidavit to the International Court of Nuremberg or any of its institutions, you knowingly and willfully lied.
>
> Kastner: (yelling) I deny that! What *you* are doing is a national crime!
>
> Tamir: (quietly) Well, let us consider this matter of national crime. And this is my last question to you, Dr. Kastner. You have agreed with me that any intervention by a Jewish official in behalf of a high S.S. officer, including Becher, is a national crime. Now that it has been revealed that you did exactly that, do you agree with me that you are a national criminal?
>
> Kastner: (his voice almost a whisper) That is your version.
>
> Tamir: He is your witness, Mr. Cohen.[42]

The Israeli press shook off its inhibitions and let the news be known. That is a fine thing about the Press—in a showdown, news and not authority is its idol. It will hurl its headline spears at High Priests and Oracles and set up a clamor for their scalps. And "truth must be served" becomes its battle cry.

But it is an easily winded champion of truth. All High Priests and Oracles in distress know this. They have only to keep their alibis and denials clacking away until the derogatory noises subside. And then their alibis and denials will become news again, the preferred news, the news from the highest sources —authority's spokesmen. After which the editorial writers will take over and work their magic of turning black to white again and rodent-gray to royal purple. And who knows if that isn't the best way for things to be. What a nuisance it would be to wake up every morning if truth were always on the front pages beside our breakfast coffee. It is better and more relaxing to read about earthquakes, airplane disasters, and adolescents shooting down their parents.

Now the Israeli press pointed out gloomily that it would seem that a Nazi collaborationist sat among the Jewish Cardinals of Israel. And it would seem, also, that the government of Israel was spending a fortune now trying to clear his name. Why? Wherefore? Was it also trying to clear its own name?

And other dour queries sprinkle the journals—why doesn't the State of Israel forget about Malchiel Greenwald, the inconsequential one, and go after the self-confessed Nazi helper, Rudolf Kastner? What keeps Chaim Cohen, Ben-Gurion, Moshe Sharett and all the V.I.P.'s of Jewry defending this muddy hypocrite from Kluj? Why not scuttle him? Not hang him completely, but at least put him on trial. Simple, logical questions these, which the government of Israel will never answer. But I will— at the proper time when all the evidence and documentations are in the record. I enter here only one more document that has to do with the Kastner-Becher story.

It is an affidavit signed by Walter H. Rapp, lieutenant colonel of the American army, legal officer of the State Department, and head of the Evidence Counsel of the War Crimes Council in Nuremberg; and also Deputy Chief to Brig. General Telford Taylor, Chief American Counsel in the Nuremberg tribunals. It concerns Kastner's responsibility for the S.S. officer's release.

Becher was listed as a war criminal in the American war criminal file, 221259. His listing read, "Kurt Becher, Lieutenant General S.S., Place of crime—Budapest, Mauthausen Camp. Reason wanted—torture." [43]

Advocate Rapp says:

"Kastner approached me as an official of various prominent international Jewish Agencies."

(Kastner had boasted that General Taylor had sent for him

and offered to pay his expenses as an expert on Jewish extermination matters.)

Attorney Rapp continues:

> To the best of my knowledge Kastner arrived in Nuremberg as a voluntary witness on behalf of S.S. Colonel Kurt Becher . . . and I gained a definite impression that his visit was aimed solely to assist Becher. Until the arrival of Kastner, it was highly probable that Becher would be tried by us.
>
> As a result of Kastner's pleadings and endeavors on behalf of Becher, many of my staff came to regard Becher with increasing sympathy, and personally went out of their way to assist him in every possible manner.
>
> Thus on numerous occasions I observed interrogations in friendly if not warm conversations with Becher, which conduct on the part of my staff was unprecedented and contrary to our rule in so far as members of the S.S. were concerned. Upon my inquiry for such apparently unwarranted conduct, I was given to understand that this case was an exception to the normal rule.
>
> It was the first and only time that we were furnished proof with regards to a high ranking S.S. officer; that Becher was personally instrumental in saving the lives of tens of thousands of Jews . . . at a great personal risk to himself with self sacrificing, if not heroic, acts . . .
>
> Becher's ultimate release . . . *was solely the result of Kastner's pleadings and the contents of his sworn testimony.* His affidavit regarding Becher was the main, if not the sole reason underlying our decision to free him.[44]

In the shocked court room Chaim Cohen starts striding through a re-direct examination of Dr. Kastner. He must induce witness Kastner to unsay his words that make the hierarchy into rescuers of Nazi mass-murderers.

He succeeds, after a fashion. Chaim Cohen's authoritative tones, his Torquemada bald head, his flaring black gown—symbol of learning and justice—bring courage back into Kastner's pummeled soul. What has he to fear? Chaim Cohen is on his side. So are all the solid leaders of Israel.

Kastner answers the Attorney General with his voice in order again.

> Kastner: (to Cohen) I don't think I phrased my testimony in the most truthful manner. If under the pressure of demagogic cross-examination I said here and there a few things, for which I am truly sorry today—it doesn't change my basic attitude in the matter.

What basic attitude? That it is correct to intercede in behalf of a high-up slaughterer of Jews? And that it is correct to lie about it in an Israeli court? Yes, that is Kastner's basic attitude.

> Cohen: Let's return to the affidavit you made. Had you a chance to make this affidavit today, would you make it or not?
>
> Kastner: Yes, but without the last sentence. I wouldn't make it in the name of the Jewish Agency.

Chaim Cohen's eyes flash. He has won a big point. Kastner is a liar. But only about the Jewish Agency. About everything else he tells the truth. And Chaim Cohen proceeds next to prove Dr. Kastner is the soul of honor.

> Cohen: Would you make it (the Becher affidavit) in your own name?
>
> Kastner: (proudly) Yes.
>
> Cohen: Do you think it is the duty of any honorable man to do the same, under the circumstances?
>
> Kastner: Every honorable man would do the same as I did.[45]

Presto, legal wizard Cohen has turned a shabby deed into a deed of honor. Poor Kastner, blushing and stuttering a few minutes ago as the most transparent of rogues, is again a politician talking proudly through his hat.

Item: the Chaim Cohen who considers Dr. Kastner's rescue of one of the deadliest S.S. officers "the duty of an honorable man" is the same Chaim Cohen who drafted the law making Nazi collaboration the only crime to merit the death penalty in Israel.[46]

"IN QUESTA TOMBA OSCURA?"——Dante

The shock and news value of the Becher scandal have taken their effect as Tamir expected, and the Humpty-Dumpty Government of Israel totters on its wall. But it hangs on.

All Israel may look at Kastner as if a swastika birthmark has come out on his forehead, but Ben-Gurion, Sharett, and those involved by Kastner in the "Help Becher" affidavit—the Jewish Agency, the Zionists, and Kastner's chief defender Chaim Cohen —all stand staunchly at their boy's side.

There will be many more court sessions—three years of them— other cross-examinations and "re-direct examinations," etc. But I step out of time context to fill in the Becher portrait here. A wobbly but still pompous Kastner is in the witness box.

Tamir: Of what department was Kurt Becher an official?

Kastner: The Economic Department of the Waffen S.S.

Tamir: Are you aware that the Waffen S.S. used to appropriate the clothes and belongings of the exterminated Jews?

Kastner: (angrily) I *never* heard of it! As a systematic procedure it is absolutely untrue!

Tamir: Is it true that the people of the Economic Department plucked out the gold-filled teeth of the murdered Jews?

Kastner: You are an ignoramus! That is a lie!

But it is hardly necessary for Tamir to go on with the Becher questions and Kastner denials, screams and perjuries which Lawyer Chaim Cohen obviously can't figure out how to stop. Of the small-scale robberies, and the big ones of Chief of the Economic Department, S.S. Col. Kurt Becher. Of the evidence that Becher received suitcases containing two million dollars' worth of jewelry and cash, that Becher was personally in charge of shaking down the Manfred Weiss family—the richest in Hungary and almost as rich as the Krupp clan in Germany.

It is hardly necessary for the Israeli populace—or even for the journalists engaged once more in valiantly white-washing the addle-pated rogue, Kastner.

For the Jews of Israel know the meaning of "Economic Department." Back of such German titles is a Black Encyclopedia of disaster. The Jews of Israel are its scholars. They know it by heart.

Their eyes have been profaned by the porcine Germans rooting among their holy loves, their honored dead. They know the unholy doings of the "Economic Department" and its head man—Kurt Becher.

And where is Kurt Becher now? In what place of exile, under what alias, is he hiding—as his Nazi associate Eichmann hid?

No exile, no alias, and no fears are Becher's. Kurt Becher, still tall and handsome, is one of the great men of the new Western Germany. He is one of its richest men.[47] The riches are for the most part the loot extorted and tortured out of myriads of Jews—before their slaughter. He is president of many corporations and loaded down with honors.[48]

Among the many enterprises he heads up is the sale of wheat to the government of Israel. Becher's firm, the Cologne–Handel-Gesellschaft, does a fine business with Israel's government.[49]

Herr Becher, a nobody before the Nazi war, rose to affluence as head of the S.S. Economic Department. But his wealth is no longer in gold teeth. He is associated with the great German banks that are the friends of Ben-Gurion's antique pal—Chancellor Konrad Adenauer.

WHEN THE WALTZES ENDED

I leave the court room for a while to remember the first wave of refugees from Budapest in the 1930's. They were a little world of song writers, story and play writers, actors, journalists and bon vivants that fled its beloved cafés and brought its intrigues and its goulash pots intact to the United States.

They seemed hardly refugees, for they seemed to have brought their homeland with them. Their homeland was an ego surrounded by wit and good cooking, sad waltzes and a touch of gout.

The great playwright Ferenc Molnar was one of them. A pink-skinned. gray-haired, sophisticated man with a childlike friendliness in his face. His name at the time was a symbol of the rue and irony that were truly Hungarian. Except that they were not Hungarian, at all; they were Jewish. Molnar, born Neuman, and several boat loads of fellow epigram fanciers, were Jewish talent on the run from Hungary's anti-Semite renaissance. The Germans were still in Germany, listening to speeches.

Among them, one speech by Adolf Hitler, "When we Germans are done with the Jews of Europe, no Jew will ever laugh again." [50]

I can see Germans today reading this Hitler promise and smiling contentedly. Whatever happened to Germany's other bold aims, that one about the Jew was not entirely unsuccessful.

I shall speak for myself about this German crusade to end my laughter, and let other Jews bear me out or not, as they wish.

The Germans did not end my laughter, but they changed it. Not by torturing and killing off six million Jews. Earthquakes and bacteria can do that, too. But by bringing into the open the fact that humanity has no respect for itself; that its response to human desecration is vague and even irritable; that mankind is full of passionate loyalty for its governments, and only fitful loyalty for itself.

That I belong to a species that thinks like an ant-heap in terms of its ant-heap politics and ideals; that my fellow humans are full of sickly enthusiasms for the wonders of Speed and Power, and look on God as an unpopular nuisance and on life, itself, as a secondary gift—these factors have taken the innocence out of my laughter.

I write here as a man not as a Jew; but it is from the vantage point of Jewishness that I have noted and felt the decay of decency in the world. It is the Jew who was first to lose some of his laughter, not because he must sorrow over his slain people. But because he looks into the faces of the killers and of their collaborators, and sees in their hundreds of million faces the diminished soul of the species of man. He looks and sees in them the face of tomorrow—the Atom-death face.

The unlaughing, the oddly laughing Jew—first. I am one of these. I see the meaninglessness of human tragedy in the eyes of the world, including even the eyes of its Jews. Tomorrow, all laughter will change, perhaps end. Hitler was a visionary, and visionaries are often confused by what they behold. It was not the Jew without laughter that Germany's Fuhrer saw, but the human being, laughless.

MY ONE MEDAL

It is futile, I know, to write in this fashion—of tomorrow and goodbyes to the human race. Here is one of my lighter reports on the Hungarian story.

At his favorite New York lunching place on 58th Street, that served no goulash and was innocent of paprika, Molnar once said to me,

"I find it difficult to be a Jew. It makes me feel unfaithful to something."

"To what?" I asked.

"To all the things I thought I was," said Molnar.

I have a Molnar anecdote in which I am the hero, of a sort.

During the years I worked as a spokesman for the slaughtered Jews of Europe and the fighting Jews of Palestine, I received a minimum of awards or honors—practically none.

This was no surprise, since my work entailed attacking *all* the enemies of the Jews, which included at the time, the Germans, the British, and the grand Kleagles of organized Jewry with their heads in a British sack. President Franklin D. Roosevelt was another target. Our great humanitarian had a curious blind spot toward the Jews and their problem of evading extermination.

Of the few honors that came to me for my work, the one I liked the best was from Molnar.

I was in especial public disfavor at the time for some anti-British, anti-Roosevelt and anti-Jewish Agency outcries I had helped loose in the press. I dropped in that night at the home of journalist Leonard Lyons whom I could trust never to turn up his nose at me, whatever my troubles. Leonard and his wife Sylvia were not alone. They were giving a party. Some sixty literary, theatrical, and financial luminaries sat dining at a dozen tables.

Standing in the entrance, I wondered which table group I might join and cause the least distress. I noted in the minutes I stood musing that, although I knew most of the luminaries fairly well, no eyes had been raised to me in greeting, let alone invitation. The guests were mostly Jews and Jewesses, with a few Britishers—all Top Drawer.

One figure stood up at the end of the room and walked slowly and a little dramatically toward me. It was Molnar. He took my hand, bowed over it, kissed it as if I were a dowager, and said, "Thank you."

Thus Ferenc Molnar, who found it difficult to be a Jew; but having to be one, he ran up his colors under the enemy's nose—and saluted a comrade.

"ALL, ALL OF YOU DO I REMEMBER YET—"

Farewell, Molnar and all the deft and chuckling disillusion that was Budapest once. How so whimsical a pessimism ever came to flower in so grim a place as Hungary after World War I is beyond me. Nevertheless it did. It bloomed, and Budapest was famous for a time because bright Jews joked in its cafés and filled its air with a confetti of the arts. I know, of course, that Jews are never more in danger than when they start winning medals and applause. But how blame the bird that has to sing, even though the song brings the snake to swallow it.

Farewell to that Budapest, and here's another Budapest—the Budapest of Kastner and the Jew-swallowers called the Arrow Cross; the Budapest of yellow Stars of David stitched on the left side of two hundred and fifty thousand Jewish coats.

Hungary's final Jewish difficulties began in the late 1930's.

There was a growing uproar against Jews in the Balkans and the adjoining lands of Rumania, Bessarabia, Poland, and Slovakia. The voice of the new Germany proclaiming in the language of Goethe and Schiller that Jews were fair game for murder raised anti-Semitism from hooliganism to statesmanship. And the Jews started running. They ran to Hungary, where Jews seemed safe and full of merriment.

In the 1940's the Hungarians still had two faces toward the Jews. When Regent Horthy and his regime were in power it was a benevolent face, not actively benevolent, but moodily benevolent. Although it saved no lives, it soothed the doomed.

In 1941, the "Eaters of Jews" as the Arrow Cross statesmen were fond of calling themselves, made their debut as killers. Twenty thousand Jews were gathered up from the towns and villages by this Hungarian gendarmerie (in imitation of the German S.S.), deported to Galicia, and shot to death.

Thereafter, the Jew-killing cooled off and Hungary seemed again a haven to the menaced Jews of Europe.

In 1943, Premier Kalai declared, officially, that any Jew who could obtain a visa to Palestine would be permitted to leave with his family.[51] This policy continued for almost a year. Because of the lack of visas from Palestine, only nine Jews a week were able to escape.

When Premier Sztojay and his Arrow Cross regime came to power in 1944, it was a butcher boy face that whistled for Jewish blood, abetted by the butcher faces of Imredy, Baky, Endre, Hain, Jaross, Ferenczy.

Admiral Horthy, Regent of Hungary, and his official Hungarian army were always vastly more powerful than the Arrow Cross anti-Semites. But Regent Horthy permitted "the Jew-eaters" to put on the robes of state. The noble Horthy loved God, but feared the Germans more. Throughout the bedevilment and extermination of Hungary's Jews, he remained verbally opposed to that project.

Timorous of world opinion, Horthy refused Hitler s order that Hungary slaughter its Jews.

Hitler to Horthy: "The Jews are parasites undeserving of any forebearance. They must be dealt with like tubercular germs. I see no cruelty in this, when I see that innocent animals like deer and hares are killed by the hundreds of thousands to satisfy the hunger of man. Why then should we suffer these Jewish brutes to live?" [52]

Regent Horthy retired to his palace to remain a champion of the humanities, but with his head under a pillow. There were many fine heads, including Jewish ones, under the same pillow.

In Budapest, the leaders of the Jewish Council, Shamu Stern and Pinchas Phillip von Freudiger, submitted pleas to their invisible champion, Admiral Horthy. They were, as yet, hopeful pleas:

"Just as the trials of bygone centuries, whether by fire, stake or scaffold, were unable to shake us in our faith and our loyalty, so shall we stand by our Hungarian country whose language is our language and whose history is our life."

The Jews were not quite alone in their pleading. Prominent Hungarians joined them. But none of it helped.

THE ANGUISH OF KASTNER

Among those affected by the Jew-eater edicts of 1941 was Dr. Kastner of the ancient city of Kluj. This once renowned home of Magyar royalty had doubled its Jewish population during the Rumanian pogrom. In 1941 some twenty thousand Jews and more lived in Kluj and its vicinity.

Hebrews were ousted from their Christian vocations. Kastner went to work collecting money for the Keren Hayessod (United Jewish Appeal) on a percentage basis.

But Dr. Kastner was more than a mercenary. He knew that doom had sounded for Hungary's Jews. He went to work not to make a living, but to help his people.

This is a fascinating factor about villains—that villainy was not always in them. There are some among the wicked who are born for outrage. But most are like Kastner, kindly bred, and maturing with their humanness intact.

How decency darkens into villainy, how a man's ego can drive him into the Devil's arms—these Lucifer antics are part of Kastner's story. And it is not a story out of my head. It comes out of the recorded proceedings of the Government of Israel versus Malchiel Greenwald. I add only a few stage-directions.

Unlike the Jews of Budapest, the twenty thousand Jews of Kluj were "eastern" Jews—more Jewish than Hungarian. They busied themselves with Zionism and all manner of Jewish activities.

Dr. Kastner came to Budapest and with a few friends set up a small outfit to help Jews escape from Hungary. Kastner worked at this for three years. From the beginning of his philanthropic work, however, he showed a remarkable talent for making friends with the enemies of Jews. The gendarmerie chiefs cozened to him. This popularity was to raise Dr. Kastner above the other Jewish helpers, who were liked by nobody.

Thus Kastner elbowed Komoy and other Jewish Agency officials out of his way. Leader Kastner's two chief colleagues were Joel Brand and his wife, Hanzi Brand.

Before the arrival of the Germans in 1944, the bulk of Hungary's Jews remained full of optimism about their future, and proud of their Hungarian nativity. Hadn't the gallant Premier Teleki declared (before shooting himself) that Jews were no longer Jews, but Magyars?

Dr. Kastner from Kluj had a clearer eye. As a journalist he had buzzed around German agents and Rumanians, spoken their languages, noted their ways of thought, but never deluded himself that he was one of them. Kluj had stamped him as a Jew.

Religion had nothing to do with it. Kastner had grown up in a climate of Jewish organizations. The Jews of Budapest had grown up in the climate of its cafés, theaters, sporting and social events.

In normal times these assimilated ones were a stronger and more sophisticated people than the Kastner kind of Jew. The world was their home, not Jewishness. Driven back into Jewishness, they became bewildered and pathetic.

This predicament of the assimilated Jews is part of Kastner's testimony. It will be used by him as an apologia. Later, he and the government of Israel will make it into a heartless apologia—to "explain" why eight hundred thousand Jews of Hungary had to be abandoned.

90

But now the Rudolf Kastner of 1942 is still innocent. His savvy as a journalist does not include the knowledge that the Jewish leaders of Palestine wear a British gag, that come what may Weizmann will not embarrass his British masters by crying out the news of the massacre.

In 1942, he and his colleague, Joel Brand, bombard the Jewish Agency officials in Switzerland, Constantinople, Tel Aviv, with cablegrams. They send detailed accounts of the slaughter in Europe, and of the slaughter yet to come.

In the court room, despite his dependence on the regime and Attorney Chaim Cohen, Kastner testifies:

"I learned that the Jewish Agency and Joint Distribution Committee Representatives in Switzerland, Moshe Schwalbe and Saly Mayer, did not give out information to the press about the mass killings. They failed to give the press the news I sent from Budapest. I sent cables also to the Istanbul Rescue Committee (of the Jewish Agency). They were also kept secret from the press. I informed them almost daily by cables about the pace of the extermination. My cables were never published anywhere."

Give Kastner his due. The "innocent" Kastner, beseeching that the German nightmare be publicized, begging that the world be roused by cries of moral outrage so that the killing orgy of the Germans may be stopped, was sadly correct.

If the "official" representatives of Jewry, and Franklin Roosevelt, Winston Churchill, and Joe Stalin had raised such an outcry when the killings of Jews got under way, the Germans might have let up on their gas ovens.

In fact, the first Nazi attitude toward the Jews (in the early 1930's) was one of caution. The Nazi propagandists believed then that Jewry was "a powerful world force," more potent, even, than Catholicism. They were fearful that any Jew killing would bring an avalanche of world rage on German heads. For several years the German leaders worked away trying to be rid of the Jews by shipping them off to Madagascar and even Palestine.

At the same time hundreds of books and treatises from the brain pans of Germany's finest thinkers proclaimed and demonstrated the foulness of the Jew—with no rebuttal to speak of from the philosophers of other lands. Noting this, the Germans began to suspect the potency of world Jewry and the world's affection for Jews. A conviction finally came to the Germans that Jews were wretches whom nobody loved, or would defend.

In the late 1930's, the Germans began to test this discovery. The S.S. started beating up Jews in Berlin, Munich, Frankfurt, Cologne, and other towns. Then they tried killing a few hundred here and there.

Their hunch was upheld. The killing of Jews, openly and brutally, produced no moral thunder or even noticeable objection—not from the United States, Great Britain, France, Russia. And not even from world Jewry. The Jewish Agency and World Zionism were officially silent.

THE SILENCE—AND THE DRUMS OF DEATH

There will be many witnesses to testify about this silence during Greenwald's trial, among them Professor Aktzin, dean of the Law Faculty of the Hebrew University in Jerusalem. I quote from the trial record:

> Tamir: Is it true that the Joint Distribution Committee and the Jewish Agency did suppress the news of the extermination in the United States up to and through 1944?
>
> Professor Aktzin: The Zionists, Jewish Agency and Joint Distribution Committee did refrain from publicizing in the American press the massacre of Jews.[53]

While the war was still on in 1945, a Jewish mission of survivors from Poland came to the annual meeting of the World Jewish Congress. They came with accusations, and the leaders of the Jewish Congress listened stoically to their plaint. The survivors from Poland accused these leaders of Zion of having failed to arouse the nations of the world to the fact that the Jews were being exterminated. The mission accused the leaders of Jewry of having neglected practical possibilities of rescue and help. The leaders stated that the omissions were the result of a deliberate decision. They offered as explanation "the opinion of the executive board was that it was inadvisable because of our diplomatic ties with these governments." (Of the Free World.) [54]

And so, in March, 1944, the Germans came to Budapest. They placed Regent Horthy in "castle arrest" and restored the Fascists to power under the guidance of a Nazi named Vezenmayer. Herr Vezenmayer was Hitler's personal representative, with full instructions on what to do. His job was to kill the eight hundred thousand Jews of Hungary.

It is something to look at—this German persistence in killing off a last million Jews at this time. (There were another two hundred thousand in adjoining territories.) The war was going badly for Germany. The great Allied offensives in the West, in the East and in the air, were pounding German cities into the ground, blasting German armies out of commission.

Yet the German appetite for dead Jews increased.

Never having wanted to murder people myself, I can only guess at German psychology. I make this guess. The Germans are habituated as Jew-killers. It is not too abnormal an activity for any Europeans. It has gone on for centuries, the tom-toms beating a hate for Jews. Why? Don't ask me. I am a Jew. Ask the tom-tom beaters.

As a Jew I have grown bored long ago with plumbing the minds of Jew-haters. Of this ancient line, the big-bottomed, knock-kneed, eunuchoid Hitler, screaming his Jew-hatred to millions of enraptured Germans, seemed the most mindless. Not Jewish talents, ideas or even religion were his targets—but its blood stream. If the Jewish blood were allowed to mingle with the refined Hitlerian blood, it would ruin the Germans' chances of becoming supermen. Although there were only three hundred thousand Jews in a Germany of sixty million people, the Germans agreed that the peril was acute. They decided, too, that they would not only save themselves, but all of Europe, by killing all the Jews in it.

Although these German thoughts sound as preposterous as the musings of a cuttlefish, they fired the soul of Teutonia. It was as "idealists," not murderers, that the Germans went after the Jews.

Such is their "thinking." There is a cold spot obviously in their souls that needs warming. It is a cold spot that only murder can warm.

In 1944, with their Reich collapsing, the Germans actually felt hot with triumph as long as they could continue killing Jews faster than ever before.

And so the Commandant of Auschwitz, Col. Rudolf Hoess, comes to Budapest. Col. Hoess has personally supervised the killing of more than two million Jews and Jewesses. He is a hard liquor man. Drinking with the other S.S. colonels, he gabbles about the new incinerating ovens and the new "Cyclone" gas chambers that are ready for action, thanks to German science. The day he left Auschwitz, for example, he watched twelve hundred Jews being gassed. They were dead in a few minutes. No convulsions. They just dropped dead like poisoned flies. As usual, a dozen infants survived the gassing. Their naked mothers always managed to hide them in the piles of clothing. After a gassing the Commandant and several guards had to hang around listening for tell-tale infant squeals.[55]

In a half hour the infants would be all removed from the hiding places in which their mothers had stuck them. Gas wasn't necessary for the infants. A small caliber pistol bullet in the back of the head finished them off. Sometimes, more sportively, they threw the noisy infants into a bonfire.

And after the twelve hundred were killed, Commandant Hoess gossips on, they were dumped into the new ovens and burned to an ash. General Himmler, himself, has inspected and approved the new Jew-disposal devices. Now it is up to the S.S. colonels in Budapest!

So goes the night revelry between Kameraden Hoess and Krumey, Eichmann, Becher, and Von Wisliczeny.

The colonels send Hoess back to Auschwitz with the promise that his modernized ovens will receive another million guests in the next few months.

THE MURDER CHESS GAME

Most of what I write now is in the protocol of the trial of Malchiel Greenwald in Jerusalem. I continue—as a court reporter.

The Germans could spare only a few thousand troops for their Hungarian adventure. To impress the Hungarians and the Jews, officers marched these troops in duplicate. A regiment at the end of the parade would hurry back to the starting post and appear again in the line of march as another regiment. Thus the five thousand soldiers managed, by running back and forth, to look like an endless army of Wehrmacht.

I should have thought this a childish trick. But the Germans are better militarists than I am. It worked. The anti-Nazi Hungarians (how many, I don't know) and the two hundred and fifty thousand Jews in Budapest were impressed.

The Final Solution was decided on in Berlin in 1941—total extermination of all Jews before the German military defeat put an end to the opportunity.

The S.S. Colonels in Budapest had a knotty problem to solve in carrying out their end of the work speed-up. How to capture and deport eight hundred thousand Jews for killing in Auschwitz with only 150 S.S. as foremen? And only five thousand Hungarian gendarmes.

Here in the record, as entered in the archives of the Jerusalem District Court, is the monstrous answer to this dilemma.

The only possible way of getting Hungary's Jews to Auschwitz on schedule was to keep them ignorant of their fate. Even more, to do everything possible to spread the delusion among them that the Germans in Horthy's Hungary were human folk with no murder in their eye.

The S.S. Colonels wanted no repetition of the Warsaw ghetto business. Particularly at a time like this, with no armored divisions to spare for battling Jews, defeats in Stalingrad and Africa, the Allies in Italy, the forces of Tito and Mikhailovich not far from Hungary's borders, and British and American bombers in the German skies day and night.[56]

In the trial, Dr. Kastner will admit that Eichmann told him he wished to avoid a second Warsaw. In Warsaw, in 1943, news of the destination of the deportees had seeped through the ghetto wall to them. A savage death. Whereupon, all the suffering Jews not yet slaughtered—some thirty thousand weary men and women—hurled themselves against the might of an undefeated German army numbering hundreds of thousands.

For twenty-seven days these last Jewish souls of Poland had stood with pistols and clubs and broken bottles in their hands, against German tanks, cannon, machine guns and the Luftwaffe. The Germans suffered many dead. There was a handful of Jewish survivors. The ghetto was reduced to a peaceful area of ashes and corpses.

Therefore in Budapest mum must be the word. No hint must get out of the new scientific equipment waiting in Auschwitz. The eight hundred thousand Jews must be speeded to their end —full of the delusion that pleasant employment lay before them in various farming and industrial centers.[57]

There was, also, another factor that made furtiveness a necessary technique for the quick killing of Hungarian Jewry. Unlike Poland, Hungary was no German-conquered territory. It was a semi-independent land. Five neutral embassies had their eyes open in Budapest's heart. A special representative from the Pope was on the scene, and a special mission of the International Red Cross was there. The joys of open bloodletting were impractical with this audience seemingly on watch.[58]

A last impediment to the immolation were the Jews themselves, almost a million of them who had been neither starved nor tortured into submission, but were still full of vigor, hope, and courage.

Eichmann concedes this in his confessions in 1954, while he was still at large, and published after his capture.

"With Hungary we were particularly concerned. The Hungarian Jews had lived through the war relatively untouched by severe restrictions. We wanted Hungary combed with a tremendous thoroughness before the Jews could really wake up to our plan and organize partisan resistance." [59]

The S.S. launched their Delusion offensive at a first get-together with Hungary's leaders of Jewry. Colonels Krumey and Von Wisliczeny presided. They were both shorties, under five feet six, and not intimidating to look at.

Colonel Krumey, a quick smiler, a hearty beer drinker, thick around the middle, blonde, blue-eyed and button-nosed, spoke to the Jewish leaders,

"We are here. There will be severe security degrees leveled against Jewish properties, Jewish freedom. Jews will wear yellow badges. But if you cooperate, the bad things will not happen." [60]

Again, the amiable S.S. Colonel Krumey addressed a meeting of 200 Jewish "delegates." Colonel Von Wisliczeny and Jewish leader Stern sat on each side of Krumey as he spoke:

"Everything will continue as before. Nothing must be allowed to interfere with your work or religious services. I want the rabbis to reassure the members of their congregations."

The delegates listened and grasped at the straw of life offered by this unusual S.S. colonel. They had heard of the "bad things" —firing squads, lime pits, gibbets, the mass killings. But that was in other lands. It might even be Allied Propaganda, at least in part. And they raised eyes full of hope to the smiling Krumey and Von Wisliczeny. And even to the third Colonel, Adolf Eichmann, who addressed them in his elegant Hotel Majestic headquarters. Said Eichmann:

"I will not allow Jews to be molested because they wear the Star of David, and will punish any persons involved in such outrages. I am a friend of straightforwardness, and I ask the Jewish Council to inform me frankly of any complaint it has. I, for my part, will be equally frank in my reply. I have had great experience in Jewish affairs, and it is therefore useless to try to mislead me. All I wish is to play fair with the Jews." [61]

This with the deportation and extermination of Hungary's Jews only two months away.

The German anesthetic worked on most of the Jews. There were, however, some hundreds of disbelievers in German mercy. These killed themselves.

With the Jewish leaders properly drugged, the Germans started the Jew-roundup cautiously.[62] Their objective was to concentrate batches of five to twenty thousand Jews in ghettos within easy reach of the railroad line to Auschwitz.

But the Germans smelled trouble ahead. Reports were coming in that Jewish groups were meeting in secret, trying to organize armed resistance. Other Doubting Thomases were escaping across the border to areas that offered haven for Jews. The exodus might grow.

The S.S. Colonels Becher, Krumey, and Eichmann knew what was needed to make the Final Solution deportations possible. Germans alone could not keep the doomed ones unsuspecting. A more potent drug than Nazi smiles was needed. For this Jews were needed, important, highly-connected Jews; authoritative Jews whose words could soothe Jewish fears and hog-tie the myriad of Jewish men, women and children for delivery to Auschwitz.

Enter, here, an answer to the German problem—Rudolf Kastner.

THE TENETS OF SATAN

The S.S. Colonels in Budapest invite Dr. Kastner to their headquarters. He arrives boldly, briskly, ready to make deals for Jews. He is a man of punctilio. He bristles with authority.

The Kastner personality is definitely a plus in Nazi eyes. It can be utilized. But more important than who Kastner is, is what he is. He is the representative of the Jewish Agency of Palestine, and a member of Ben-Gurion's Mapai Party.

The S.S. Colonels in Budapest, whatever their other cultural shortcomings, are up on the activities of modern Jewry. They know that the religious Jews of Hungary are a minority and that even a much smaller minority are Zionists. More, they know that only a minority of the Zionist Jews belong to the Mapai Party.

Yet, knowing these things, they select Rudolf Kastner who represents almost no Jews at all in Hungary, as the man with whom to deal. Their selection of Kastner is one of the not too-frequent evidences of German political brightness. Kastner represents the party that controls Jewish Palestine—the Mapai.

This Party has already showed that it kept its mouth shut about the slaughter of Jews in Europe—in deference to the British, who want no hullabaloo endangering their closed Palestine ports.

Head Rescuer Kastner, selected by Mapai chiefs and now also selected again by the Nazis, will serve everybody as they wish—except the eight hundred thousand Jews. He will continue the "Elite policy" of Weizmann and, after some modest protests, will be satisfied with the rescue of a selected group of six hundred.

And so, in the eyes of Hungary's Jews, the Nazis succeed in creating a great Jewish leader—by treating him as one. But another factor, independent of Nazi plotting, helps raise the little Kastner of Kluj to the great Kastner of Budapest. Hungary's assimilated Jews, the bulk of its Jewry, realize now that they are an isolated mass. They have no connections. But Dr. Kastner and his Mapai forces! Connections everywhere. Chairmen, meeting halls, executive boards in Constantinople, Geneva, Jerusalem, London, New York.

Not dreaming that the Mapai and its Zionist connections will keep silent about their catastrophe, the Jewish leaders of Hungary step aside. They give their places to Dr. Kastner.

Here is an excerpt from the trial, revealing the overnight change in Kastner's status from Jew-pleader to the mysterious figurehead. Two witnesses, Joel Brand and Bondi Gross, testify that a secret courier from Switzerland tried to bring Kastner important letters and 290,000 Swiss francs, and 59,000 (American) dollars for his rescue work. Gestapo men caught the courier with his money and letters, and turned him over to Colonel Eichmann. And Eichmann restored the money in full to Dr. Kastner. With these funds Dr. Kastner could own a car, pay wages to secretaries, finance couriers, and generally add pomp to his comings and goings as a Rescuer. He could also supply a little food and clothing to refugees.

And thus the S.S. Colonels, Eichmann, Becher, Krumey, Wisliczeny, using their 150 S.S. men, their 5,000 Hungarian gendarmerie, plus Rescuer Rudolf Kastner, start the plot that leads to Auschwitz.

The Colonels begin their work on the Hungarian boundaries away from Budapest. One of their first concentration traps is the town of Kluj, Kastner's home town. Here a batch of twenty thousand Jews is held ready for shipment. They have been moved out of their city homes into a single ghetto area. Assurances have been given them that nothing sinister is involved. All that is going to happen to the twenty thousand is that they are going to be taken by train to the German-occupied area called Kenyermeze. This is a prettily-named district. Kenyermeze in Hungarian means "Field of Bread." There they will be given jobs in factories and fields. And every Jew will be permitted to take his entire family with him.

The Germans explain that their new leniency toward Jews is a practical matter. They have learned from experience, they say, that a Jew will work harder and produce more if he has his family around him. Therefore, each Jew who goes to Kenyermeze will have with him wife, parents, sisters, grandparents and children down to his newest born.

The twenty thousand Jews cooped up in the Kluj ghetto believe this German fairy tale. They discuss it day and night. The Germans are evidently hard-pressed in the war. They need to step up their war production. And they have decided that live Jews are more helpful than dead ones. A wise decision, and an understandable one. There is tension, hardship, anxiety in Kluj —but not great fear of death.

A first twelve hundred leave for Kenyermeze on the special trains the Germans have provided. And the Jews of Kluj wait tensely to hear news from them. The news comes on postal cards, in brief letters. Kenyermeze is a fine place. The work is fine. The food and lodging, fine. And love to all.

The letters are forgeries. There are no Jews in Kenyermeze. The twelve hundred who rode off eagerly on the first train are ashes in Auschwitz.

In Budapest, the S.S. Colonels promote Dr. Kastner to full status as a human being, no yellow Star of David, an automobile, telephones in his home and office, and freedom of travel in Budapest.[63]

Despite the promotion, a mishap occurs. Kastner is arrested by the Hungarians. They do not like the picture of a Jew without a yellow badge darting around Budapest in an automobile, apparently helping Jews.

KASTNER INTO FAUST

Hitler's personal representative in Hungary, Herr Vezenmayer, intercedes and gets Kastner out of jail.[64] No fool, Kastner. He makes a good guess at the meaning of this sign of Nazi good will. He will later write in his report to the Jewish Agency in Tel Aviv,

> Against our will, we had to tell ourselves that if Eichmann helps, if he does us small favors, if Hitler's personal representative, Vezenmayer, intervenes for us with the Hungarian Government, it is certain they do not do it on their own decision. It must be that they are obeying a higher German authority. It is obvious that we, the Rescue Committee, have a place in their plans.[65]

Kastner has spotted Satan's forked tail, and now stands transfixed.

He has closed a deal with Krumey, Eichmann, and Wisliczeny. They have agreed to let him pick out six hundred Jews for rescue; three hundred from Budapest, three hundred from outlying towns. The six hundred will be sent off to the Free World.[66]

With Eichmann's approval, Dr. Kastner alters the original deal somewhat. Instead of picking Jews from any "outlying towns," he picks three hundred and eighty-eight Jews from Kruj alone. They are the "best," the most important members of Kluj Jewry—mainly Zionists. He includes also his own family.

The news of Kastner's first victory is hailed by the Jews—religious, unreligious, organized, unorganized. Kastner has breached the Nazi wall of Jew hatred. He has liberated Jews.

It is at this hour of triumph that the "good" Kastner begins to dim out. Or maybe he has already vanished in smoke. I don't know. Kastner's own tortured admissions in Jerusalem will offer no date of the change. Worse, no psychological explanation. They will offer only the following facts:

Krumey sends him to Kluj on a mission to reassure and cheer the doomed ones.

Rudolf Kastner knows the truth about the death trains to "Kenyermeze." Kastner knows the truth about the Final Solution, about the S.S. plan to deport all the eight hundred thousand Jews of Hungary to Auschwitz for cremation.

I am not guessing here at what Kastner knows. It is what he will admit in the Jerusalem Court. He will say that when he came to Kluj he knew that the deportation of his townsmen to Auschwitz was about to begin.

This incident has great mystery in it, chiefly the mystery of Hermann Krumey. Colonel Krumey knows that Kastner is aware of the S.S. program for deporting Hungary's Jews to Auschwitz for extermination. Krumey is aware that Kastner knows that the twenty thousand Kluj Jews are headed for the "Cyclone" gas chambers. And the Jews in Kluj are cut off from telephone, transport and all information media.

If Kastner breathes a word of this truth to a single condemned Jew in Kluj, the entire Final Solution will be wrecked. The twenty thousand Jews of Kluj will knock over their handful of guards and escape to Rumania, three miles away.

Yet Colonel Krumey sends Kastner to Kluj, to move alone among the twenty thousand doomed men, women and children.

I stare at this moment of leavetaking between Kastner and Krumey. The Jerusalem Court record has nothing to offer on the mystery of Krumey's incredible trust in Kastner, other than that it existed.

Is Krumey so brilliant a Mephistopheles that he can see to the bottom of Kastner's soul—in so brief an acquaintance with it? Or did Kastner assure Krumey on his honor as a Jew that he would drop no hint in Kluj of the shameful death awaiting his fellow Jews? And if Kastner made such a vow, why should Krumey believe he would keep it?

What is the hellish truth behind not only Krumey's certainty, but the certainty of Eichmann and all the other Jew-killers who let Kastner ride off to Kluj, convinced that he will keep his mouth shut?

Rudolf Kastner comes to Kluj. What a welcome! For weeks the Kluj people have been talking about "their" Dr. Kastner. He i their own, born in Kluj, reared among them If only he woulc come and tell them what was true, what was untrue, everybody could sleep better.

Hope fills the Jews of Kluj. Rudolf Kastner has not forgotten his own. Famous though he has become, he is here to help them!

Kastner walks among the twenty thousand Jews in the town. He sits among the old Hebrew scholars and their young students. He attends meetings, renews old friendships.

And here is an item from which my pencil shrinks. There are only twenty Hungarian gendarmes and one German S.S. officer guarding the twenty thousand people in the ghetto.[67] And there are thousands of able-bodied young Jews among the condemned. The border, and freedom, are only three miles away.

Hopeful Jews of Kluj with their great man back among them. Now, thank God, they will find out the truth.

There is a little trouble hatching here and there in basements. Hotheads are talking resistance and escape to Rumania. The Rumanian hussars are no longer occupied in slaughtering Jews. They are getting their own heads blown off on the Russian front. Escape is easy. There are only twenty-one guards to overcome.

Dr. Kastner, moving among the muscled young ones of Kluj, helps cool the trouble makers down. He has the Zionist organization to help him. In Kluj the Zionists are the leaders of Jewry. And the head man of all the Kluj Zionists is Dr. Joseph Fisher, father-in-law of Rudolf Kastner.

Kastner takes no chances on the Auschwitz death plan leaking out. He does not even confide it to his father-in-law or to the group his eminent relative assembles to help cheer the waiting ones. Kastner tells this elite number that they have been selected to go to "a better place" than the one to which the remaining 19,620 Jews are to be taken.

Dr. Fisher and his select group might have alerted their townsmen to action, but Kastner and the German strategists succeed. They fool them.[68]

I was far away from Kluj at the time, but I can hear Kastner's words to the young, hotheaded Jews; and the oratory of his fellow Zionists. They are like the speeches that Weizmann and Ben-Gurion uncorked at their rallies in Tel Aviv, about how to behave toward the British enemy in Palestine. No resistance. No gangster terrorism. A hand raised against the British is a hand raised against the Jews. Any violence jeopardizes the very existence of Jewry! Will bring ruin to all the dreams and achievements of Zionism.

Thus in Palestine. And here, now, in Kluj—again, no resistance! We are your leaders. You have nothing to fear. Everything is under control. Do not listen to the hotheads. We, your leaders, are the only ones who can save your lives.

Authority speaks. The wise tongues wag. The respected ones dazzle their twenty thousand listeners with their respectability. And the day is saved—for authority. They will ride off to life, their twenty thousand listeners to death.[69]

"THE SERVICE OF HIS PEOPLE"

A remarkable monster of a Kastner returns to Budapest. He has done what he had guessed, despairingly, the Nazis would try to make him do—help exterminate the Jews. His silence in Kluj was a death sentence for twenty thousand, minus three hundred.

Yet there is no despair now in Kastner. No guilt.

He does not pale or hang his head. He does not find it hard to sleep at night. He walks as briskly as ever, and he is full of pride. For he is a greater man than ever before in Budapest.

The Jews in Budapest shake his hand. They know nothing of their own future travels. The ride to Auschwitz is a secret between Kastner and Eichmann, between the Jewish Agency chieftain and the Nazi chieftain.

The twenty thousand Jews of Kluj are jammed now into a brick factory. And now Kastner soothes them from Budapest— over the telephone. The Nazis allow him to make ten phone calls to his father-in-law, Dr. Fisher. The Nazis let him talk to Kluj, and still he gives no warning. This is the last contact, before going to their deaths, that the twenty thousand Jews of Kluj have with their Jewish Agency rescuer.

But here is Israel's Attorney General Chaim Cohen summing up before Judge Halevi, after all this evidence is in: "There is not an iota of proof that Kastner became a collaborator. The good intention never left him to the end. Not only did it not leave him, it was not even lessened an iota. It has been proven beyond any doubt, from the first moment to the last, including his testimony given for Becher, that Kastner had in his heart one thing only—the service of his people." [70]

"NOW FORGE THYSELF A HEART, O MAN, AND COME AND WALK THE TOWN OF SLAUGHTER."
Bialik

The betrayal of Kluj comes by accident into the trial. Tamir has heard that the Israel police once quizzed Kastner about his rescue work in Kluj. The police files on the matter are unavailable. But Kastner is available. Tamir piles question on question and pulls part of the truth out of Kastner. And the name KLUJ begins to grow.

As the incredible tale takes form, Tamir fills it with living characters. He finds twenty witnesses who are among the few of Kluj who escaped Kastner and the ash barrels of Auschwitz. The twenty of Kluj tell their stories from the witness stand.

Jacob Freifeld of Kluj testifies. Freifeld and his family went on one of the early trains to "Kenyermeze." They arrived in Auschwitz. Freifeld escaped. His family was incinerated. He tells Judge Halevi:

> Freifeld: After the first train load left Kluj, all the Jews were assembled in the ghetto. Kohani [one of Kastner's group] jumped up on a platform and read aloud a letter he said was from a Jewish family in Kenyermeze. The letter said the whole family was working at good jobs and were all in good health and being well taken care of.

105

I had a friend, Hillel Danzig. We worked together earlier in the Ukraine camps. In Kluj I asked him, "What's the truth about those letters Kohani read in public. Are they really true?" He told me, "Yes, they're true." And he gave me a tip I should try to go to Kenyermeze as soon as I could. Because the first arrivals there would get the best places. So I decided to go on the next train—instead of waiting for the last one. Yes, we all hurried to get to Kenyermeze.

Tamir: Were you taken to Auschwitz on the train?

Freifeld: Yes.

Tamir: Did Hillel Danzig go to Auschwitz?

Freifeld: God forbid. How could such a thing happen! He was a member of the Jewish Council—working hard with that clique. So he remained with the saviors—safe. My own whole family—ten people—were exterminated.

Judge Halevi: You believe that your friend sent you intentionally to your death, and the killing of your whole family?

Freifeld: It is hard to believe he would do such a thing. But he did. They all did it to save themselves.

Judge Halevi: Knowingly sent you and your family to death?

Freifeld: I can't imagine that the people with whom I suffered would send me intentionally to die in Auschwitz. But I don't know what Danzig's political aim was in separating the masses from the leaders.

Danzig was a Zionist big shot in Kluj. He was taken to Budapest and later to safety, with the 388 saved ones. At the time Freifeld testifies, he is a leading Israeli journalist, one of the literary stars on Ben-Gurion's paper, *Davar*.

A peppery Danzig writes a letter to Judge Halevi denying the whole Freifeld story: "I do not know a man named Freifeld and I can remember no such incidents." [71]

The Israeli government remains uninterested in Mr. Danzig, the alleged collaborator. It is Judge Halevi who invites the perturbed journalist to back up his letter in court under oath.

Danzig, short and suave, enters the witness box.

106

The Judge asks Jacob Freifeld to stand up. He does, and identifies the witness as the Hillel Danzig he knew, to his sorrow, in Kluj.

Halevi asks Danzig, "Do you know this Jacob Freifeld? Can you identify him as the man you knew in Kluj?"

Journalist Danzig faces the man who has accused him of helping murder his family of ten to save his own skin. After a pause, Danzig answers in a manner which affirms, denies and befogs a topic in a single sentence.

> Danzig: I never knew him in Kluj, and I don't remember any such name. But now that I see him I remember him as one of the men with me in the labor camp in Russia [a German camp].
>
> Judge Halevi: Your letter denies the truth of his testimony.
>
> Danzig: I can only repeat what I said in my letter. Freifeld's charge that I hurried him and his family to their deaths is preposterous.
>
> Tamir: Freifeld said that you definitely told him that the trains go to Kenyermeze.
>
> Danzig: That is a lie.
>
> Tamir: What reason can Freifeld, who suffered with you in the labor camp, have to lie?
>
> Danzig: The circumstances by which he came to give this testimony require clarification. I don't think it was he who decided to testify.
>
> Tamir: Was he bought? Was he bribed with money? What is your assumption, Mr. Danzig?
>
> Danzig: I don't know.
>
> Tamir: I put it to you that Freifeld tells these facts about Kluj and about you to his friends everywhere for the last six years.
>
> Danzig: How does it happen that such talk did not reach me?
>
> Tamir: You have refused to hear many things, Mr. Danzig.

Under persistent querying by Tamir, Danzig reluctantly admits that he knew he was being taken "to a safe place," and he knew, also, that people like Freifeld would be taken to "a place much worse."

Tamir pursues this important point—Danzig's information.

Tamir: You met Kastner when he came to Kluj. What did you hear from him?
Danzig: That the situation was grave.
Tamir: Drop your editorial clichés. Did Kastner tell you they were going to the gas chambers of Auschwitz?
Danzig: No.[72]

When Danzig has departed the court room, the fact has been clarified—Kastner told no one, not even his Agency chum Danzig, of Destination Auschwitz. But, just as witness Freifeld said, the Important Ones peddled the Kenyermeze myth.

Jacob Freifeld sits glaring after the dapper Danzig, and all the dead of Kluj glare out of his eyes.

The same fact is established by the next witness, Yechiel Shmueli—from Kluj. He is now an official in an Israeli Army camp.

Dark-haired, calm of manner, but with staring black eyes, Shmueli, from Kluj, answers Tamir's questions in a soft voice.

Tamir: When were you taken into the Kluj ghetto?
Shmueli: May 23, 1944.
Tamir: Did you know at this time that Jews were being exterminated in Auschwitz?
Shmueli: No.
Tamir: Did you oñer ny resistance when you were put on the train?
Shmueli: No. Because we had all been told we were being taken to Kenyermeze to work. The Jews in charge of the ghetto said to us, "Brothers, you should know that the Hungarian authorities have decided to empty Kenyermeze of its population, and all the Jews of Hungary are going to be placed there until the end of the war."
Tamir: What happened to you and your family in Auschwitz?
Shmueli: They separated us. I was sent to Warsaw to work in a factory. My mother, wife, daughter and six-year-old grandson were murdered by the Germans.[73]

Joseph Katz, a lawyer from the town of Nodvarod, four miles

from the Rumania border, testifies. He says the twenty thousand Jews of Nodvarod knew nothing of the extermination program. He had been told the Jews were being resettled, for their own good, in Kenyermeze.

> Tamir: Did you know how to use arms?
>
> Katz: Yes. It was easy to escape into Rumania. Jews were safe in Rumania at that time. Some skeptics did escape —because they didn't like the Nodvarod atmosphere. I was sent to Auschwitz and put to work in a large tailoring shop.
>
> Tamir: What sort of a tailor shop was it?
>
> Katz: The clothes of the exterminated Jews were stored there. We were given the clothes to repair.[74]

David Rozner, a steel mill owner from Kluj, now a member of Ben-Gurion's party, Mapai, testifies:

> Tamir: When you returned to Kluj after the war, what was the general opinion there of Dr. Kastner?
>
> Rozner: There was a violent feeling against Dr. Kastner. If he had showed himself in the street he would have been killed.
>
> Judge Halevi: Why do you say that?
>
> Rozner: Because he was the man who misled the Jews to believe in the good intentions of the Germans.[75]

Witness Levi Blum has some additional details. Blum is a workman and a member of the Zionist party. He tells of a celebration for Kastner held in Tel Aviv in 1948, by the List People of the train. Blum had stood listening to speeches lauding the "heroic Jew-rescuer, Dr. Kastner."

> Blum: Finally, I couldn't stand it any more. I jumped up and yelled out, "You people are making a big mistake about this Kastner. He was the only Jew who was a close friend of the Nazis and Eichmann." And I yelled at Kastner, "You were a Quisling! You were a murderer! You can sue me for what I say! I'm too poor to take you into court. But I dare you to take me." I also told him, "I know that you, Kastner, are to blame for the Jews of Hungary

109

going to Auschwitz. You knew what the Germans were doing to them. And you kept your mouth shut." Kastner didn't answer me. I asked him, "Why did you distribute post cards from Jews supposed to be in Kenyermeze?" Somebody yelled out, "This was done by Kohani, one of Kastner's men."

Kohani was also in the hall. He jumped up and yelled, "Yes, I got those post cards." I asked him, "Who were they from?" He answered, "That's none of your business. I don't have to explain what I do to you."

Judge Halevi: All this happened in public?

Blum: Yes, several hundred people were there.[76]

The little parade of Kluj survivors continues to stare at Kastner from the witness box, curse and revile him as a Nazi collaborator and the dark Angel of Death.

LOOK HOMEWARD, DARK ANGEL

On March 1, 1954, a day of unusual frost for Israel, Dr. Kastner enters Judge Halevi's court room. Tamir cross-examines.

It is a different Kastner than the one who opened the trial, but not too different. Exposure as a liar, and as the Jewish official who saved Himmler's chief aid, S.S. Lieutenant General Kurt Becher, has not taken the steam out of him. People may scowl at him in the street, in the court, but Dr. Kastner has his admirers. Who? The finest people in Israel—the ministers, caliphs, cardinals, satraps and politicniks. They are on Kastner's side, to a man; behind him like the spirit of his Fathers, around him like a Roman phalanx. So what matter exposure, dead Jews, lies, Nazi palship, Becher, Krumey, more dead Jews, more lies—what matter these things if a man has fine, true friends who will never desert him, who may even reward him with a higher post when this stupid trial is done?

Nevertheless, there is some change in our Kastner. His smile

110

looks a little insincere, like the pugilist's smile of assurance before
his eyes begin to glaze.

Now the assault.

Tamir: Is it true you were interrogated by the Israeli police,
Dr. Kastner?

Kastner: Yes.

Tamir: When?

Kastner: Three years ago.

Tamir: Did they ask you about the ghetto of Kluj?

Kastner: Yes.

Tamir: Why did the police question you three years ago
about Kluj?

Kastner: I wasn't interested enough to ask them their reason.

Tamir: Don't you know that it was exactly at that time
that the Israeli law against Nazi criminals and their collaborators was enacted? [The law provided a death penalty.]

Kastner: Oh, yes, I knew such a law was enacted at the
time.

Tamir: Weren't you interested in a possible connection
between that new law and your police interrogation?

Kastner: I wasn't at all interested in this subject.

Tamir: Is it true that the police interrogated you about the
accusations that as a result of your activities the Jews of
Kluj did not escape over the border?

Kastner: No, it is not true.

Tamir: What, then, did the police question you about?

Kastner: They asked me if I knew what had happened in
the Kluj ghetto—and why some people think there was a
connection between the deportation of the Jewish community from Kluj and the rescue of this group. [The 388
Zionists.]

Tamir: Dr. Kastner, I put it to you, that while the 20,000
Jews of Kluj were being shipped to the gas chambers,
your Rescue Committee in Kluj was busy compiling its
list of 388 who would be saved.

Kastner: True.

Tamir: And I further put it to you, that you and your

111

Rescue Committee in Kluj never advised the Jews to resist with weapons or without?

Kastner: (rather eerily) I never heard of such a thing.

Tamir: And you knew at that time the true significance of the deportation to Auschwitz?

Kastner: I knew.

Tamir: And when you talked to the leader of the Jewish Committee in Kluj did you advise him to organize resistance?

Kastner: No, I did not.

Tamir: How do you account for the fact that more people were selected from Kluj to be rescued than from any other Hungarian town?

Kastner: That had nothing to do with me.

Tamir: I put it to you that you specifically requested favoritism for your people in Kluj from Eichmann.

Kastner: Yes, I asked it specifically.

Kastner had "nothing to do with that," and he "asked it specifically." Prosecutor Tell scowls nervously at the contradiction, but says nothing.

Tamir: Was there a branch of your Rescue Committee in Kluj, Dr. Kastner?

Kastner: Not formally, but a few people were active.

Tamir: Their names?

Kastner: I remember Dr. Marton and Hillel Danzig.

Tamir: They were under your guidance?

Kastner: Yes, morally. All the local Rescue Committees were under my jurisdiction.

Tamir: Committees! You speak in the plural.

Kastner: Yes—wherever they existed.

Tamir: Where else except in Kluj was there such a committee?

(Kastner stares at his past made of lies and vainglory. The sharp voice of Tamir frightens the fantasy out of his head.)

Kastner: Well, I think the committee in Kluj was the only one in Hungary.

(With this answer, ten years of Kastner's bragging of his widespread Rescue Committees all over Hungary take the count.

In the court room, not in the offices of government. Sharett and Ben-Gurion will revive the Kastner boast as soon as they feel that people have forgotten its clobbering.)

> Tamir: Did your Budapest committee contact other towns on the telephone?
> Kastner: I didn't personally. But there was a special sub-committee which dealt with these matters.

(The Kastner eyes clear for a moment and his political strut returns as he talks of "sub-committees" and "dealt with these matters." When a politician can throw a few pompous phrases into the chopper, he feels he is on solid ground.)

> Tamir: Did the members of your sub-committee telephone to the other towns of Hungary?
> Kastner: I don't know.
> Tamir: You were able to telephone Kluj?
> Kastner: Yes.
> Tamir: And what about telephoning to all the other Hungarian towns in which a half million Jews were about to be deported?
> Kastner: Maybe some other members of my committee were able to telephone other towns. I don't know.
> Tamir: Did your sub-committee in Budapest report to you on their activities?
> Kastner: Yes, of course.
> Tamir: Was the telephone of the sub-committee at your disposal?
> Kastner: What for?
> Tamir: I wish to know, could you talk over the phone with the towns and villages of Hungary?
> Kastner: What for?
> Tamir: I put it to you, Dr. Kastner, that you could have used the telephone to call the towns and villages of Hungary.
> Kastner: Yes.
> Tamir: Did you talk to any other town than Kluj?
> Kastner: I? No, I didn't manage to. I couldn't do everything myself. So I concentrated on Kluj, for obvious reasons.

Tamir: Dr. Kastner, you could have phoned the other towns, just as you phoned Kluj?

Kastner: Yes, that's right.

Tamir: Then why didn't you contact the Jews of all these towns on the phone to warn them?

Kastner: I didn't because I didn't have time enough.

Tamir: If you were so busy with your political activities, why didn't you assign the task to another Rescue worker less busy than yourself?

Kastner: That was impossible.

Tamir: Let us sum it all up—you had the opportunity of communicating with all the towns of Hungary.

Kastner: Yes.

Tamir: And you, Rudolf Kastner, head of the Hungarian Jewish Agency Rescue Committee, do not know if any of your assistants tried to warn the Jews of Hungary.

Kastner: (wildly) I can't remember.

(Kastner's voice is a scream. His eyes roll and he looks like a man about to jump out of a window. Prosecutor Tell rushes in with the smelling salts.)

Tell: (jumping to his feet) This is torturing a witness! This man will have to be carried out of here on a stretcher. It is pure torture!

Tamir: If simple questions become torture because the witness is struggling to avoid answering them truthfully, the fault is not mine.

Judge Halevi: Don't you feel well, Dr. Kastner?

Kastner: I'm nervous.

Halevi orders the court recessed. When the hearing resumes in a half hour, the Judge instructs Court Clerk Shlomo to fetch a chair for the witness.

Judge Halevi: You may proceed with your questioning.

Tamir: How many times did you visit Kluj?

Kastner: Twice.

Tamir: You could go to other towns, if you were able to go twice to Kluj?

Kastner: A Jew was not allowed to travel.

114

Tamir: But you traveled to Kluj?

Kastner: I received a special permit to go to Kluj.

Tamir: From whom?

Kastner: Once from Krumey and once from the Hungarians.

Tamir: What arguments did you offer to get these special permits?

Kastner: I said I had to go for personal reasons.

Tamir: And that was enough to persuade them?

Kastner: Yes.

Tamir: In that case you could have asked for a permit to go to other towns as well.

Kastner: Yes, it was possible.

(Tamir leaves the admission hanging in the air.)

Tamir: Is it true, Dr. Kastner, that some people in Budapest warned you that all your negotiations with Eichmann were only for the purpose of distracting the Jews from the knowledge of their extermination?

Kastner: Yes, there were such opinions expressed. And I also felt the same thing in my heart.[77]

(Not "knew it in his brain" but sensed it in his heart. The contents of a heart cannot be used as evidence against its sensitive owner. Kastner is trying to spar with Tamir, but his sweating forehead and rolling eyes betray his near collapse.)

Tamir steps away.

He has proved this part of his case—that Kastner knew the doom awaiting the Jews of Kluj, and gave them no hint of warning—no hint even to his father-in-law or to eminent Klujians like Hillel Danzig. Tamir does not want to give Kastner a chance to deny his guilt, and withholds therefore, the question that must bring a final confession or denial.

115

A JUDGE SPEAKS IN ISRAEL

Not so, Judge Halevi. His Honor knows the missing question. He will have a verdict to deliver, not only on Greenwald, but on Witness Kastner. Halevi wants to be certain that Kastner is given every chance to deny his guilt, as well as affirm it. Who knows but what in the labyrinth of the Kastner mind there may be a hidden fact of his innocence?

Judge Halevi asks the question:

> Judge Halevi: (slowly and distinctly) Did you tell anybody in Kluj what you knew about the extermination that was going on in Auschwitz?

All Israel has been waiting for the answer, from Kastner and from nobody else; did Kastner warn any of the eight hundred thousand Hungarian Jews of their impending annihilation?

Kastner pales. His throat dries. His eyes stare, as much into the future as into the past. They both have the taste of death in them.

> Kastner: I beg the court's permission to explain. I cannot answer in one word. Those whom I contacted heard me say what the Germans were doing to Jews in Poland and Russia.
>
> Judge Halevi: (sternly) That was not my question. Did you tell anyone that the Germans were preparing the deportation of Hungary's Jews to Auschwitz?
>
> Kastner: I had no definite knowledge. I heard rumors in Budapest spread by the Germans and Hungarians about resettling the Jews in Kenyermeze. We all tried to check these rumors.
>
> Judge Halevi: But you said yourself that at the end of April you knew that the gas chambers and crematoria were ready in Auschwitz. And that the train schedule for deportation to Auschwitz had been fixed.

116

Kastner: I couldn't check all the rumors.

Judge Halevi: But Joel Brand, who left Budapest on May 17, told everybody in Istanbul that twelve thousand Jews were being deported daily from Hungary to Auschwitz.

Kastner: I don't know on what he based that statement.

Judge Halevi: It was based on what Adolf Eichmann had told him on their meeting, after which you met Brand.

Kastner: But Eichmann said he would wait two weeks for Brand's answer before doing anything.

Judge Halevi: (intently) And then start the extermination after two weeks at the rate of twelve thousand a day.

Kastner: Yes. I don't know whether he knew the rate.

Judge Halevi: He testified in court that he knew it. And that you knew it as well.

Kastner: My hopes were dispersed only at the end of May. Until then I thought—maybe not—maybe not so many.

Judge Halevi: Every day a train left after the middle of May—sealed trains that went to Auschwitz. Did you know that?

Kastner: Yes. After the middle of May I knew that as a fact.

This is Kastner's second admission to shake Israel. Kastner, himself, says he knew! (And warned no one!) Judge Halevi carefully rephrases the ominous question.

Judge Halevi: Why didn't you inform the Jews of Kluj of what you knew? I want to hear your answer, Dr. Kastner.

Kastner: (faintly) I told them everything I knew—when I was in contact with them—later I was in contact only with my father-in-law. And I dared give only one clear hint. He had to know that there was deportation and that extermination would follow.

Judge Halevi: Then why didn't the Jews of Kluj know about all that?

Dr. Kastner breathes unevenly.

Kastner: Your Honor asks me—

Kastner stops before the monstrous question. There is pathos in his pause. His Honor asks him if he is an evil man, a Jew

117

who helped Nazis slaughter his own people. How can one answer such a question without giving the wrong impression of himself and of all the Great Ones of Israel's government? But suddenly, Kastner's double talk dries up in his mouth, and he is too frightened to lie any more. A panic-headed politician is left in the witness box, full of wobbly alibis, horrid confessions blurted out, and followed by screams of innocence.

> Kastner: Your Honor, I think that my colleagues in Kluj, including my father-in-law, did not do all in their power —did not do all that could have been done—all that they had to do.

The buck is passed by Dr. Kastner to his mysterious underlings, who took orders only from Dr. Kastner, according to his own testimony. Kastner, himself, recognizes the stupidity of his answer. He tries another.

> Kastner: On the other hand, Your Honor, I am sorry to say that the witnesses from Kluj who testified here—in my opinion, I don't think they represent the true Jewry of Kluj. For it is not a coincidence that there was not a single important figure among them.[78]

ENTER A HEROINE, THANK GOD

But I am weary of writing of evil and human rot—at least for a time.

I invite the reader to look at Hanna Senesh with me and smile as one smiles gratefully at the glow of valor that heroes and heroines bequeath us.

Battlefields provide us with enough young heroes dying bravely, and often even for their convictions. But the count is meager of those whose spirits survive brutality in isolation and who stand up to death in loneliness.

Here is the story of Hanna Senesh, born in Budapest in July, 1921, and executed by a Hungarian firing squad in November,

1944. Her young bones lie in Israel with one of the poems she wrote as her epitaph:
"Happy the match,
Consumed kindling a flame." [79]
The facts of the story, and its Kastner epilogue, are part of the Jerusalem trial. I add a few grateful words in my report. Hanna's parents were of old Hungarian stock; Jews, but nevertheless Hungarians. They owned a silverware and jewelry shop, but business was a minor issue in their lives. Literature was their world. Hanna's father, Bela Senesh, was a writer; not quite a playwright, but the next best thing—a critic. He wrote for *Theater Life*, an exuberant periodical run by the wittiest of Hungarian editors, Sandor Ince—also a Jew.

Ince, a New Yorker since 1939, told me about the Senesh family. His friend, Bela Senesh, was a humorous writer, gentle and ironic, who died in 1929. His wife, Catherina, was a woman of elegance and fine looks. Ince remembers their daughter Hanna—a poetic face, a wand-like body and long brown hair.

In 1939, when things began to look bad for the Jews of Budapest, fifteen-year-old Hanna surprised her friends by announcing that she had become a Jewess. The Seneshes had always been Jews, but without taking notice of it, as with most of the sophisticated ones who were their friends. It is not unpleasant to be a Jew when Jewishness is only a flower in your lapel, and not yet a yellow badge.

Hanna recorded the announcement in the diary she was to keep until the days of her martyrdom. She wrote:
"I am a Zionist. I feel now that I am a conscious Jew. With all my heart I am proud of my Judaism and I plan to migrate to Eretz-Israel to participate in its up-building. I will begin to study Hebrew." [80]

A year later Hanna migrated and arrived in Palestine to help its up-building. Her mother remained in Budapest, lonely for her daughter, but happy that she was out of danger.

From her diary, poems, and the memories of those who knew her, comes a picture of a pretty face, a merry voice and the somewhat smug seriousness of the convert. Disdaining a life of ease for which she had funds, pioneer Hanna found delight in digging soil and scrubbing floors in a Kibbutz. My apologies for the word *smug*. I have almost forgotten that patriotism is like that when we are young. We add to our joy of life the name of a country, as we add to our gratitude for earth and sky the name of God.

In these days of celebration Hanna wrote a poem titled "Walk to Caesarea." It reads:

> Dear God, that these should never end—
> The world, the sand, the sea,
> The sound of water, the prayers of men,
> The thunder of heaven.
> Oh, Lord, that these things shall never end—
> The sand and the sea,
> The sighing of the little river,
> The lightning in the skies—
> And man's belief in man-to-be.[81]

All youth is half verse. It sings away of its bright hopes until hurt comes. Letters from Budapest began to disturb Hanna. They were gallantly phrased letters, particularly those from her mother; no clamor in them.

But Hanna read that there were new anti-Jewish edicts in Budapest, that the Arrow Cross was gaining power . . . Regent Horthy was due for another eclipse . . . in which case the anti-Semitic devils would be loose in the streets . . . and there was the nightmare rumor about the Germans coming.

Though there was silence in Eretz-Israel on this subject of Hungary's menaced Jews, Hanna understood the horror that was a short time away. Politicians can ignore the peril of others, but not a poetess whose heart responds to the sighing of a little river.

The dream of the up-building of the new Jewish land gave place in Hanna's soul to something móre insistent—a need to go back to Budapest and help save the luckless ones. Hanna saw all its Jews in her heart—the old ones of the synagogues whom she had hardly known; the bright ones who had debated in the Senesh house on Molnar, Altenberg, Schnitzler, and the wonders of Lili Darvas' voice crossing the footlights; and the thousands of girls like herself, bright with youth and waiting for love. All these would be brutally killed. A need to go to them grew in

120

Hanna until there was no other thought or dream in her. But how?

God was good. News came to Hanna that the British were training Jewish parachutists in Cairo to rescue the Jews of Hungary and the Balkans. Some of the parachutists would be dropped secretly near the Hungarian border, make their way into Hungary, and function as a British underground for the rescue of Jews.

This was an odd thing for the British to be doing at a time when they were driving Jewish refugees from the shores of Palestine with shot and shell. But the British are never entirely insensitive. Their manners are usually correct even if their policies aren't. And something, decidedly, was called for—in the way of a decent gesture, eh what?

Thus it befell that the British Army undertook to train seventeen Jews as parachutists—to save the million Jews still alive in Hungary and the Balkans. The sarcastic note is mine, not Hanna's. Miss Senesh would have been grateful if the British had undertaken to train only one Jew—herself.

A happier parachute-trainee than Hanna was never seen at any army base. She made her practice leaps out of the clouds as if she were learning a new hop-scotch game. She sat bearing in her Cairo quarters, uniformed and impatient. Her training done, Hanna awaited orders for the parachute mission. She writes in her diary at this time:

I may be called very soon. I often ask myself, how can I leave the country and our freedom? I must drink in as much fresh air as possible so that I may be able to breathe in the stifling *galut* atmosphere, and spread the air among those who have not had a whiff of liberty for so long. I am fully aware of the hardships and dangers involved, but somehow I believe I shall be able to fulfill my mission.

I consider all that has happened up to this point merely a preparation for my task. I am waiting to be called. I can think of nothing else.

It seems to me that those about me do not sense the change in me. I go on with my daily work, but it seems as if everything that surrounds me were so distant. I don't want to have too much contact with the people around me. It will make it easier to leave.

No, that is a lie. Now, especially, I would like to have someone close.

I have only one desire—that the period of waiting shall not drag out.

I am afraid of nothing. I have confidence in myself and am ready for anything. I am a soldier. I want to believe that all I have done and will do is as it should be.[82]

The orders suddenly came through. If the parachutists are to accomplish anything, they will have to enter Hungary before the Germans occupy it; once the Germans take over, goodbye to everybody.

Before flying off on her mission, Hanna wrote in her diary:

A minute—
Farewell to you; farewell.
Who knows if I return,
Yes, who?
But I am content.
Eternity has kissed me,
A kiss that shall linger on my burning lips.[83]

Hanna and two young men parachuted out of a British plane to a landing in Yugoslavia—among the partisans. The two young men were Joel Palgi and Peretz Goldstein.

They landed safely, reconnoitered, and learned that they had arrived a little late. The Germans were already in Budapest.

Joel Palgi argued sensibly that the three of them should spend more time picking up all the information they could before entering Nazi-infested Hungary. Young Peretz agreed. They were both brave youths, but there was no point in throwing away their lives by dashing blindly into enemy country. They would cross the border in a few days, and know what they were doing.

But such sensible considerations are not for Hanna. Palgi will write later in a book of Hanna's impatience. She argues that every hour they delayed was a betrayal of their mission. The rescue of Jews must begin at once, before the horrors piled up for them.

Two young Jews and a Jewess arguing in the night how to enter the land of Jew-killers, how to steal into their midst and pull victims out from under their noses—there's a plot turn to linger on. If only Hanna Senesh will listen to the brave but more cautious Palgi, and to the daring but wiser Goldstein. But Hanna listens only to her heart. She stops arguing, smiles and says goodbye to the two young men crouching in the dark field. It is not a sensible goodbye. But heroines are never too sensible.

And this whole parachute business is not to be judged by its logic or its results. There is something more than sense in it. There is the courage that leaves its signature on lost causes. It is a signature mankind treasures.

Hanna Senesh met up with two Jewish partisans and crossed into Hungary with them. Hungarian gendarmes spotted and captured them. Hanna tried to rid herself of the military transmitter she carried. Her captors found the transmitter. It was by this transmitter that the parachutists were going to keep in touch with each other, and contact their British bases.

The transmitter identified Hanna as an important catch—an enemy spy. It revealed also that there were other spies with whom she expected to communicate. Arrow Cross Gestapo official Peter Hein was notified. He issued orders.

Hanna was taken to the prison in Budapest, stripped naked, strapped into a chair, and whipped and clubbed for several hours. The Hungarians wished to learn from her the code signal which would bring her fellow parachutists out of their hiding places into arrest.

Hanna spoke no word to the men who beat her into unconsciousness. The beating and defilement of Hanna Senesh continued for several days. Its extent is unknown. Hanna entered no record of it in her diary. Its pages remained proudly blank of torture and pain.

After many beatings, the officers in charge brought Hanna's mother into her cell. Mrs. Senesh saw a Hanna with her face lumpy and swollen, her eyes black and closed.

But Hanna could still speak. She embraced her mother and said, "I'm sorry, mother, that I had to do this to you."

Hanna wept in her mother's arms, and then said, "Don't stay. Don't look at me. I can't bear your pain, mother." [84]

The Hungarian officials arrested Mrs. Senesh later and put her in a cell. They told Hanna that her mother would be tortured unless Hanna gave up her code information.

The beatings continued, with Hanna strapped in a chair. Screams came from her before she blacked out, but never the transmitter code signal that would trap her fellow parachutists.

Mrs. Senesh was finally released from her prison. She visited Hanna at once. Hanna told her that she was going to be put on trial. She asked her mother to find a lawyer to defend her.

And Mrs. Senesh rushed through Budapest seeking help for her daughter. She learned from Jewish and Hungarian officials that there was only one man who could do anything for Hanna —the one Jew who had the power to move the Nazis—Dr. Rudolf Kastner. She learned also that Dr. Kastner was the only Jew allowed to see the imprisoned Jews whenever he wished, and to get parcels of food to them. The Hungarians sometimes forgot for days at a time to feed their Jewish prisoners.

Mrs. Senesh tried day after day, and then week after week, to see Dr. Rudolf Kastner. She spoke to Dr. Kastner's secretary, to his assistant, Mrs. Hanzi Brand, and to as many of his other aides as she could find. She sent pleas through them to Dr. Kastner, begging for an appointment, a conference, a lawyer, a parcel of food to be brought to her daughter.

Kastner was not entirely indifferent to the brave parachutists. Two of them had arrived secretly and safely in Budapest, and reported to Dr. Kastner. They had been instructed by the Haganah in Palestine that Dr. Kastner was to be their "base" in Hungary. Their rescue work would be done with his cooperation.

Kastner induced Joel Palgi to come out of hiding and surrender to the German Gestapo chief Klages. Later he lured Peretz Goldstein out of hiding to surrender to the Hungarian gendarmerie. He assured both young men that their gesture of surrender would mean clemency for them. He told them also that these same German and Hungarian authorities would allow them to join him in saving Jews.

There was another persuasive factor—young Palgi and Goldstein were natives of Kluj. Dr. Rudolf Kastner had been their leader in the "Zionist Youth Movement" of Kluj.[85]

The young parachutists obeyed Kastner and gave themselves

124

up. Both were put to immediate torture by the S.S. officers and Hungarian gendarmerie. After months of torture, they were shipped aboard a sealed train to one of the German death camps. Palgi managed to leap from the Jewish cattle car and escape. Peretz Goldstein was never seen again.[86]

Their torture and sentencing did not imperil the safety and comfort of their confidant, Dr. Kastner.

Now revealed as the "base" of the enemy spy operations, Dr. Kastner remained the trusted pal of the S.S. Nazis and Hungarian gendarmes who continued to help him "save Jews."

Hanna, waiting in a solitary cell, wrote in her diary:

One, two, three—eight is the length.
Two steps are the width of the wall.
My life flutters on a question mark—
One, two, three—perhaps another week.
Over my head—nothingness.
In this month of July, I shall be twenty-three.
I played a number in a game,
The dice have rolled. I have lost.[87]

After three months in solitary, Hanna wrote another line in her diary,

"I loved the warm sunlight." [88]

Satisfied that torture would not make her talk, the government ordered Hanna moved into a general cell to await her trial for treason. There were four other prisoners in the cell. Two of them were children. They had been imprisoned for years.

Beaten-faced, Hanna Senesh went to work teaching the two children to read and write. Her spirit moved into all the cells where Jews were waiting trial and execution. She loosed joyful rumors through the prison. Showing herself in her barred window, Hanna held a finger across her upper lip as if it were a small mustache. She moved another finger slowly across her throat. The rumor swept the prison that Hitler had been assassinated.

She flashed mirror signals to the Jews in other cells, and held up large Hebrew letters in her window spelling out words of hope for the other doomed ones. And when the guards forbade this and closed the window, Hanna continued to communicate with her fellow prisoners. She drew the Star of David in the window dust for them to see.

Unable to win an audience with the all-powerful Dr. Kastner, bewildered by the misinformation pompously offered her by his Jewish Agency assistant rescuers, Mrs. Catherina Senesh finally turned in desperation to a Hungarian for help, a lawyer who agreed to defend Hanna.

Soon after, Mrs. Senesh was summoned to a government office. Its anti-Semitic official told her that her daughter's trial was over and the sentence pronounced and carried out a few hours ago. The official said,

"Your daughter did not wish to see you again. She said she did not want to bring you pain. I must bow my head to your daughter's behavior before her death. Her last words were that she was very proud to be a Jewess." [59]

I shall finish Hanna's story in Judge Halevi's court, but my comment is here.

Hanna could have saved herself months of torture and disfigurement by giving her captors the code signal that would bring her fellow parachutists into their hands. She might also have saved her own life by betraying her comrades.

That in a time such as hers, a time of slaughter of harmless humans—there was one human being who preferred to die rather than bring pain to others—is an important historical fact.

That Hanna Senesh sacrificed herself not so much for patriotism or idealism as for the simplest of human reasons—a respect for other humans—is another important fact. It stands like a white monument in the dark century.

One such as Hanna Senesh makes me proud to write of my fellow Jews, to be one of the biographers of the girl who wrote—

"Eternity has kissed me,
A kiss that shall linger on my burning lips."

GHOSTS SPEAK OUT IN COURT

The parachutist story comes leaping into the trial unexpectedly.

Tamir: Was there any other inquiry concerning your past activities?

Kastner: I can't recall any.

(Tamir pauses, a memory of long-ago gossip in his head.)

Tamir: Dr. Kastner, in the Haganah . . .

Kastner: (nervously) Yes, yes, there was some inquiry in the Haganah.

(Tamir sees suddenly—a target has been hit.)

Tamir: Let's hear. What was it all about?

Kastner: (the patriotic) I do not know whether I am allowed to reveal the details of the inquiry in the Haganah. And I refuse to answer any question about it, unless I receive the required power of attorney.

An argument starts. Prosecutor Tell is firmly opposed to more "smearing" of the government "rescue hero," Dr. Kastner. And wild horses can never drag out of patriot Kastner any information which might be harmful to the military security of the nation. Tamir persists. Judge Halevi finally asks Witness Kastner, "What was the subject of the Haganah inquiry?"

Kastner: The inquiry touched on the parachutist story in Hungary. But anything relating to the parachutists is secret. I shall have to consult with the proper authorities.

Two days later Kastner faces cross-examination on a new and morbid episode of his past. It took days of quizzing to uncover the story of Kastner's betrayal of young Palgi and Goldstein, and his turned back on Hanna Senesh.

Tamir: What did you do to help Hanna Senesh?

Kastner: We held meetings of the committee over what steps to take. We decided on a long series of steps. To

127

find out from the Hungarian authorities if it was possible to release her; to find out from the German authorities if this was possible and to raise money for a lawyer to defend her.

Tamir: Was she defended? Did you get a lawyer?

Kastner: As far as I recall, we did.

Tamir: What was his name?

Kastner: Some Hungarian lawyer, a young military man. I don't remember his name.

Tamir: Did this lawyer get in touch with Hanna Senesh?

Kastner: I don't know.

Tamir: You weren't interested?

Kastner: I was. I think Offenbach told me he was handling the matter.

(Offenbach was a member of Kastner's Rescue Committee.)

Tamir: Did the lawyer visit Hanna Senesh in jail or not?

Kastner: I don't know.

Tamir: Did you ask whether Hanna sent any message to you through this lawyer?

Kastner: No.

Tamir: Did you inquire whether Hanna had any food in prison?

Kastner: I did not.

Tamir: Did you inquire whether she was being tortured?

Kastner: No.

Tamir: I put it to you, Dr. Kastner, that you were not interested in the fate of Hanna Senesh.

Kastner: That is not true.

Tamir: I put it to you that you never looked for a lawyer for Hanna Senesh.

Kastner: You are wrong.

Tamir: I put it to you that your aides advised Hanna's mother not to get a lawyer.

Kastner: That is not true.

Tamir: Did you meet Hanna's mother?

Kastner: No.

Tamir: Did the mother ever ask to meet you?

Kastner: To the best of my knowledge, never.

128

Tamir: Is it true that Hanna Senesh was a British officer in addition to being an emissary of the Jewish Agency?
Kastner: Yes, that is true.
Tamir: Is it true that British interests in Hungary were represented by the Swiss Consulate?
Kastner: Yes.
Tamir: Did you notify the Swiss Consulate that a British prisoner of war was being held by the Hungarians?
Kastner: No.
Tamir: Why didn't you?
Kastner: I think I had my reasons.[90]

A sweating Kastner waits for the all-out assault on his Hanna Senesh lies. This is one of Kastner's worst crimes in the eyes of Israel's public. For Hanna is no vague dead Jewess lost in a mountain of corpses. She is one of the greatest of Israel's heroines. Her poems are read widely. Her memory is as alive as if she had died a day ago. There is a kibbutz named in her honor— "Yad Hanna."

Tamir makes no final assault. He has a better answer for Kastner's lies. He has a witness to testify how the Jewish Agency in Hungary turned its back on Hanna and let her die without a finger lifted in her behalf. Tamir calls Hanna's mother to the witness box.

Mrs. Catherina Senesh is now a house mother of a girls' school in Israel.

Government officials had tried to argue Mrs. Senesh out of testifying. They had warned her that she might lose her job and remain in the disfavor of the rulers of Israel if she appeared as a witness. Nevertheless, Mrs. Senesh appeared. She entered the court with her loyal son, Giora, at her side.

Tall, poised and handsome, Mrs. Senesh speaks from the witness box. She tells her story calmly, proudly, in language her daughter would have admired.

Mrs. Senesh: Hanna asked me for only one thing—to get her a lawyer for the trial that was coming. I asked one of the active Zionists, a Mr. Grossman, to appoint a lawyer. I pleaded with him and told him Hanna had asked for a lawyer. The man said to me, "There is no need for a

129

lawyer. We have everything in hand. Go home. She may be waiting for you now." I hurried home. My daughter wasn't there. I called on this same Grossman day after day until people said to me, "Why do you bother with Grossman? Why don't you go to Kastner? Kastner is the one to help you."

Tamir: Did you ask Grossman to arrange a meeting with Kastner?

Mrs. Senesh: Yes. He said, "That is impossible. Dr. Kastner is too busy. Anyway, he is not home now." He always had a different excuse.

Tamir: What else did Grossman say to your plea for engaging a lawyer for your daughter?

Mrs. Senesh: He said there was no need for a lawyer, that everything was fine. I told him that if I could engage a lawyer, the lawyer could at least bring my daughter a parcel of food. Grossman insisted I did not need a lawyer for that. Kastner had a right to visit every prisoner. I asked, "Why hasn't he gone to my daughter?" I asked for Kastner's address. Mr. Grossman said, "No, that is impossible. I cannot give it to you." Later I got the address from someone else.

I went to the address. There I spoke to a woman. I told her who I was. I said, "I have heard that Dr. Kastner is the only one who can help. My daughter is one of the parachutists from Palestine." The woman said, "Yes, I know. We know of the case. Dr. Kastner intends to see her tomorrow. I'll give you Dr. Kastner's office address. You can talk to his secretary there. She will arrange it." Years later I met this woman and learned she was Mrs. Hanzi Brand.

Tamir: Did you take a food package to the secretary?

Mrs. Senesh: Yes. She would not accept it. She asked me to bring it back to her tomorrow.

Tamir: Did you try again to meet Dr. Kastner?

Mrs. Senesh: I tried again and again for many days.

Tamir: Did you finally get a lawyer?

Mrs. Senesh: Yes. While I was trying to see Dr. Kastner, I met Dr. Komoy who was in the same building. He knew our family and Hanna. I told him what I had been doing and how they had told me I didn't need a lawyer. Dr. Komoy was surprised. He had not heard that Hanna was in Budapest. He said, "You must get a lawyer today." It was October 12th. I rushed out and hired a lawyer. He was my daughter's only lawyer.[91]

But it was too late. Mrs. Senesh's faith in the Zionists had kept her from looking for help elsewhere.

Mrs. Senesh speaks in court of the morning she was told by a Hungarian official of her daughter's execution. The Hungarian said: "I must bow my head over your daughter's behavior before her death. Her last words were that she was very proud to be a Jewess."

Tamir: Mrs. Senesh, did you meet Dr. Kastner at all before your daughter's execution?

Mrs. Senesh: No, never.

Tamir: Have you met Dr. Kastner in Israel?

Mrs. Senesh: Yes, once. I was in Jerusalem taking care of some matters for my school. I went to a Government office. Dr. Kastner heard I was there. He walked in quickly and greeted me. I said to him, "Dr. Kastner, I'm not prepared to meet you." He answered, "Why? If you were prepared, what would you tell me?" I said, "There were times when I tried desperately to meet you. I was not successful." Dr. Kastner said, "Believe me, it was only in Switzerland the next year that I heard how often you'd come looking for me."

I said, "How is it possible that in such a crucial time you had such an irresponsible secretary who failed to tell you that I came constantly to the office asking for you?"

Dr. Kastner answered, "Believe me, what happened pains me more than it does anyone else."

I said, "I believe it is painful to you now, Dr. Kastner, but at that time, when something could have been done, I could not find you." He said, "No, we did everything. One day I shall come to you and tell you how much we did."

I said to him, "I know it is not true. I don't say that you

could have saved my daughter Hanna, but that you didn't try—it makes it harder for me that nothing was done."

He said, "Truly, we did everything. Believe me, we did everything and I will call on you and tell you someday."

I said to him, "I know the contrary to be true. If you wish to tell me, Dr. Kastner, that the matter of my daughter Hanna was so dangerous that it was better not to touch it, I'm willing to accept that as an explanation."

He said, "Dangerous for me? Dear Madame, I dealt only in danger."

I said to him, "Then perhaps the matter was not important enough or interesting enough for you."

He said, "No, you're mistaken. As a veteran Zionist I'm one to appreciate fully your daughter's heroic deeds. No, believe me, we did everything and tried everything."

I said, "How is it possible, if that is the case, that on October 12th I saw Komoy, your colleague, who didn't even know Hanna was a parachutist? At that time Hanna was in prison. There was nothing to eat in prison. At least a parcel of food could have been sent to her. More than that, my daughter Hanna waited for a sign that someone outside was thinking of her."

Dr. Kastner said, "I really don't understand how it happened that none of the food parcels I sent your daughter arrived."

I said, "It is a little difficult to understand why the food parcels my friends sent arrived and yours did not, Dr. Kastner."

This was my only meeting with Dr. Kastner.

Tamir: Did he offer to visit you and explain matters further?

Mrs. Senesh: Yes. I said to him, "I don't see anything to be gained by such talk. I think it is unnecessary, Dr. Kastner. I see no reason for any further discussion between us." [92]

Attorney General Chaim Cohen waives cross-examination. Every word added by Mrs. Senesh would be further proof of Kastner's turned back on Hanna.

132

No newspaper in Israel, not even Ben-Gurion's *Davar*, challenges Mrs. Senesh's testimony.

Sleep well, Hanna. it was not in vain. Whoever looks for belief in humanity and faith in its goodness will find your name.

REBUTTAL

Here is Attorney General Chaim Cohen's explanation and rebuttal for all these matters. He declaims in his summation to Judge Halevi:

"The only thing the Defense could prove was that Kastner did not receive Mrs. Catherina Senesh for an interview, or send parcels to prison, and that he did not put himself out enough.

"Supposing this is true, which it is not, *what does it prove?* It proves that because of Kastner's great heavy work and responsibility for the lives of thousands of Jews, he was not active enough in behalf of one Palestinian Jewess. Therefore he is a traitor and collaborator?" [98]

What does it prove? Come with me, brother Jews, and look on Kastner's work.

SLAUGHTER IN SUMMER

In the Budapest of June 1944, you would never know that Germany had started its nose dive into disaster; that the Allies were blasting their way toward its vitals. The War that is going *kaput* is a lesser event than Jew-killing.

Trains full of Jews (and how full!) are roaring to Auschwitz. Hungary is emptying its Jews into the German gas ovens. It is a massive, headlong operation—this clubbing and bayoneting of a half million humans into ghettos; packing them into train compartments, which requires more clubbing and bayoneting; and getting them to Auschwitz in time.

133

The Jews are deported to Auschwitz daily, on schedule. They leave from the ghetto embarkation depots, on schedule. Conductors signal, "All aboard." Brakemen wave lanterns. German and Hungarian guards shoot a few reluctant travelers, club and bayonet a last group of mothers into the compartments. The engineer opens his throttle. And the train is off for Auschwitz, on schedule.

Eighty Jews ride in every compartment. Eichmann told Kastner the Germans could do better where there were more children. Then they could jam one hundred twenty into each train room. But eighty is no reflection on German efficiency.

The eighty Jews must stand all the way to Auschwitz with their hands raised in the air, so as to make room for the maximum of passengers.

There are two buckets in each compartment. One contains water. The other is for use as a toilet, to be shoved by foot, if possible, from user to user.

I wonder here, why the water and toilet buckets? One water bucket, one toilet bucket for eighty despairing men, women and children plastered against each other as in a packing case, and riding to death. Why? One water bucket, one toilet bucket are not enough to relieve the misery of these barely living ones. Jammed together, how can they use any buckets? They must urinate and defecate in their clothes. They must continue to burn with thirst until they arrive at the gas ovens. But the buckets are there.

I look at these two buckets as at some curious souvenirs. Of what? I answer hesitantly; of the fact that humanity is hard to stamp out completely. It persists. It sneaks a token of itself into each foul-smelling, Jew-jammed compartment. The two buckets are like the spoor of some wounded thing—a German memory of humanity not quite dead.

Arrived in Auschwitz—a hiss of gas, a roar of flames, and the multitude of lives are ashes.

The news of Jews turned into cattle, of Jews being rushed to Poland for slaughter, is out now in Budapest. The Jews of Budapest have been moved into a Jewish quarter. Rich, poor, learned, ignorant, religious, skeptical are all together in one district, huddled seven and eight in every room. Every child and adult wears a yellow Star of David on his or her coat front. Jews who had converted to Christianity are permitted to wear a Cross alongside the Yellow Star.

The two hundred and fifty thousand waited their turn. Death sat on their doorsteps. Nazi boots clanked in their Jewish streets. Hungarian shouts of "Eat the Jews!" rose in the night. And each hour brought murderous tales of twelve thousand a day killed in Auschwitz.

We know now that there was little hysteria among the doomed. Rich, poor, learned, ignorant, the yellow-badged Jews walked quietly in their streets, held their heads up, smiled at each other, dreamed of saving their children, and still tried to arouse the human conscience of their fellow citizens. A group of Budapest's Jews printed and distributed this leaflet:

> In the last hours of our tragedy, we, the Hungarian Jews, ask for help from the Hungarian Christians. We turn to those with whom we have shared good and bad in the land which holds the graves of our ancestors.
>
> Death trains are leaving from every part of the country. A half million persons have been deported; old, young, sick, babies, pregnant women, cripples; all beaten and driven into freight cars. And they do not ride off to work, but to annihilation. The Christians of Hungary have no idea of what is going on. There is no mention of atrocities in the press.
>
> Friends, should this appeal for our lives be in vain, we ask, then. only one thing—spare us the horrors of deportation and end our suffering here, so that at least we can be buried in our native land.[94]

Thus the Jews of Budapest—their last proud request.

Thus the fifteen thousand Jews in the ghetto of Kassa waiting their ride to Auschwitz; the thirteen thousand Jews behind the barbed wire of the gypsy camps on the Ronyva River; the twenty thousand Jews under guard in the ghetto of Miskolc; and the other thousands on thousands waiting in the disposal depots of Tizhorod, Tesco, Beregszaz, Felsoviso.

Typhus spreads through these camps. Peter Hain and his Hungarian gendarmes invade them to torture information about hidden valuables out of the doomed. The Jewish Council reports on their technique:

> The wife was beaten before the eyes of her husband. And if this showed no results, children were tortured in front of their parents. The methods favored by the Hungarian Gestapo in obtaining a confession of some sort were—fetterings, rubber truncheons, use of electrical appliances, blows and kicks in the face and belly, and driving sharp objects beneath their finger nails.[95]

Concerning these same disposal camp statistics from the Dracula's land in which he was then Regent, the great Admiral Horthy has a curious statement to make—in the summertime of July, 1944.

Says the famed Horthy, renowned as a "good" Hungarian:

"My Minister Laszlo Endre has visited the new ghettos and found everything in perfect order. The provincial ghettos have the character of sanitoria. At last the Jews have taken up an open-air life, and exchanged their former mode of living for a healthier one." [96]

I omit the Hitlerian gloatings of "my Minister Endre" issued in the same slaughter-month of July, 1944. Only to wonder where were these proud Magyar blood and torture exulters when Hungary was recently invaded by the Commies? Did they fight, did they hide, did they cry out for world pity?

The 1944 Nazi-Hungarians held the last leaflet published by the Budapest citizen Jews to be a crime. They arrested those responsible for the printing, and tortured and executed them. Among the executed were Rabbis Fabian Herschkowitz and Niklos Pehnes, and Professor Philip Greenwald, director of the Jewish Museum. Professor Greenwald was the brother of Malchiel Greenwald, "the defendant" on trial before Judge Halevi.

Escape was now impossible. Machine guns ringed the ghetto zones. Electrified barbed wire enclosed the embarkation depots. Thousands of Hungarian guards led by S.S. officers, guns in hand, clanked through the starving, unarmed multitudes of Jews. The Delusion-Strategy had fooled the Jews; Kastner and his official Jewish bosses had led them into the barricaded ghettos. Fooled by their enemies and by their own, the Jews waited stoically for extermination. Knowing they were doomed, why didn't they hurl themselves on their captors and die in a hail of bullets? Some of them did.

Hundreds of men and women refused to enter the deportation trains. They threw themselves on the rails and clung there. They were shot and killed by the gendarmes.

Toward the end of the Slaughter Summertime, when the Auschwitz garden of Camp Commandant Colonel Hoess was "a paradise of flowers"—he writes in his book—and his "children played peacefully with their pets, which included tortoises, kittens and lizards"—in that autumn, lavish of golden leaves—the methods of travel to Auschwitz changed for the tortured ones of Hungary.

The Russians moved into Poland. No more piling Jews into trains. The way to "the paradise of flowers" is cut off, with the Russians driving hell-bent for Vienna. The Colonels—Eichmann, Krumey, and Becher—return to their post, and organize a death march from Budapest to Vienna.

And here is a sop to the Christian citizens of Budapest! To tell the truth, they are a little queasy about a couple of hundred thousand Jews being murdered in the streets of their capital. And so—the hour is late, and there is little time for controversy about Jews joining their ancestors in what they foolishly call their native soil—the doomed Jews will be marched on foot to Vienna.

From the waltz-city of Budapest to the waltz-city of Vienna is a march of one hundred and fifty miles. It will be the kind of outing that few will survive. Hunger, beatings, illness and bullets will dispose of many Jew hikers en route through the autumn-smelling fields. The thousands are clubbed into line—gun butts and bayonets beat them toward Vienna.

Hoess, the flower-lover of Auschwitz, is present to inspect the walk. He finds the latest Jew-disposal tactics prolonged and messy, but workable. Without food or water, marching day and night, with gun butts cracking at their bones and bellies, Jews fall in silence, and are shoveled into the summertime fields by their exhausted co-marchers.

Nevertheless, the death march is not a success. The Russians have cut off the road to Vienna. The Hungarian government of

Jew-killers, who have assisted the Germans loyally, now issues a call for volunteers to be called Death Brigades.

Thousands of the brave breed of Hungarians who so recently (1960) pleaded for United States compassion when the Commies came along to grab their country, answer the call. Grinning, they stand in the streets while officers deal out rifles, and pin on their sleeves the skull and crossbones arm bands that make it a patriotic duty to pop off Jews. (The yellow badges on the left breast make good targets.) Jewish corpses fill hallways, synagogue pews, and temple steps.

In the palaces of Budapest, their beer steins at their elbows, the merry Colonels, their Hungarian cronies with them, sit and chat. Often at their side sits the Jew, Kastner, busy abetting the do-nothing, say-nothing policy of the Jewish leaders toward the dying last Jews of Hungary.

One of their favored gathering places in the home of the seductive Eve Kosytorz, Col. Krumey's mistress.[97]

He has set her up in a large apartment glittering from floor to ceiling with Jewish loot. La Kosytorz is a busy shopper. Whenever she hears of a Jew or Jewess owning something she fancies, she orders the owner arrested and executed. Some sixty Jews have contributed to the décor of the Krumey love nest.

Here Krumey, the beer-bellied, button-nosed shortie with his blue eyes, pink cheeks and blood-shot hands, is fond of drinking a few beers, reminiscing about Jew killings he supervised in Poland and Austria, and boasting that he is the greatest living authority on extermination camps. He boasts also of helping to wipe out the town of Lidice, where he was personally in charge of the killing of children.

While the skull-and-crossbones Christian Hungarians are roaming the Jewish quarter and egging on the death march, Dr. Kastner sits.

During the Witches' Sabbath of Budapest's slaughter summer, the Jewish Agency factotums of Palestine sit. They sit until the Jews of Hungary are done in and destroyed. Their tongues and right arms remain useless, pledged to the Nazis in Budapest and the British in Jerusalem.

Only one exception to the do-nothing, say-nothing policy of official Zionism—religious Zionist Moshe Kraus, who left the

Jewish-Agency-Zionist Party Line and its ranks of "rescuers," and, almost single-handed, raised a fairly audible outcry. Heroic Moshe Kraus enlisted the support of the 'Swiss consul in Budapest, Charles Lutz, the Swedish Representative, Raoul Valenberg, and representatives of several South American countries. He headed up an Underground that turned the city's basements into hideaways, and outwitting the Nazi and Hungarian killers, saved forty thousand Jews.

A stirring thing!

(In the time I write of—the Trial days when the Government's arm is staunch around Kastner's shoulder, Moshe Kraus eats his dry bread in limbo. The doors of Government employment are closed against him—which, in Mapai-land, means most doors.)

But—why didn't the last two hundred thousand unrescued ones fight back? I return to this often-asked question . . .

I change the scene to New York City, the Jersey flats across the Hudson, and understand it better.

All the Jews of New York City have been driven into Hoboken and are waiting to be taken off to the stock yards in Chicago to be exterminated. Imagine the blankness that would come into our minds when we realized that we American Jews, with all our energy, culture, talents, love of our country and of our fellow Americans, were suddenly as undesirable to our government as if we had turned into so many mangy alley cats and disease-breeding sewer rats; that suddenly our humanity had no existence. And the old query of "Hath not a Jew hands, organs, dimensions, senses, affections, passions?" had been answered by the American President and both Houses of Congress with a thunderous, "No!"

And how—if at the same time—the free and safe Jews in the world, the rich and great ones, and most of all the Elite Hierarchy of Eretz-Israel, were to concur, in silence, to the death sentence? What then?

Waiting in the Hoboken Meadows, we American Jews would not be numbed by fear of death. We would sit stunned because we had been insanely deprived of our human faces.

As my friend Molnar said, we would be no longer all the things we thought we were.

139

THE SILENCE

Out of this shell-screaming, fire-gutted 1944 Europe comes a letter from a man hiding in a cave on the bank of the Danube river. It is one of the most potent missives ever put in an envelope.

Its writer is a strong, profoundly religious man named Rabbi Michael Dov Weissmandel. This bearded and mystic man was one of the heroic rescue workers in the time of Jewish catastrophe. His headquarters were a cave outside his native town of Bratislava, Slovakia. Making sorties out of this cave, he plucked doomed Jews from under the Nazi noses and rode them to freedom. He worked as a one-man army of the Lord.

The Jewish leaders in Turkey, Switzerland and Palestine had received a number of communications [98] from the indomitable rabbi in the cave. This one, written on the day after the deportation of Hungary's Jews to Auschwitz started, read:

May 15, 1944—In a cave near Lublin. Sholom and Greetings.

We send you this special message to inform you that yesterday the Germans began the deportation of Jews from Hungary. It is the beginning of deportation of all the Hungarian Jews.

Every day, twelve thousand souls are being taken off.

Four deportations of forty-five such train-loads move daily out of Hungary. Within twenty-six days all that area will have been deported.

The deported ones go to Auschwitz to be put to death by cyanide gas. A great number are dead on arrival.

The Germans allow a few of the strongest to stay alive.

Those who are allowed to live are branded with a number burned into their arm and the Star of David burned into their chest.

Most of these privileged ones die within a month. Others take their place.

Those who go directly from the train to the gas chambers to be suffocated are not branded. They are completely consumed in the ovens and leave no evidence behind. These are 95% of each transport.

The dead bodies are burned in specially made ovens. Each oven burns 12 bodies an hour. In February there were 36 ovens burning. We have learned that more have been built.[99]

Information supplied us by a few eyewitnesses reveals that in February there were four disposal buildings. We have learned that more have been built since then.

Formerly, the Germans killed and burned the Jews in the Forest of Birkenwald, near Auschwitz. *Now the killing and burning take place in the buildings shown on the enclosed map.*

In December, the Germans built special trains to transport the Jews of Hungary to their extermination.

This is the schedule of Auschwitz, from yesterday to the end; twelve thousand Jews—men, women and children, old men, infants, healthy and sick ones—are to be suffocated daily and their bones and ashes are to be used to fertilize the German fields.

And you—our brothers in Palestine, in all the countries of freedom, and you, ministers of all the kingdom—how do you keep silent in the face of this great murder? Silent while thousands on thousands, reaching now to six million Jews, were murdered. And silent now while tens of thousands are still being murdered and waiting to be murdered?

Their destroyed hearts cry to you for help as they bewail your cruelty. Brutal you are and murderers too you are, because of the cold-bloodedness of the silence in which you watch.[100]

Because you sit with folded arms and you do nothing, though you could stop or delay the murder of Jews at this very hour.[101]

In the name of the blood of the thousands of thousands who have been murdered we beg, we plead, we cry out and demand that you take action. that you do deeds now— at once!

That the Ministers of Kingdoms and all the Lands raise a loud and piercing outcry that must enter the ears of the world, the ears of the German people, the ears of the Hungarian people. Let them cry out a warning to the German murderers. Let them proclaim that they know all that has been done in the past, and that which is still being done.

And the Pope, himself, should join in this cry of outrage against the German murderers.

Let this outcry be heard over all the radios and read in all the newspapers of the world, that unless they stop at once the deportations of Hungary's Jews—then will Germany be forever exiled from civilization.

We ask that the crematoria in Auschwitz be bombed from the air. They are sharply visible, as shown on the enclosed map.

Such bombing will delay the work of the German murderers.[102]

What is more important—to bomb persistently all the roads leading from Eastern Hungary to Poland and to bomb persistently the bridges in the neighborhood of Karpatarus.

Drop all other business to get this done. Remember that one day of your idleness kills twelve thousand souls.

You, our brothers, sons of Israel, are you insane? Don't you know the Hell around us? For whom are you saving your money?

How is it that all our pleadings affect you less than the whimperings of a beggar standing in your doorway?

Murderers! Madmen! Who is it that gives charity? You who toss a few pennies from your safe homes? Or we who give our blood in the depths of Hell?

There is only one thing that may be said in your exoneration—that you do not know the truth.

This is possible.

The villain does his job so shrewdly that only a few guess the truth.

We have told you the truth several times. Is it possible that you believe our murderers more than you believe us?

May God open your eyes and give you heart to rescue in these last hours the remainder.

142

Most important is that which I write about the bombing of the Auschwitz Crematoria and the bridges leading to them.

Such bombing can vitally delay the evil work of our slaughterers.[103]

And God who keeps alive the last remnant of Israel will show His mercy for which I pray. I pray as I write out of the sea of tears of the people of Israel. We wait God's help.

One from the Market who witnesses the woes of his people.[104]

In August, 1944, Rabbi Michael Dov Weissmandel received an answer, of sorts, to his letter. He was captured by German S.S. Jew-hunters and put aboard a train headed for the German ash barrels. On the train to Auschwitz the religious one stood silent in Bedlam. Packed in with the other human garbage marked for disposal, Rabbi Weissmandel held in his hand a crust of old bread. In the bread was a coil of emery thread that could saw through steel. At night, the Rabbi cut a hole in the sealed car and leaped out into the darkness.

He resumed his rescue work, although no answer was made to his letter.

A decade later, and Tamir repeats in the court room the accusing S.O.S. of "one in the market place" who, hidden, watched his people being tortured.

Tamir questions Menachem Bader of the Jewish Agency in the witness box of Judge Halevi's court room:

"Did you receive this letter from Rabbi Weissmandel?"

Bader, now General Manager of the Government Development Bureau, and pinpointed by other witnesses as the Jewish Agency rescue worker on the scene to whom the letter came, answers:

"Letters like this came to us every day."

Tamir addresses Judge Halevi on the reply to Rabbi Weissmandel's call for help—silence. He sums up:

"In answer to the wild outcry of twelve thousand Jews going daily to be murdered, what does the organized Jewish community reply? What action does it take?

143

"What answer is made to the ways of rescue listed by the Rabbi writing from his cave?

"There are no answers. There are no deeds."

Tamir takes up the silence (in obedience to the British) preserved by the Weizmann Zionists toward the massacre of Europe's six million Jews—the silence and indifference that then hardened into Policy.

"Our charges are that here, in Eretz-Israel, the official institutions have submitted to the British Government. They were not willing to endanger themselves and they were caught by narrowmindedness, and an utter refusal to give up the internal rule, and because of all these came that which I am forced to define as the abandonment of European Jewry in the most horrible hour to befall it.

"The witness Katz described how the Jews in Auschwitz were standing and watching the British bombers, who bombed military targets and omitted the gas chambers and the crematoriums. Had these gas chambers been bombarded, the extermination could have been delayed, and tens of thousands of souls saved. But they were not bombed.

"In this situation, what action is taken, not by the Kluj ghetto, but by the organized Jewish community of Palestine? Six hundred thousand people, not men who 'had no spirit' but a community with a tradition of Nili,[105] of HaShomer,[106] of the Hebrew legions, of the Gallipoli corpus, of the Haganah, of the Underground, of the Palmach—what does this Jewish community do in view of the enemy of its people who are thus helping extermination?"

Here Tamir quotes the secret message which Rabbi Michael Dov Weissmandel sent to the Jewish leaders of Palestine and the free world, and continues,

"It is far too easy for the organized Jewish Community in Palestine to say in 1944: the British didn't want to permit rescue and immigration. In 1946 the Haganah knew well how to follow the Irgun and Lehi and to blow up bridges so that the British would be forced to permit it. How is it that in 1944 they didn't come out to fight for the opening of the gates of Palestine to the victims of Hitler? In 1944 the coming results of the war were clear. And then we had to wage war on all fronts. Then the whole attention, the whole soul, the nerves and body alike, had to be concentrated on one matter only—the rescue of hundreds of thousands of remaining Jews.

"But let us not talk of blowing up bridges in Eretz-Israel. Let us not talk of so-called 'extremism.' Let us refer to legitimate, legal actions. Let us talk just of the most conventional, traditional Jewish activity: fund-raising for rescue.

"Izaak Greenbaum, head of the Jewish Agency Rescue Committee, writes in his book, 'If I am asked, "Could you give from the United Jewish Appeal moneys to rescue Jews," I say, "No!" And I say again, "No!" In my opinion we have to resist this wave which puts the Zionist activities in a secondary line."

Continues Tamir,

"Izaak Greenbaum is not a private individual. He is the man appointed by the Jewish Agency as chief of its Rescue Department. What does this mean except knowingly neglecting and sacrificing the Jews of Europe?"

Bader—this same Bader who passed on to Palestine the letter of Rabbi Weissmandel—has testified that they forwarded to the Jewish Agency chiefs "every particle of news and fact of the massacre."

Tamir to Judge Halevi:

"Yet, in Palestine, these facts remained almost unnewsworthy. Silence continued. Complete suppression.

"Look at the small tucked-away items (in the Press) about Jewish troubles in Europe. And note how absent from the editorial pages are comments on rescue problems.[107]

"During this time, there appear in the Jewish Agency press, long speeches by Ben-Gurion and Sharett—speeches made in Palestine and abroad. All Zionist official minutiae are reported in full, all the huffing and puffing of the Histadrut and Mapai parties are offered the public under staggering headlines. Local problems, strikes, the cost of living, political quibbling—all receive full coverage. But of the horrors and details of the extermination of Jews, and of the rescue problems—almost no mention.

"More than that, in Davar, official Jewish Agency paper, appears this editorial. I quote: "The Nazi denial of extermination has a good foundation. Not as many were annihilated as was feared.'

145

"Let us come to the hour of the extermination of Hungarian Jewry.

"Two days after the Nazi occupation of Hungary, headlines, editorials, denunciations, fill the columns (of *Davar*)—not against the terror of the Hungarian Fascists, not against this terror of Eichmann, but against the terror of the Irgun Zvai Leumi, and the Jewish Fighters for the Freedom of Israel.

"In the fatal months of April, May, June of 1944, during which scores of thousands of Jews were taken to Auschwitz daily for slaughter, the suppression continues. There is a speech by Ben-Gurion [carried in full by the Jewish Agency press]. No mention of Hungary is in it.

"*Sir—11 of April*—They begin the concentration of the Jews in Hungary. Ben-Gurion delivers a speech. Not a single word about Hungary. An editorial appears in *Davar*. Again, against the Terror, the Terror against the British.

"*9 of May*—The deportations to Auschwitz at the rate of twelve thousand per day are about to start. The General Assembly of the Jews of Palestine assembles. Their agenda: paragraph 1—election of parties. The British could afford to go without elections at that decisive time, but with us the whole turmoil was around the elections. And this also is the topic of the General Assembly.

"*11 of May*—The last days before commencement of the deportations. Again a speech of Ben-Gurion. Not a word about the Hungarian situation.

"*15 of May*—The full-scale deportations to Auschwitz start. Twelve thousand a day, Sir. Mr. Sharett delivers a speech. Not a single word about Hungary. Not a word about the extermination in general.

"*21 of May*—The seventh day of the deportation, which will be finished and done with in a few days. Ben-Gurion delivers a speech. Not a word about Hungary. The first information appears on the *23 of May*. Ehud Avriel sends a cable from Turkey about the danger to one million Jews and it appears in *Davar*. Let's see what follows the alarm information of Avriel. *On 2 of June*, eight days later, and by then almost one quarter of a million Hungarian Jews have been burned in Auschwitz, the

General Council of Mapai (Ben-Gurion's party) assembles. Not a single word of reaction.

"On July 10, 1944, *Davar* publishes coolly and with no hint of emotion, a small item of news—Kraus' report from Budapest. (Kraus is the lone-wolf rescuer who saved forty thousand Hungarian Jews without an assist from the Jewish Agency.)

"This *Davar* chilly item is the first authoritative news that the deportations have reached so big a scale.

"And the story appears after the deportations were over, and the near million already slaughtered!"

(I intrude on Tamir—it is now safe for *Davar* to mention deportations. Dead Jews cannot embarrass British policy to get into Palestine.)

"Here's another date. Six days after the Kraus bit of news was published, Berl Katznelson, central figure of Ben-Gurion's Mapai party, delivers a speech. He speaks not a single word on the subject [of Hungary's massacred Jews]. Not one word on the general topic of extermination.

"Ben-Gurion also speaks at length at the Histadrut convention that same week—about 'the great tasks facing the Jewish nation.' And he says not a word about the eight hundred thousand Jewish souls and their extermination.

"Until mid-July, six weeks after the killing of twelve thousand a day had begun, still not a single authoritative word is uttered by the Jewish Agency or any Zionist officials that the deportation had started—that already half a million were exterminated.

"The Jewish Agency had by then the best and most exact informative source [108] on the fate of the Jews of Hungary, and on the deportation, and there was no British censorship of such items, as was proven in Court. But from the end of May until the 16th of July, for a full month and a half, when 12,000 Jews are being killed a day, still not a single authoritative word is uttered by the Jewish Agency or any Zionist officials that these deportations have started and are continued; that already half a million Jews were exterminated. For a full month and a half, Mr. Sharett and the Jewish Agency are knowingly and wilfully suppressing all the news known to them.

"Yes, instead of blazoning it in headlines, instead of arousing the world's Jews and non-Jews to some action—the dreadful news

147

is suppressed, knowingly and willfully—by orders from the British, with whom our Jewish leaders are so proud of collaborating.

"The Attorney General dared to ask—and I don't know why, for it is irrelevant—'Where were those in the time of war against Hitler who come now with accusations?'

"If such a question is asked by so high a dignitary, I owe an answer. The people about whom he inquires were, in those days, in the small huts of Latrun,[109] in the Prison of Acre, in the African detention camps, and hanging from British gallows in Cairo; they were fighting to open the ports of Palestine for the Jews of Europe, not yet murdered.

"And why this suppression of the dreadful news by Ben-Gurion, Sharett, Weizmann and all the official leaders of Jewry? Because, had the masses in Palestine known then what was happening in Hungary, and known then the stony hearts of their leaders, a storm would have risen in our land. Power would have fallen out of their hands. And this, it seems, was more important to them.

"There is no other explanation. Therefore I said: 'Collaboration here, parallel to collaboration there. But if the collaboration there has developed under German pressure, here we talk of men who lived in the free world, whose discretion could be more balanced, who were in control of good youth, wonderful youth, which awaited a command. The fact remains that the moral and historical responsibility, as far as Jews are concerned, lies first and foremost on those who lived in the free world. And though I am here to prove the guilt of Kastner, I say that his responsibility is lesser than that of the leaders of our free Jewish world."

EPITAPH

The Jews who were killed in Hungary for being Jews were among the brightest of Europeans. The fame of their wit and charm still lingers in endless anecdotes. Their courage in meeting the insanity that wiped them out is also recorded in hundreds of annals.

Nevertheless, their character will receive sneer and belittlement from the Government of Israel that seemed to echo the voice of the Nazis who slew them.

Nazi chieftain Dr. Joseph Goebbels wrote: "The Jews deserve the catastrophe that has now overtaken them."

In 1954, Chaim Cohen, Attorney General of Israel, declaims to Judge Halevi about these same slaughtered Jews:

"For those and millions of Jews like them there came true the old curse, 'And, lo, they were meant but to be taken like sheep for slaughter, for killing, for destruction, for crushing and shame.' There was no spirit in them. The Jewish masses in Warsaw were in the same condition."

In 1937, Dr. Chaim Weizmann, President of World Zionism, said of Europe's six million Jews,

"They are dust . . . in a cruel world . . . They must meet their fate . . . Only a branch shall survive. They must accept it."

Dr. Goebbels, in 1943, seconds this Zionist attitude. He writes in his diary, "In our Nazi attitude toward the Jews, there must be no squeamish sentimentalism."

There is another scribble on the tombstone of the exterminated —by Karl Marx. The founder of Socialism wrote in the 1830's that the Jews of Europe worshipped only money as their God, that they were as worthless humanly as fleas; and that the Jewish religion was:

"Contempt for art, history . . . Even the relations between the sexes become an object of commerce. The woman is auctioned off . . . The social emancipation of Jewry is the emancipation of society from Jewry." [110]

The present government of Israel is based on the theories of Karl Marx. I don't imagine it ever believed with its philosophic parent that "the Jews of Poland are the smeariest of people;" or that it ever shared with its patron saint (Marx) his emotional distaste for Europe's Jews. Karl Marx's father was an orthodox rabbi, and Christian convert Karl had to alibi his apostasy by fouling the nest he had abandoned. There was no apostasy in the government clique of Israel to echo this phase of Marxian theory.

149

But there was Socialist obsession enough in Israel's leaders to cool their eyes and hearts toward the Jews of Europe and deem their fate less important than the building of their little Socialist experiments in Palestine.

All these theories come to the same thing at last—those of the Nazis, of the Socialists, of the official Zionists and of the Arab-fancying British. They come together at last to chisel one line on the tomb of the Exterminated,

"You were unwanted."

END OF A MYTH

I recall an anecdote out of my Chicago newspaper days.

"Go back—" the city editor said to his reporter who had phoned in that he had just been kicked downstairs by an irate official: "Go back and tell that bastard he can't kick one of *my* men down the stairs."

Thus Kastner is back in the court room, a bit wobbly and glassy-eyed, blinking but defiant.

The last denuding of Dr. Kastner, official in good standing in the Israeli Government, begins.

> Tamir: Let's turn to your travels. What passport did you have for your travels?
>
> Kastner: Well, I had a passport issued by the German embassy in Budapest.
>
> Tamir: What was your nationality on that passport?
>
> Kastner: Unknown nationality. It seems this was the maximum they would grant even me.

A wistful note. Great man though he was in Nazi eyes, they could not quite bring themselves to crown him with: "Nationality—German."

> Tamir: What sort of clothes did you wear?
>
> Kastner: I was always in civilian clothes. The story that

I wore an S.S. uniform towards the end of the war is untrue.

There is a widespread tale of Dr. Kastner a-strut among the Nazis in one of their military costumes. But Tamir has no photographs. He, therefore, drops the subject, on which Kastner seems a bit eager to linger. Tamir takes Kastner over his Nazi travel route instead. On these travels Kastner is accompanied by S.S. high officers. He is escorted to Switzerland, allowed to meet Allied officials in Switzerland. Kastner is a gold mine of military information on the German war machine—its strength, positions, morale. Yet the Nazis let him mingle with the Allies—not a bit of worry that he will betray them.[111]

His Nazi chums pay his fare back from Switzerland to Vienna.[112] There are hardly any Jews in Vienna to save—only some five hundred in all. In Budapest there are still some two hundred thousand living left.[113] (Moshe Kraus is busy there violating the Jewish Agency Party line by rescuing thousands on thousands.) [114] Although more than half a million Jews of Hungary are dead now, Rescuer Kastner's friendship with the Nazi Colonels suffers no setback. On the contrary, it thrives and deepens, particularly with Kurt Becher, Hermann Krumey, Wisliczeny, and Eichmann.

The spectacled Krumey, top man in the "de-Jewification of Budapest" work, becomes a violent fellow. He snarls at any Jewish rescue leaders who come near him—except Dr. Kastner. He likes Kastner. So does the siren, Eve Kosytorz.

But at this time, forgetting Budapest and the two hundred fifty thousand in mortal danger there, Kastner sits in Jew-less Vienna, in a plushy suite in the Grand Hotel [115]—where all the best Nazis are holed up—and saves nobody.

Though that is not exactly his story. Questioned by Tamir about all the Nazis who liked him, Kastner doesn't deny their patronage. He feels good, back on his pedestal as a Nazi pal, and even smiles in the court room, for the Kastner myth was—and is—that all this brudershaft with the Jew-killers was a fine thing. In his report addressed to Agency official Eliezer Kaplan, on file now in the Israeli court, Kastner boasted of his friend Kurt

151

Becher, "who served as Liaison Officer between Reichsfuhrer Heinrich Himmler and myself . . ."

Tamir goes after this vision of his greatness that Kastner offers his fellow nabobs in Palestine.

> Tamir: You say here that Himmler issued an order to stop the exterminations on a certain date. Supposing there was such an order, will you agree with me that it was not a result of your talks with Becher? That it was because the Russian, American and British armies beset him from all sides?
>
> Kastner: No, I don't agree.
>
> Tamir: You state that your talks did it. Don't you realize that you are a megalomaniac—to make such a statement?
>
> Kastner: Not *I* am a megalomaniac, but you are ignorant of history.
>
> Tamir: Very well. Then, according to you, the war situation had no influence on Himmler's action.
>
> Kastner: (suddenly nervous over the whole thing) Well, that it contributed to his calculation, I can't argue. But the war situation was very far from causing him to issue the order.
>
> Tamir: Well, let's sum it up. Your meetings with Becher were more important for the Jews than the strategic situation of Germany towards the end of the war.
>
> Kastner: Yes, I have no doubts in making that statement.
>
> Tamir: (quietly) To sum up, Dr. Kastner, Becher helped you save Jews.
>
> Kastner: Yes.
>
> Tamir: And Himmler helped you save Jews.
>
> Kastner: (firmly) Yes.

I call a pair of Christian ghosts as witnesses in Rebuttal—Colonel Rudolf Hoess, Commandant of Auschwitz, and Reichsfuhrer Heinrich Himmler, creator of the S.S., the Black Soldiers' Corps, and the creator also of the extermination camps. Ghost Hoess was hanged by the Poles. Ghost Himmler dodged the noose by getting himself shot while escaping.

Ghost Hoess, in his autobiography, completed in Cracow in

1947, quotes Himmler after the Reichsfuhrer's inspection of Auschwitz in the fall of 1944. Said Himmler:

> Every Jew we can lay our hands on must be destroyed now, during the war—without exception. All the mass graves must be opened and the corpses burned. In addition, the ashes must be disposed in such a way as to make it impossible in the future to calculate the number of corpses that were burned.

Tamir: Did you meet S.S. Colonel Hoess?
Kastner: Yes.

Hoess is a name all Israel knows. He testified in Nuremberg that he was in direct charge of Auschwitz and that he personally supervised the murder of 2,500,684 Jews. The exact figure is the Colonel's. He testified also that it was his duty to watch the killing of the myriad of Jews through a peep-window in the gas chambers, to make sure "that nothing went wrong."

Other observations offered by Ghost Hoess at Nuremberg: that the Cyclone B gas used in the speed-up killings was supplied by the excellent German chemical firm of Tesch and Stabenaw; that the doomed Jewesses "stumbled about like ghosts," and their men waiting their turn to be slaughtered "stumbled about like lines of skeletons." Colonel Hoess told also of difficulties in keeping order while children and infants were slaughtered with their mothers. The mothers often screamed, explained Colonel Hoess, and went mad—"they would even sit with their dead babies in their arms singing to them." And, testified Colonel Hoess, the work was always full of details which his superior Reichsfuhrer Himmler did not fully appreciate:

> After gassing, the bodies had to be taken from the gas chambers, the gold teeth had to be extracted, the hair cut off to be sent to German upholstery firms; and the bodies had then to be dragged to the crematoria. There the fires had to be constantly stoked, surplus fat had to be drained off the bodies for use by soap manufacturers, and mountains of burning corpses had to be constantly turned over so that the draught might fan the flames.

Added Hoess, like the poet and philosopher of the New Germany that he was: "The Jews' way of living and dying was a true riddle that I never managed to solve."

Kastner answers again:

> Kastner: Yes, I met Colonel Hoess in the Budapest office of Dr. Bulitz, one of Colonel Becher's aides. Krumey was also present.

It is at this point that Tamir hesitates. Should he give chronic name-dropper Kastner a chance to rehabilitate himself in Israel by asking about his association with Hoess and eliciting from him a late-day denunciation of the German head-killer? Judge Halevi takes up the questioning.

> Judge Halevi: What did you talk about?
>
> Kastner: We talked about the Death March of the Jews from Hungary to Austria.
>
> (Not about the twenty thousand Jews of Kluj whom Colonel Hoess had converted into ashes.)
>
> Judge Halevi: (slowly) What did Hoess say about the Death March?
>
> Kastner: Hoess said he thought the whole thing was swinish. He said he thought the things he saw happen on the road between Budapest and Vienna were utterly swinish.

A hush is in the court room as Kastner pins his valentine on this vilest of Germans. But Kastner, as always, is unaware of any flaw in his attitude. His loyalty to the good name of the Nazis seems a spontaneous one. Loyalty to evil and simultaneous boasts of virtue are the Kastner schizophrenia, not unusual in politics. Now the boasts again:

> Kastner: I confirmed what Colonel Hoess said about the Death March. And I provided him with the details of how many of the marchers were dropping dead at the roadside every day. And he stated to me he would take immediate steps to have the Death March stopped.
>
> Judge Halevi: (who seems to feel he wasn't hearing aright) What was Colonel Hoess' job?
>
> Kastner: He was Commander of Auschwitz.

154

Judge Halevi: Commander of the Death Chambers of Auschwitz?

Kastner: Yes, he, himself.

His Honor looks in silence at Kastner; and Kastner anwers the look.

Kastner: Strange and tragi-comic as it may seem, it is true.

Tamir again: You have stated, Dr. Kastner, that Himmler issued an order through Becher to ease the situation of the surviving Jews.

Kastner: Yes.

Tamir: When did he issue this alleged order to stop the extermination of the Jews?

Kastner: Between October and November of 1944.

Tamir: Is it true that after Himmler's supposed order, tens of thousands of Jews were still exterminated in the German camps?

Kastner: I know that after Himmler's order tens of thousands died, but I don't know if they were exterminated.

Tamir: Would you agree with me, Dr. Kastner, that those who died were exterminated—that some food, clothing and human treatment would have kept them alive?

Kastner: Yes, that is true.

Tamir: Is it true that even in May 1945 [the last days of the war] Jews were exterminated?

Kastner: I heard so.

Tamir: Back to the Bergen-Belsen camp. You were there and I wasn't. [In Kastner's alleged do-good travels with the Nazis.] Nevertheless, I tell you that never to the very last moment of the war was the fate of the Jews improved in that camp.

Kastner: (indignantly) That is untrue!

Tamir: Very good. Now tell us when it was improved.

Prosecutor Tell: Your Honor, I object. Tamir is merely fishing.

Tamir: Correct—but look at the big fish I'm landing.

Judge Halevi: Objection overruled.

Tamir: Are you willing to admit now, Dr. Kastner, that the

155

catastrophe never changed for the Jews, from the beginning to the end?

Kastner: According to the results, it was catastrophic.

(Is there any other way of judging the killing of six million than "according to the results?" By what other measurement was the killing not catastrophic?)

Tamir: Then why do you dare say that it's untrue that the position of the Jews was *not improved?*

Kastner: I had heard of attempts to improve—but when I went to the camps I saw no evidence.

Tamir: When the British entered Bergen-Belsen in April 1945, there were still bodies in the ovens.

Kastner: Yes, I heard so.

Tamir: (grimly) Will you agree with me that there was no improvement in Bergen-Belsen?

Kastner: True.

Tamir: And in the Terezienstadt Death Camp—no improvement either.

Kastner: There, too, the situation remained unchanged.

Tamir: Would you agree with me that in no German concentration camp was there any letup in the killing of Jews, despite this alleged order?

Kastner: The question is too general.

Tamir: Why is it general?

Kastner: The change varied in different camps.

Tamir: Do you mean to say there were camps in which Jews were well-treated by Germans?

Kastner: I was not asked about Jews in your question.

Tamir: We talk only of Jews.

Kastner: Well, not only Jews were in the camps.

Tamir: I repeat and ask only about Jews—were there any cases of Jews being favorably treated in any camp?

Kastner: There was no favorable treatment of Jews.

Having pulled this admission out of the fogs and fantasies in Kastner's skull, Tamir goes after the story of the Rescuer's final "work" among his Nazi *companeros.*

156

Tamir: Where did you go from Vienna?

Kastner: To Berlin.

Tamir: At the climax of the war, in April, 1945, where did the representatives of the Jewish Agency live in Berlin?

Kastner: In the apartment of one of Becher's aides. After I had spent one night in prison by mistake.

[Typical Nazi blindness—mistaking Dr. Kastner for one of their enemies.]

Tamir: How long did you stay in the Berlin apartment?

Kastner: Four to five days.

Tamir: What did you do while you were in Berlin?

Kastner: I sat in the apartment or took walks in the neighborhood. I waited to meet Himmler and Becher.

Tamir: Where did you eat?

Kastner: In the apartment.

Tamir: Who gave you food?

Kastner: The wife of Becher's aide.[116]

Tamir's questions show him obviously fascinated by this almost legendary picture of a Jew living the life of Riley in Hitler's own city, just as it is having its guts blasted out of it by the Allies. I am also fascinated. A Jewish official in Jew-clean Berlin! With the speed-up of Jew-killing in all the death camps! I stare at this little Red Riding Hood of a Kastner beaming and chatting with all the S.S. wolves, and mysteriously immune. He makes no mention of any bombs falling, or streets flying apart. He seems to remember only the nice side of his Berlin visit—the friendly Becher, the fine hospitality all around . . . . . No mention now of any "philanthropic" work, even though Kastner will linger among his Nazi friends during the finale of German resistance, and take his "heroic" part in a few grimly ludicrous episodes of the Third Reich's final hours.

But these episodes have an entirely different meaning from the inane doings described in the Berlin apartment—the walks, the talks, the food, the beer steins on the table . . . Fascinating though it has been, the tale of Kastner's picaresque travels in Nazi Germany is obviously finished. And the myth of Kastner as a power for good among the German killers lies dead in a court room.

157

And with it the myth of the Jewish Agency rescue work by means of the power of that pompous rogue, Kastner. That myth lay dead too.

OPERATION WHITEWASH

The Allies are a ring of might around Germany's vitals. Russians and the Allied Armies move toward the rendezvous at Berlin. And Becher, Krumey and Wisliczeny are more eager every day to save Jews. They manage to pull a few emaciated and tottering victims out of the death camps.

These saved ones are distributed through Switzerland. They will serve as a sort of window dressing for Nazi "goodness," a proof of the "good will" toward the Jews shown by Becher, Krumey, Hoess, Jutner, Klages, Wisliczeny and all the S.S. chieftains trying to elude the postwar gallows.

The window-dressing Jews will work not only for the S.S. Colonels after the war; but for Kastner, also. They will help whitewash him.

And not Kastner alone, but the Jewish Agency and Zionist leaders of Palestine will benefit. A new myth of Jewish Agency philanthropy is in the making. Attorney General Chaim Cohen, making his summation before Judge Halevi, cries:

"My friend [Tamir] says Kastner was a guest in Berlin in the apartment of a Nazi officer, put at his disposal by Becher.

"Where should he live in Berlin—in the Embassy of the Jewish Community?

"Kastner went to Berlin on a certain mission. What is more natural than that Becher gives him sleeping quarters?

"There is another charge: that Kastner lived in the Grand Hotel in Vienna, the headquarters of the Nazi officers. Where then should he spend his stay? There were no hotels in Berlin or Vienna for transients. About all these charges, that it was a special pleasure for him to mingle with the Nazis—I do not envy Kastner these pleasures." [117]

And so on and on . . . that there "is not one iota of proof" that Dr. Kastner did or thought a wrong thing "in his great and heroic rescue work of Jews from the Nazi Hell."

The Government mouthpiece cites one of these heroic deeds —the ludicrously transparent Jewish Agency rescue operation in Bratislava, Czechoslovakia, in April, 1945. And here is Dr. Kastner on the witness stand again, sweating and blinking through a cross-examination on this grim piece of heroism, and trying to sound as honorable as the Government Attorney General says he is.

Tamir: Dunand, the Red Cross representative, states [in his published book] that when the Gestapo left Bratislava and the Russians were about to enter it any minute, you were nervously searching through the caves [outside the city] collecting Jews to transfer to Switzerland. Is that true?

Kastner: Yes.

Tamir: Why should you be, Dr. Kastner?

Kastner: Because they were already bombing the outskirts and I still had my rescue work to complete. I wasn't nervous for my own life.

Tamir: How many Jews did you rescue from Bratislava?

Kastner: I took twenty-six or twenty-seven Jews out of there.

Tamir: Dr. Kastner, the Germans have left. The Russians are about to occupy the city. Why would it be very important for you to hunt up twenty-seven Jews and take them to Switzerland?

Kastner: It was very important. The Jews thought so too.

Tamir: In his book, Dunand describes how these Jews in their caves on that Friday night were full of rejoicing over the arrival of the Russians and terribly fearful after months of hiding to entrust themselves to the Gestapo. But you persuaded them. You told them it wasn't a matter of rescue, but that they would be able to enjoy a convalescence rest in Switzerland. After which they could come back to Bratislava, if they wished.

Kastner: Yes, it's true they were afraid to leave their caves and entrust themselves to the Gestapo. In fact, I was worried over that myself.

159

Tamir: But you persuaded them.

Kastner: No, we persuaded each other it was the better thing to do.

Tamir: Dr. Kastner, you needed twenty-seven Jews to take along when you got to the Swiss border with Krumey. You needed 'them as an alibi for him and for yourself as well. And you were ready to dig Jews up from under the earth or anywhere to furnish you that alibi.

Kastner: (wildly) This is one of your typical savage lies! It is not true! Never! Not true!

But Tamir is done. He feels he has battered enough truths out of the Rescuer from Kluj, enough confessions, admissions, contradictions, screams. Enough for this trial. For it is true Tamir is dreaming of the time when Kastner is put on trial for his crimes. Tamir believes this will happen. It must happen.

For the people of Israel are everywhere asking bitter questions. A revolt of some sort seems to be in the making. In the schools, the army barracks, the cafés, parlors, synagogues—the questions arise hourly.

Ben-Gurion, an old hand at riding out storms, has some time ago, retired to his Kibbutz and announces wistfully that he has returned to his first love—sheep-herding. Photos of the Jewish leader walking in a meadow with a lamb on a string appear in the press. His suspenders hang down, the wind ruffles his moujik mane. He is a man of the people, with a tender heart. See the lamb.

When Tamir informs the court he is done, Judge Halevi turns to the unfortunate Kastner.

Judge Halevi: Do you have anything to correct, or add to all your testimony here? If you have forgotten anything important or were mistaken as to something important I give you the opportunity to say so.

Kastner: Your Honor, will you give me some time to think?

Judge Halevi: Please do.

Judge Halevi's face offers no hint of his mood. But the slow, careful utterance of his questions make it obvious. He has heard astonishing and damning confessions of viciousness from Kast-

ner. His Honor wishes to give Dr. Kastner a last chance to uncover some fact of innocence that may be hidden away in the
labyrinth of his mind. Kastner does his thinking with a ball-point pen in hand. He
makes notes on paper. He finally dictates his notes to Judge
Halevi's secretary. It takes an hour. Judge Halevi asks, "Is that
all?"

Kastner: I cannot refrain from expressing again my sorrow
over the impression which may have been made in some
people regarding the phrasing of my testimony about
Becher—comma—and the result of it—full stop. Neither
I nor my friends have anything to hide in this whole
affair—and especially we do not need to regret that we
acted in accordance with our conscience, despite all that
has been done to us in this trial.[118]

The government press sums up the story of Kastner's lies and
confessions in a triumphant headline. The *Jerusalem Post* informs
Israel in a streamer across the front page,
"Kastner—'My Conscience Clear.'" [119]

THE ODDITY OF GUILT

It is not a pleasant spectacle to see the truth ripped out of a
man. A guilty man exposed suffers often more than an innocent
one misjudged. I used to note this when I covered murder trials
in Chicago—that guilt was sometimes harder to bear than injustice.

It is odd that a man should be suddenly hurt by something
he has known for a long time—his guilt. There are many reasons
for this. One of them is that a man does not feel his guilt deeply
until the world sees it, or until he has to pay for it.

Individuals accustomed to private lives are often crushed by
becoming visible to others—as what they are. Not so with public
figures.

Guilt does not make a politician outcast—be he Jewish, British,

161

or Nazi. For the politician is never guilty as a wrongdoer; only as a wrong thinker or wrong guesser. Even if his thoughts and guesses set bonfires raging in the world and rain disaster on large areas of it—he is still immune from guilt in the eyes of the law, and in the eyes of his contemporaries. History will sometimes take a look at him, dead in his grave, and give him a bad mark. But the contemporary verdict is nearly always the same —not guilty by virtue of serving an ideal.

Although shaken and embittered by the continuing revelations in Halevi's court room, the statesmen of Israel offered no visible or audible sign of any suffering.

There's the thing I find most ominous in my day—the rhinoceros hides that encase politicians' hearts. They will not react to the truth that exposes them any more than to a drop of rain. For they are never exposed. The evils proved against them reveal only that they were devoted servants of an ideal, a party, a national destiny.

Exposed in the Kastner case, the Israel politicians do not need to disprove any of the facts in order to prove themselves not guilty. They need only to flash into the eyes of their constituents the "ideal" they served. Who attacks them, attacks Zionism. Who attacks Zionism attacks the finest development in two thousand unhappy years of Jewish history. Tyrants, dictators, and all power-drunk leaders operate always behind the screen of some Ideal. The Ideal exempts them of any guilt for what they do. More, it magically converts their connivings and wicked deeds into proof of how valorously they served the Ideal.

"I understand Kastner," Eichmann writes in his autobiography, published in *Life* magazine. "He is an idealist like I am." [120]

CHAIM COHEN "STANDS BEFORE GOD"

The Attorney General of Israel offers a rather brief summary of his admiration of Dr. Rudolf Kastner. It is lyric, sardonic and tempestuous, but it takes only one day. This would be almost a distance record for United States court oratory, but in Israel it is only once around the track. Particularly for so leading a silver tongue as Chaim Cohen.

At the finale of the trial, Judge Halevi's court room is no longer the teapot chamber in which the proceedings began. When Attorney General Cohen took over the case for the Government, the proceedings were moved immediately into Israel's largest court room, with the largest seating capacity. And the government pulled two of its stenographers out of the Knesset to take over the recording.

Now the large court room is jammed. All the top journalists of the land are on the job. The largest assemblage of trial fans ever beheld in a Jerusalem court since the Romans left around 300 A.D. packs the scene.

I cut the day's oration down to its vital statements; but though I cut, what I quote is a literal translation of Chaim Cohen's Hebrew sentences.

Israel's Attorney General speaks as follows:

"Your Honor, I feel like a representative of the public before God. I pray to you that the man I have to defend will not suffer because of my unworthiness. It is presumptuous of me to try, with my dull words, to do justice to these great heroes who stood as a holy guard during the most tragic hour to befall our people."

(The great heroes are Rudolf Kastner, and his co-workers in Budapest.)

"I am not worthy of the task," says Chaim Cohen, "I can only hope Your Honor will not be deaf to my humble efforts. My prosecution today will be more firm and more grave than it ever was before in an Israeli Court."

There follows a ringing affirmation from Attorney General Cohen (and author of the law) that any Jew who collaborated with the Nazis during the extermination deserves to be hanged by the neck until dead. After which, the Attorney General orates: "There is not an iota of proof that Rudolf Kastner became such a collaborator. His honorable intentions never left him to the end.

"My learned friend [Tamir] says that the Germans played a vicious trick, using Kastner to help them induce the masses of Jews to avoid resistance, avoid escape.

"What masses? Escape—where to? Revolt—by whom? . . . These were Jews behind whom there were many long years of

163

persecution, torture, endless suffering, who had returned from forced labor in the Ukraine—who saw with their eyes what the Germans had perpetrated there; they were the Jews who were tortured in quizzings for their property, who were jammed in brick factories without a pillow for their head, without food, without dress . . . For those and millions of Jews like them there came true the old curse, 'And lo, they were meant but to be taken like sheep for slaughter, for killing, destruction, crushing and shame.'

"These should escape? They had no feet on which to run. They should revolt? They had no hands with which to fight. No spirit was left in them. . . .

"Even the Warsaw ghetto was no exception. The masses in the Warsaw ghetto were in the same condition and the revolt there was waged only by a few extraordinary characters."

(Item: the few extraordinary characters were thirty-three thousand Jews who stood off three hundred fifty thousand Wehrmacht troops and thirty thousand S.S. troops—their tanks and cannon—for twenty-seven days in the Warsaw ghetto. None of the Jews surrendered.)

Attorney Cohen makes a small concession. He fails to support Government official Kastner completely in his testimony about Becher: He argues:

"I am willing to assume that Kurt Becher was a vicious criminal, a man not to deal with. Kastner did not lie [about Becher] and there was even no contradiction in what he said. But let us assume for a moment that he did lie.

"Supposing Kastner forgot after a lapse of ten years [it was only six years] to whom he gave the testimony. [The pro-Becher affidavit.] This may justify my learned friend, Tamir, in claiming that Kastner had a weak memory, and that one cannot rely on his testimony.

"The question, therefore, of whether or not Kastner tells the truth or has a reliable memory has no bearing on the accusation at issue here. My friend [Tamir] has asked some of his witnesses, 'Would you give a sworn affidavit in favor of a Nazi?' All of them answered in chorus, 'Amen, we wouldn't have done it.'

"There may well be a divergence of opinion between such people and Dr. Kastner as to what is correct and what is incorrect. And he who thinks it is a national obligation [to help S.S. Colonel Kurt Becher with an affidavit] does not become a worse Jew or a traitor. If Dr. Kastner thought his way was the right way, then it was right for him, and nobody has the right or the authority to say to Dr. Kastner, 'You had no right to testify for a Nazi.' There is no one who can sit in judgment on Dr. Kastner, but Dr. Kastner's own conscience, his sense of values, of duty, and his sense of national responsibility.

"There is nobody who can invent standards by which to measure a man's sense of national responsibility. If my learned friend [Tamir] wants to teach this court or me a lesson in national responsibility, pardon me if I look for a teacher somewhere else.

"My friend attacks Kastner because he did it [the Becher whitewash] in the names of the Jewish Agency and the Jewish World Congress. I don't understand the aims of this attack. If it is intended to prove that Kastner pretended to a standing he didn't have, or if it wishes to prove that Kastner used the name of respectable institutions in order to raise himself above anyone's criticism—be that as it may—I hold that Dr. Kastner's explanation for his act is reasonable and wise. And I don't want to go into the question of whether he did or did not have such power of attorney.

"But let us assume again that he did not have such power. Since he had power of attorney to negotiate with Kurt Becher in the past [in Budapest] why should he think he has no power to testify for Becher as he did?

"Let us assume that Dr. Kastner was being boastful here [about claiming Jewish Agency backing—or a Nazi whitewasher?], as he seems often inclined to be, because he likes to pose as a man of high standing. What does it prove—using the name of the Jewish Agency and the Jewish World Congress? I say that as the man who negotiated with Becher in the name of the Jewish Agency, and found out that Becher's reaction was good and beneficial for those Jewish institutions and for the people of Israel, I say Dr. Kastner had the right to do what he did—was, in fact, bound to do what he did.

"I think that the crime of the Defendant is as grave as actual bloodshed. He took upon himself the right to put a sign of Cain on the forehead of a man on whom neither the Defendant nor his lawyer is authorized or able to express any legitimate opinion whatsoever." [121]

Such is the gist of Chaim Cohen's address to Judge Halevi. It re-affirms the Israeli Government's contention that Dr. Kastner did the correct thing in not warning the twenty thousand Jews of his native Kluj, when there were only 21 guards to keep them from escaping the ash barrels of Auschwitz.

But I'll let Tamir make the rebuttal.

THE DEFENSE SUMS UP

I offer a longer account of the Defense Summation, since it takes seven days to deliver.

Another reason is: the Defense Summation is a fine mark for Israel. It is a denunciation of the Government of Israel, made in an Israeli Court room, by a citizen of that new land. When such a denunciation as this one is tolerated by a government and given ear to by a judge, it is a bright proof of a people's honest soul.

Tamir addressing the District Court of Jerusalem is more than a Jewish voice. He is the voice of an individual who can still assail the sins of the State in which he lives. This voice sounds the difference between government's triumph over man, and man's non-defeat by government.

Tamir begins:

"Your Honor, a cruel and inevitable duty was imposed on us in the trial. Every step taken had to be made through Jewish blood. And now a great human, moral and historic task commands me. Our nation raises its eyes to the high seat of justice and waits the sound of truth from it.[122]

"From the great butchery of Jews until a year ago our land was given to forgetfulness and perfidy.

"The bones of the slain millions of Auschwitz had been plowed into German soil as fertilizer. And these plowmen had regained their freedom and become leaders of the new Germany. The murderers and their collaborators had returned to the bosom of human society.

166

"In payment for Jewish blood, money has been offered and accepted [123]—by the state of Israel. And memorial forests were planted in our land in honor of the exterminated Jews of Europe. "But memorial forests did not silence the voices of the slaughtered. The voices entered finally a court room in Jerusalem and compelled us to open the book of extermination, and study it, and see its truth.

"I heard the Attorney General's cry in this court room, 'Who are we and what are we to judge public officials who worked in that Hell of death?'

"I heard that question. I ask another. Who are we and what are we who dare avoid facing the truth in our souls—the truth of why and how catastrophe came to our people? Out of all the shames and agonies which smote us during the slaughter of Jews, there is one shame we can remove today—the shame of hiding the truth.

"The Attorney General said, 'Nothing is proven—not a single fact—it is all a baseless series of charges—all whipped up for political reasons.' Your Honor, if our charges were so groundless, why the great anxiety which seized the Attorney General, and those he represents? Why did he rush to take over the prosecution from his assistant? Why did he start pleading for long recesses to bring witnesses from abroad? [124]

"And why did important public figures like Avriel, Danzig, Bader, Rafael,[125] Palgi, appear here and make themselves a laughing-stock in their efforts to conceal what they knew?

"Was all this due to the mud-slinging tactics of some irresponsible lawyer? And did this court allow us to waste its time with that sort of chicanery?

"If the case of the Attorney General is so pure, why is it so dirty? He cries out the dirt is in my accusations. The dirt is not in them, Your Honor, but in what they have exposed.

"I have heard it said, 'Even if it is true, why expose it? Can it restore the dead? It can only damage us. We are all in a very small boat in a stormy sea. Exploring these matters can only damage all the Jews of Israel and of the world.'

"There is a factor more important than any temporary damage that may be done by exposing the truth. There is a young generation in Israel that must know the full story of what happened

167

to its brothers, its fathers, its kith and kin. This young generation must know the full truth in order that it may have a true scale for its judgements.

"I shall not insist that Rudolf Kastner is a born criminal, or a man entirely black. I shall not say, 'Death to Kastner!' [126]

"I say this: just as Kastner's brothers were exterminated bodily in Auschwitz, his soul was destroyed there. He, too, was a Hitler victim—a victim who became a wild danger to the Jews of Europe—but a victim nevertheless.

"I shall try to show Your Honor how an idealistic, Zionist youth like Kastner, owning a few flaws, but full of talent, deteriorated into a trusted chum of the Nazi leaders in 1945.

"In explaining Kastner's activities I shall offer many facts in his defense. But how dare anyone stand in this court and say we are not to judge Kastner? And who says it? The Attorney General of Israel—four years after our parliament has enacted the law against Nazis and their collaborators, the same law under which this same Attorney General prosecuted scores of offenders in our courts.

"And whom did this Attorney General bring to justice? Little people, always. A jewish policeman who had beaten a woman in a concentration camp in order to save his own life. The whole force of the state of Israel was mobilized against such small, pathetic offenders. And the Attorney General thundered for conviction.

"Are the legal nets of our country only for the catching of little fish? Are there big holes specially left in them for the escape of the big sharks?

". . . The Attorney General's words shocked my heart. Because it was not a privately hired lawyer who orated here. It was the representative of the government of Israel.

"I charge, Your Honor, that his whole speech from beginning to end, was an oratorical screen to cover evils that were exposed.

And when they wish to cover up any of their own actions, they are willing to defame all of Jewry. It is about one million Hungarian Jews that the Attorney General said, 'revolt—by whom? They had no hands. They had no feet. There was no spirit in them.'

"Moshe Sharett is o.k., Rudolf Kastner is o.k., Hillel Danzig is o.k., but the Jewish masses in Kluj, Nodvarod, Budapest—they had no spirit, no hands. They were without courage and reason. Therefore they had to be slaughtered. It was heaven's decision, said this Attorney General of Israel, a decision not to be altered that they must go like sheep to the slaughter pens.

"The Attorney General said, 'Who is he and what is he who dares defame public officials who worked in the Hell of Death?' [Kastner *et al.*]

"And I say: Who is he and what is he who dares defame our own good Jewry which was so badly smeared by the Prosecution witnesses in this trial? Who is he and what is he who dares utter this defamation of the Jewry of Herzl, Nordau, Dov Gruner, Jacob Weiss, Hanna Senesh—and all the heroes and martyrs who sacrificed their souls?

"The Defense in this trial defends not the accused alone. It defends all Jewry that has been berated and cursed by ruthless men—it defends the Jews who have been called dust, called 'Jews without spirit or hands,' called 'the frozen hearts,' called non-Zionists.

"I call upon Your Honor to decide that, in the choice between Hungarian Jews and Kastner and his clique, it was Hungarian Jewry that was fine, great and tragic.

"But in their tragic hour they had no true honorable leaders— only little egoists, self-seeking and narrow-minded—who aided in their destruction.

"I call on Your Honor to agree—that there was no reason on earth for these men, women and children of Hungary to go like sheep to the German butchers.

"It is a sin against God and against Jewish pride and human dignity to say that these near million Jews had to go to their deaths the way they went—and that it was impossible for them to do other than they did—that a man had to go with his wife, children and parents like an animal to butchery by the Germans.

"Guilty for their deaths are first the German murderers. Next, the criminality of the nations who aided the murders, actively or passively—Hungary on the one hand and England on the other. Guilty next are the other great civilized nations, whose acquiescence and indifference spurred on the slaughter.

"But guilty also is the small-souled, criminal leadership and

169

cowardice of our own Jewish leaders. They knew only how to grab power. Courage and ability and decision were beyond them.

"All these apologetic chants about Jews having to go to their deaths without protest, these hymns of acquiescence for . the death-industry of Auschwitz, we had to hear from an Attorney General of Israel.

"No, Your Honor, this is not the morale of Jewry—the sacrificing of the many to save the few.

"Chaim Weizmann in 1937 said that the Jews of Europe are '. . . economic and moral dust in a cruel world . . .'

"True, they were not wanted. And so they remained the dust to be scattered. Now the Attorney General continues this point of view, he endorses it.

"Who is this Attorney General representing—the citizens of our state or the private interests of some officials of the state? It is not too difficult a question to answer.

"The Attorney General is not alone in covering up for Kastner. Many institutions have done the same covering-up before him. In 1946 the Zionist Congress in Basel,[127] the Haganah trial in the case of the parachutists,[128] and the Israeli police in 1951, all took a look at Kastner's activities—and covered up what they saw.

"And when all the Jewish leaders and all the powers of government had covered up for Kastner, one old man steps forward to reveal the truth.

"And why did all the powerful government institutions leave this truth-telling to Malchiel Greenwald? Why did they knowingly cover up the collaboration of Kastner with the Nazis? There is only one answer. They had no choice. They had to protect Kastner for fear he would reveal all the facts known to him about another collaboration—the Jewish Agency collaboration with the British—which sabotaged the rescue of Europe's Jews and contributed to their annihilation.

"That's how this 'show' happened in this court—a government and all its leaders did not act towards this man, Kastner, as any decent society would have done.

"After seven days of cross-examination, Kastner's lies and villainies were clear to all. Instead of abandoning the protection of such a creature and handing him over to the court saying, 'Let's look into this nightmare ourselves,' they throw all their great authority, all the prestige and cunning of their officials into the case to save him. And all these Israeli government officials came here, one pulling the other, all conspiring to conceal from this court and from the nation the truth of how the catastrophe befell the Jews of Hungary.

"I charge that all the witnesses for the prosecution lied to this court. I can say, with a clean conscience, that none of the witnesses for the defense lied knowingly.

"There was no relation between our witnesses. They had no thought of 'helping each other.' They were workingmen, clerks, refugees, people from all parties, the people of our land.

"The other side offered a united group of public figures—all culled from one party and clique.

"There you have the two sides—the ruling clique of Israel and the people of Israel."

Tamir continues about Kluj.

"Our charge against Kastner is this—a community of twenty thousand Jews, one of the finest in Hungary, of which a great part could have been rescued, was sacrificed in order to save 380 of his own friends and relatives.

"We charge that these 380 people (we are all happy they remained alive) were not an achievement but the price for sacrificing the many thousands.

"We charge that this cost was reckoned and this price paid with the same lack of conscience that the Attorney General described with such enthusiasm when he declared that the sacrificed Jews were 'without hands or spirits.' And we charge that Kastner deliberately decided it was best to rescue the 'prominents.'

"I said Kastner was not a born criminal, and not all black. It is foolish to say that he was even a bloodthirsty man.

"We have never said Kastner was a traitor who did what he did simply to receive money from the Nazis. He did not start with treason. He started with collaboration—which the Nazis preferred.

"The traitor is not the most efficient instrument for an enemy. A traitor hands over his regiment, his information, and his job is finished. The traitor's way is one act of surrender.

"Collaboration is a more effective technique. You take an important figure from the other side. And you help him play the

171

drama in which he stars as the leader of his people. You help him show success and triumphs (little ones). But the cost of these successes to the people is their destruction.

"Kastner, the collaborator, was worse than any Pétain or Quisling. Because Kastner's collaboration didn't sacrifice honor and freedom alone. It accomplished the complete extermination of the people themselves—after which nothing remains.

"It is only human for a man to save himself and his family first. Had it been an ordinary man, exploiting his connections and running away with his family, who would dare to criticize him? Who knows if any of us would behave differently?

"But this is not the case of Kastner. We deal here with a leader, a leader of rescue, a man who became a national leader. This is another story.

"And is this the motto our Attorney General wishes to give to every officer in the Israeli Army and Navy, 'When danger comes, run away first and save yourself and your own.'

"Let us grant further that even a National Leader can make mistakes—pull strings to save his own skin. It is not nice, but one can sometimes understand or forgive.

"But at what a cost! Here we don't speak of a man who runs away, who, under great pressure, deserts his people. With Kastner, it is not the running away. It is the terrible price in the blood of his people that he is willing to pay. Out of his sickly ambition to be considered a big shot, a leader of Jews, his blindness, his lies, and his terrible crimes, increase and increase.

"This is a collaboration for which there is not the routine apology, 'Other days will come and the situation will be changed.'

"No, I don't say traitor. I say collaborator. And a collaborator needs studying.

"Of course in the beginning he is trapped by the German Satan. Eichmann tells him—'Everything is lost. Your accursed Jews must all die. There is no way out. No matter what you do, they will all be annihilated.' Then he adds, 'But perhaps you can save a few. But in return for such a favor, you have to help me!'

"And here the list of train-people appears. And Kastner, the little journalist from Kluj, never too choosey a fellow—allows his sickly ambition to confuse his values. His eagerness to be a somebody outwits his conscience. He grabs at the Eichmann proposal. He hopes, he trusts, he deceives, until he is hooked on the wheel and into the mill he goes for grinding.

"The 380 prominent Jews are quartered outside the Kluj ghetto. And they will be kept there until all the twenty thousand Jews have ridden off to Auschwitz.

"Their function is to soothe these doomed ones, to keep them calm and hopeful. And this they do, until the last Jew is sealed and delivered to the gas chamber. Not until Kluj is empty of Jews and their lullaby task is done, do they get their reward. In special trains they ride through the barren ghetto, through the empty streets, and leave for Budapest.

"Until May, 1944, Kastner was a man of honest intention. He was a self-seeking, slippery fellow, but basically his intentions were to save Jews.

"From mid-May on, his entanglement deepens, his crime grows. He performs in a whirlpool of blood.

"No wonder that he will never return to his home town of Kluj when the war is over. No wonder that on October 15th all the survivors who trickled back to Kluj—Zionists, Social Democrats, Communists, Jews of every sort—try him *in absentia* in a people's court and pronounce him a war criminal.

"Kastner tells us that at the beginning the Germans talked to him about money he must pay them. But soon Kastner finds out the Germans have no financial interest in Jews. When every other Jewish group had to give money to the Germans, Kastner alone gives no great sum. He has something better to give the Germans. He gives Jews.

"And who are the Germans who help Dr. Kastner? He mentions Becher, Krumey; Wisliczeny—the killers of the Jews of Poland, Greece, Hungary. He mentions Hunshe and Novak, two of Eichmann's chief assistants.

"And Kastner has an in also with Hungarian Nazis. He meets Ferenczi, chief of the Hungarian gendarmes. He even meets Baky, who, according to all testimonies, was even more eager to 'eat Jews' than Eichmann. And he is in contact with Gerzoli, head of Hungarian anti-espionage.

"It is of Garzoli and Gestapo chief Klages that Kastner said, 'They were among those who wanted to help me.'

"Who, then, wanted to exterminate Jews? They all wanted to help, says Kastner—Klages, Garzoli, Krumey, Becher, all wanted to help. And Himmler 'helped.' Who then exterminated the Jews?

"And what was Kastner doing in Berlin?

"The Attorney General says, 'His solemn and noble duty.'

"Does the Attorney General claim seriously that there was such a close mutual interest between the Third Reich and our Jews? When hundreds of thousands were rotting in the camps, being murdered daily by the thousands, and used in laboratories for inhuman experiments—was it then there bloomed this mutual interest?

"In the last, most crucial four months of war, the Jew Kastner parades in Vienna or Berlin—among the highest Nazi chieftains. And his Nazi chums speed him goodbye as he hustles off at the climax of the war. He will arrive in Switzerland in time to meet the American representative, McClelland, there, and be able to supply McClelland with all he knows of the Nazi crimes.[129]

"Is there a deeper trust that Kastner's Nazi friends could show than this? What else do I have to prove in this case—but this alone? The Nazis would never put such trust in an Englishman or American. But they put their faith in the representative of the Jewish Agency who witnessed their worst crimes.

"—I therefore say to this court what the defendant Greenwald did not say in his pamphlet. I say that, in the last months of the war, Kastner became the agent for the whole Nazi gang—the most effective Jewish agent in their ranks. For he was now one of them, their trusted ally and apologist."

Tamir takes up Becher and Kastner's affidavit:

"Who is Kurt Becher? The head of the Economic Department of the S.S. The Economic Department meant concentration camps, gold teeth, bones for fertilizer, clothes, and above all —Jewish fat for soap. These were the functions of the Economic Department. And it was for this crime that the Americans held Becher in custody from 1945 to 1948.

"All the witnesses have testified that General Kurt Becher had always the last word, that he was responsible only to Himmler himself.

"Becher was also involved in the extermination of Slovakian

174

Jews. He decided who would be deported in the notorious death march. He decided even what women should go to their deaths. And Kastner dares to make depositions at Nuremberg declaring that Becher saved Jews in Budapest. The same Kastner who wrote in a report that Becher was among the chief Nazi criminals who worked actively in the extermination of six million European Jews.

"Sir, he who says Becher saved Jews, says Himmler saved them. He who says Becher was an honorable man says Himmler was an honorable man. There is no escape from the facts. I will go one step further and say he who says Kastner was an honorable man says the S.S. leaders Becher and Himmler were honorable men.

"Sir, the learned Attorney General had the gall to deny even Kastner's proven lies. If there were ever malicious and willful lies—perjury in a court case—admitted and corroborated—they are the lies told by Kastner.

"At least let the Attorney General keep silent, and not deny they were lies.

"I say that Kastner cold-bloodedly stood in the witness box for days and lied to this court and to the Israeli nation. And our Attorney General of the Government of Israel overflows with pathos and tells us he feels 'with all modesty and humility' his great privilege of defending the glory of this man, Rudolf Kastner.

"The Attorney General allowed himself to define the testimony of the twenty concentration camp survivors as a chorus of amens against a Nazi officer. Thus he describes the cry of agony of an exterminated people.

"But I speak no more of the time of extermination. I will speak of the years 1947 and 1953. I speak of a Kastner not under Nazi pressure, not in the dread atmosphere of the ghetto or in occupied Budapest.

"I speak of the action of a man in the free world, after he was saved from doom—of a man who knows everything—a man whose honor the state of Israel has stepped forth to vindicate—the man in whose behalf all the legal apparatus of Israel has been mobilized—while all their might was hurled against the one who dared attack this man.

"This man, Kastner, contemptuous of court and public, has brazenly tried here to cover up his own crime in delivering Kurt Becher, one of the arch-killers, from judgment in Nuremberg.

"Sir, if this is how he behaves after the war, in an atmosphere of freedom, when no danger threatens, when he has become one of the pillars of the government of Israel—how did he behave then, in a climate of terror, under the Nazis, when scores of thousands were in his keeping? If this is his morality now, what could it have been then?

"Sir, today I am allowed and am bound to call upon Your Honor not only to acquit the Defendant, not only to lay down that the Complainant and chief witness, Dr. Kastner, perjured himself maliciously in this court, not only to lay down that he and his colleagues conspired together to conceal from this court and from the whole world the historical truth—but also to recommend that this Dr. Kastner be put to trial by the Israeli Government in accordance with the law against Nazis and their collaborators.

". . . Sir, I am convinced that neither the rhetoric of the Attorney General nor the backing of the whole Israeli government will overcome the truth. Nor will they be able to make a free Israeli court exonerate even partially the enormity of the collaboration with Nazi killers that was reached by Dr. Kastner, Rudolf Kastner, the biggest Jewish agent in the service of the Germans." [130]

THE SOUL OF A JUDGE

There is a likeness between Justice of the Jerusalem District Court, Benjamin Halevi, and the girl, Hanna Senesh. They serve different causes—Hanna, the cause of human love; Judge Halevi, the cause of human justice—but they serve them in the same way—with their entire souls.

The enemy Halevi had to face and vanquish is sometimes a tougher foe than the one Hanna met in Budapest. It is the enemy of a man's own perspectives and prejudices. Halevi has to sit in judgment objectively not only on Greenwald and Kastner, but on his own complex humanity, which includes his life's dedication to Jewry and to the State of Israel.

Two men were never more apart as Jews and patriots than Tamir and Halevi at the start of the trial. Tamir was a child of revolt. He loved his country completely. But Tamir's country did not consist only of the righteous few who ran it. To the contrary, these men had offended his patriotism and embarrassed his soul since childhood. Tamir considered most of the government men in power as unproud and unworthy Jews who had come into their power through the courage and vision of others —a courage and vision they had usurped after it was safe and profitable to echo them.

Not so, Halevi. To Halevi, most of the factotums who took over the running of the new land of Israel were, often, friends, and men and women of upright character.

With 90 percent of the world's Jewry, Halevi believed in these new rulers as he believed in the great kings and prophets of ancient Judea. They, the new ones, were anointed by the long travail of the Jews. The long Jewish dream was a halo over their heads.[131]

It takes Halevi nine months to write his verdict. He does it in the loneliness of his study. He reads and re-reads the protocol of the trial. Halevi is not a slow-witted man. His mind has been long aware of the lies and villainies in the case. Then why so long at his chore? Were there doubts he must resolve? Was it clarity and logic on which he labored? Perhaps. But there was more than fastidiousness that slowed down the writing of his verdict.

I did not interview Judge Halevi in his study any more than I did Hanna Senesh in her cell. And neither of them made report on what went on in their dolorous days. Their deeds, only, speak for them.

Judge Halevi's deed is under his arm as he enters his Jerusalem court room after the nine months. It is a thick manuscript. His verdict is in it.

The court room is filled, and the land of Israel holds its breath. In the court room old Malchiel Greenwald sits staring grimly. He has been well-behaved throughout the trial, contenting himself with derogatory grunts and salty mutterings. Tamir sits beside him.

Kastner is not present. Also missing is Attorney General Chaim Cohen.

Judge Halevi reads his verdict in a low voice that is almost a whisper. But under his quiet tone, a storm is audible. Pale, burning-eyed, and half whispering, Judge Halevi reads for fourteen hours.

Said Tamir, "A nation raises its eyes to the high seat of justice and awaits the sound of truth from it."

The nation hears that sound now. I quote only the vital fragments of Judge Halevi's verdict:

> The masses of Jews from Hungary's ghettos obediently boarded the deportation trains without knowing their fate. They were full of confidence in the false information that they were being transferred to Kenyermeze.
>
> The Nazis could not have misled the masses of Jews so conclusively had they not spread their false information through Jewish channels.
>
> The Jews of the ghettos would not have trusted the Nazi or Hungarian rulers. But they had trust in their Jewish leaders. Eichmann and others used this known fact as part of their calculated plan to mislead the Jews. They were able to deport the Jews to their extermination by the help of Jewish leaders.
>
> The false information was spread by the Jewish leaders. The local leaders of the Jews of Kluj and Nodvarod knew that other leaders were spreading such false information and did not protest.
>
> Those of the Jews who tried to warn their friends of the truth were persecuted by the Jewish leaders in charge of the local "rescue work."
>
> The trust of the Jews in the misleading information and their lack of knowledge that their wives, children and themselves were about to be deported to the gas chambers of Auschwitz led the victims to remain quiescent in their ghettos. It seduced them into not resisting or hampering the deportation orders.

Dozens of thousands of Jews were guarded in their ghettos by a few dozen police. Yet even vigorous young Jews made no attempt to overpower these few guards and escape to nearby Rumania. No resistance activities to the deportations were organized in these ghettos.

And the Jewish leaders did everything in their power to soothe the Jews in the ghettos and to prevent such resistance activities.

The same Jews who spread in Kluj and Nodvarod the false rumor of Kenyermeze, or confirmed it, the same public leaders who did not warn their own people against the misleading statements, the same Jewish leaders who did not organize any resistance or any sabotage of deportations, . . . these same leaders did not join the people of their community in their ride to Auschwitz, but were all included in the Rescue train.

The Nazi organizers of extermination and the perpetrators of extermination permitted Rudolf Kastner and the members of the Jewish Council in Budapest to save themselves, their relatives, and friends. The Nazis did this as a means of making the local Jewish leaders, whom they favored, dependent on the Nazi regime, dependent on its good will during the time of its fatal deportation schedule. In short, the Nazis succeeded in bringing the Jewish leaders into collaboration with the Nazis at the time of the catastrophe.

The Nazi chiefs knew that the Zionists were a most vital element in Jewry and the most trusted by the Jews.

The Nazis drew a lesson from the Warsaw ghetto and other belligerent ghettos. They learned that Jews were able to sell their lives very expensively if honorably guided.

Eichmann did not want a second Warsaw. For this reason, the Nazis exerted themselves to mislead and bribe the Jewish leaders.

The personality of Rudolph Kastner made him a convenient catspaw for Eichmann and his clique, to draw into collaboration and make their task easier.

The question here is not, as stated by the Attorney General in his summation, whether members of the Jewish Rescue Committee were or were not capable of fulfilling their duty without the patronage of the S.S. chiefs. It is obvious that without such S.S. Nazi patronage the Jewish Rescue Committee could not have existed, and could have acted only as an underground.

The question is, as put by the lawyer for the defense, why were the Nazis interested in the existence of the Rescue Committee? Why did the S.S. chiefs make every effort to encourage the existence of the Jewish Rescue Committee?

Did the exterminators turn into rescuers?

The same question rises concerning the rescue of prominent Jews by these German killers of Jews. Was the rescue of such Jews a part of the extermination plan of the killers?

The support given by the extermination leaders to Kastner's Rescue Committee proves that indeed there was a place for Kastner and his friends in their Final Solution for the Jews of Hungary—their total annihilation.

The Nazi's patronage of Kastner, and their agreement to let him save six hundred prominent Jews, were part of the plan to exterminate the Jews. Kastner was given a chance to add a few more to that number. The bait attracted him. The opportunity of rescuing prominent people appealed to him greatly. He considered the rescue of the most important Jews as a great personal success and a success for Zionism. It was a success that would also justify his conduct—his political negotiation with Nazis and the Nazi patronage of his committee.

When Kastner received this present from the Nazis, Kastner sold his soul to the German Satan.

The sacrifice of the vital interests of the majority of the Jews, in order to rescue the prominents, was the basic element in the agreement between Kastner and the Nazis. This agreement fixed the division of the nation into two unequal camps; a small fragment of prominents, whom the Nazis promised Kastner to save, on the one hand, and the great majority of Hungarian Jews whom the Nazis designated for death, on the other hand. An imperative condition for the rescue of the first camp by the Nazis was that Kastner will not interfere in the action of the Nazis against the other camp and will not hamper them in its extermination.

Kastner fulfilled this condition. He concentrated his efforts in the rescue of the prominents and treated the camp of the doomed as if they had already been wiped out from the book of the living.

One cannot estimate the damage caused by Kastner's collaboration and put down the number of victims which it cost Hungarian Jews. These are not only the thousands of Jews in Kluj alone, but also the thousands of Jews in Nodvarod or any other community in the border area; Jews who could escape through the border, had the chief of the rescue committee fulfilled his duty toward them.

All of Kastner's answers in his final testimony were a constant effort to evade this truth.

Kastner has tried to escape through every crack he could find in the wall of evidence. When one crack was sealed in his face, he darted quickly to another.

Judge Halevi reverts to the meeting of Kastner, Becher, and Rudolf Hoess, at the time when the "new line" of rescuing Jews was revealed by Hoess. He says:

From this gathering in Budapest, it is obvious that the "new line" stretched from Himmler to Hoess, from Jutner [132] to Becher and Krumey.

According to Kastner, however, these Nazis were all active in rescuing Jews.

This meeting of these important German guests in Budapest exposes the "rescue" work of Becher in its true light. It reveals also the extent of Kastner's involvement in the inner circle of the chief German war criminals.

Just as the Nazi war criminals knew they needed an alibi and hoped to achieve it by the rescue of a few Jews at the eleventh hour, so Kastner also needed an alibi for himself.

Collaboration between the Jewish Agency Rescue Committee and the Exterminators of the Jews was solidified in Budapest and Vienna. Kastner's duties were part and parcel of the general duties of the S.S.

In addition to its Extermination Department and Looting Department, the Nazi S.S. opened a Rescue Department headed by Kastner.

181

All these extermination, robbery and rescue activities of the S.S. were coordinated under the management of Heinrich Himmler.

Judge Halevi continues:

Kastner perjured himself knowingly in his testimony before this court when he denied he had interceded in Becher's behalf. Moreover, he concealed the important fact that he interceded for Becher in the name of the Jewish Agency and the Jewish World Congress.[133]

As to the contents of Kastner's affidavit, it was enough for the defense to prove Becher was a war criminal. It was up to the prosecution to remove Becher from this status, if they wished to negate the affidavit.

The Attorney General admitted in his summation that Becher was a war criminal.

The lies in the contents of Kastner's affidavit, the lies in his testimony concerning the document, and Kastner's knowing participation in the activities of Nazi war criminals, and his participation in the last minute fake rescue activities— all these combine to show one overwhelming truth—that this affidavit was not given in good faith.[134]

Kastner knew well, as he himself testified, that Becher had never stood up against the stream of Jewish extermination, as Kastner had declared in the affidavit.

The aims of Becher and his superior, Himmler, were not to save Jews but to serve the Nazi regime with full compliance. There is no truth and no good faith in Kastner's testimony, "I never doubted for one moment the good intention of good Becher."

It is clear that the positive recommendation by Kastner, not only in his own name but also in the name of the Jewish Agency and the Jewish World Congress was of decisive importance for Becher. Kastner did not exaggerate when he said that Becher was released by the Allies because of his personal intervention. The lies in the affidavit of Kastner and the contradictions and various pretexts, which were proven to be lies, were sufficient to annul the value of his statements and to prove that there was no good faith in his testimony in favor of this German war criminal. Kastner's affidavit in favor of Becher was a willfully false affidavit given in favor of a war criminal to save him from trial and punishment in Nuremberg.

Therefore, the defendant, Malchiel Greenwald, was correct in his accusations against Rudolf Kastner in the first, second, and fourth of his statements.[135]

Judge Halevi's verdict found Malchiel Greenwald generally innocent of libel against Kastner, but fined him one Israeli pound (fifty cents) for the one unproven accusation—that Kastner had actually collected money from his Nazi partners for his aide to their slaughter program. The judge also ordered the Government of Israel to pay Greenwald two hundred pounds (one hundred dollars) as court costs.

THE MORNING AFTER

The trial had already cast a villain's shadow on the Ben-Gurion Kleagles. Halevi's verdict aggravated their problem—how to rise and keep shining as the custodians of Jewish honor in the face of evidence to the contrary.

There was a way—caution, patience, and faith in the political psychology of the mob. The new Israelites were like the people of any other nation—eager to believe in the virtues of their masters, and quick to forget any proof that these virtues were non-existent.

Halevi's verdict was an emancipation proclamation for the soul of Israel. But a soul is harder to set free than Uncle Tom. The soul of a people is no eagle soaring toward the sun, but a ground hog blinking out at it.

The Ben-Gurionites know all the tricks—how to bamboozle a people and keep the trumpets of righteousness pealing. They know also how to orchestrate the word "smear," and how to hide guilt in the strut of importance. But, chiefly, the leaders of Israel, like all leaders, know that moral indignation in the public is usually a brief passion. Usually a few headlines, a few editorials, a few denunciatory rallies and parades with hand-made posters, will suffice for its full expression. After which, the rebellion will subside to a café and parlor mutter. And, presently, to a repentance for ever having existed at all.

Thus will the Ben-Gurionites arise out of the almost-Revolution that almost filled the land. They will remain in their swivel chairs, with their names lettered on the doors of government.

Nevertheless, though no Israeli job holder except Prime Minister Sharett is booted out of office, in the hearts of Israel something has been overthrown. An illusion has collapsed. The face of the government of Israel will no longer be the face of Hebrew dreams, but the scandal-pocked winner's phiz of the politician. Not to all, but to many.

The government clique will continue, but its bloom will change, just as a love affair changes in the heart of a lover after glimpsing his Isolde between the sheets with another. Forgiveness and forgetfulness may ensue. Kissing may be resumed. But magic is out of the cuckold's bedroom.

Thus Tamir's court-room revolution does not overthrow a regime. It reveals it. And it sets the soul of Israel to brooding.

Israel's press erupted and kept erupting over the Halevi verdict as if His Honor had bombed Jerusalem.

Dr. Moshe Keren, one of the nation's leading political journalists, who had been considerably pro-Kastner, wrote in *Haaretz*— the *New York Times* of Israel,

> Kastner must be brought to trial as a Nazi collaborator. And at this trial, Kastner should defend himself as a private citizen, and not be defended by the Israeli government.
>
> . . . The manner in which the Attorney General allowed Tamir to play with them [the government] and so completely dominate the case, can only be described as a shameful show. A government official is sometimes allowed to fail, like any other human being. But such a tremendous failure calls for consequences.[136]

(Item: The consequences for Chaim Cohen—promotion to Supreme Court Judge.)

Keren continues:

184

The echoes of the Kastner trial will keep on among us for years and years to come. They will continue to poison the air above us, like those famous historical trials after which old governments fell and new governments arose. The State of Israel will never be after this verdict what it used to be before the verdict.[137]

After writing seven installments on the Kastner case, Dr. Keren flew to Germany. His intention was to interview Kurt Becher.

A few days after his arrival in Germany, journalist Keren was found dead in a German hotel. The diagnosis was "heart attack."

Dr. Keren was clasping a book on the Jewish extermination in his dead hand.

The newspaper *Herut* editorialized:

"Israel is fortunate to have an independent judge." [138]

Hatzofe, a religious paper, pronounced:

"The decision will have deep echoes in our generation and generations to come." [139]

Lamerchav, the pro-government Kibbutz paper, stated:

"Nobody can shut his eyes to the tremendous educational value and great national importance this verdict will have." [140]

Haboker, the general Zionist pro-government paper, stated:

"The public wants to know the real facts about Kastner, and not about him alone. The only way to find out the truth is to put all the Rescue Committee people on trial and give them a chance to offer their defense." [141]

Maarev, Israel's largest evening paper, stated:

"This is one of the most terrible blows ever received by the Mapai—coming as it does just before the elections." [142]

Yediot Achronot, an independent evening paper, stated:

"If Kastner is brought to trial the entire government faces a total political and national collapse—as a result of what such a trial may disclose." [143]

Davar, the Ben-Gurion party paper, stated:

"Any attempt to decide in 1955 how rescue workers should have acted ten years ago is undertaking a tremendous human and historical responsibility.

"And it is astonishing how a single judge had the courage to take upon himself this responsibility." [144]

Kol-Haam—Voice of the People—a Communist paper, stated:
"All those whose relatives were butchered by the Germans in Hungary know now clearly that Jewish hands helped the mass murder." [145]

The Jerusalem Post—English paper (pro-government)—offered:
"The most you can wish for Dr. Kastner is that now, after having been found guilty of grave crimes, he will be brought to trial by normal procedure—and will be prosecuted by the State prosecution and not by a lawyer with a political ax to grind." [146]

Mr. Argov, one of Ben-Gurion's closest friends, and chairman of the Defense and Security Committee in Parliament, stated:
"Only a ruthless judge could hand down such a verdict." [147]

Ben-Gurion, himself, was more coy in his comment.[148] He stated:
"Judge Halevi's verdict has aroused in me deep astonishment both in substance and style." [149]

Rudolf Kastner, in a radio interview, stated:
"I am a victim like Captain Dreyfus." [150]

(In the Dreyfus case a Judge was bribed and the trial proved to be a frame-up—against Dreyfus.)

Dr. Karlebach, one of Israel's brightest journalists, wrote in *Maariv*:

What is going on here? The Attorney General has to mobilize all the government power, appear himself in court, to justify and defend collaboration with Himmler! And in order to defend a quisling, the government must drag through the streets one of the grimmest stories of our history!

At 11 P.M. the verdict was given. At 11 A.M. next morning the government announces the defense of Kastner will be renewed—an appeal filed. What exemplary expediency! [151] Since when does this government possess such lawyer-genius who can weigh in one night the legal chances of an appeal on a detailed, complex verdict of three hundred pages? [152]

The whole question of the extermination of Europe's Jewry was revived by the trial and its verdict. It continued to sound throughout Israel despite Ben-Gurion's German handshaking policy.

There is one comic note in these morning-after shudders of Israel. It is sounded by Chaim Cohen—who else?

After his all-out defeat by Tamir, and with the land full of cries of "Fire Cohen!", the Attorney General draws up a new law for Israel and submits it for adoption.

It is a new evidence law, especially tailored for Israel—to prevent another Kastner case, and another government fiasco. It restrains an attorney from attacking a witness too severely, from bullying or insulting a witness, or from asking questions without advance proof of their answers.[153]

This is the same Chaim Cohen who had proposed a law allowing the use in court of a confession secured by the police by physical force.

Israel's parliament adopts Chaim Cohen's "please-don't-hurt-me-Mr. Tamir-law"—with modifications. It leaves the matter and manner of wangling truth out of government officials up to the presiding judge.[154]

This is a setback for Chaim Cohen. But a Supreme Court judge-ship for life will take the sting out of it.

MY OWN SUMMATION

Rudolf Kastner's story is vicious. But it has a human pulse in it. And there are glints of courage and pain in it. He is understandable.

But the others—Ben-Gurion, Sharett and Company—are a harder lot to plumb. Looked at as humans, they are almost preposterous. Obviously they have to be looked at as something else—not Jews, not citizens, but the Face of Authority, as old as the first cities of the world.

A hundred thousand differently named gods have spoken out of this Council Chamber Face—from Babylon and Crete to Washington and Moscow—and the Jerusalem of the new Zion. And if it is not quite gods who speak today, the voices are not a bit less all-knowing and unknowable.

The most preposterous fact at hand about the ruling clique of

Israel is this: How did it happen that these potentates were dim-witted enough to launch such a suit as must bring them to obloquy?

The Golden Calves of Israel could not have been ignorant of what lay behind Kastner. Yet they boldly launch the case that will expose what they have carefully hidden for a decade.

The answer is that authority has an unshakable faith in the image of virtue it calls itself. Authority knows the thousand lies and shenanigans out of which it was created. But authority does not regard these as its true character. Its true character is not what it is, but what it can induce people to believe it is. Thus, until it is led off to the guillotine for its villainies, its true character is always glory and beneficence.

Like the actor, authority has faith in its false whiskers.

But its deepest faith is in the human hunger for illusion. People will hang on to illusion as eagerly as to life itself.

To the people, the false whiskers are the Prophet; the actor strut of Bossism is the Patriot; the reiterated lies of power are the soul of truth.

The government of Israel launched its case against Greenwald because it believed staunchly in the stupidity of the People and the power of the Lie.

To be betrayed, misused, lied to, robbed of youth and life; to be inoculated with hates and manias never in their heads before, and to be sent forth to kill and get killed—all this has always been the lot of peoples unfortunate enough to enter history. The Jews are no exception, although there is a difference in verbs—they were not urged on to die, but permitted to die.

I have a personal involvement in this matter of how six million Jews of Europe were permitted to be slaughtered by the Germans. I worked with those in the United States—the only ones—who tried with all their might to break the Silence in which Europe's Jews were being exterminated. When the massacre had hardly more than started, the propaganda committees of the Irgun Zvai Leumi in New York City began banging out the bloody news.

Two young men of the Irgun, Peter Bergson and Samuel Merlin, came to the United States from Palestine, without contacts or funds. Occupying a hall bedroom, they used the lobbies of swanky hotels in which to hold stowaway press conferences, and in no time at all they hatched a series of propaganda committees glittering with notables. I was their co-chairman, later joined by Senator Guy M. Gillette and novelist Louis Bromfield. I list the numbers of our notables, not to show how powerful we were, but how powerful was the opposition of Jewish Agency and Zionist organizations. For the opposition of Jewish Authority won the day. Although we could break the conspiracy of Silence in large meeting halls and in coast-to-coast newspapers and magazines, we could not grab the ear of government. The slick and respectable Jewish organizations of the United States kept this ear plugged.

On our side, working for our various committees—for a Jewish Army in Palestine to help fight the Germans, for a Free Palestine, for the smuggling of German-doomed Jews into British-closed Palestine; working for us as lobbyists, helping us raise funds, stage pageants and perform in them; endorsing our conferences, proclamations and appeals, were the following categories. I take the count from a Proclamation in 1943 signed with the names of these: thirty-three U.S. senators, one hundred and nine members of the House of Representatives, fourteen reigning state governors, fourteen outstanding ambassadors and members of President Roosevelt's Cabinet, (never Mr. Roosevelt, himself), fifty-five justices and judges of various Supreme and district courts, sixty mayors of leading American cities; four hundred rabbis in all the centers of American Jewry, and almost twice as many Catholic and Protestant right reverends, priests, ministers; a score of American Army generals, colonels and Navy admirals and rear admirals; scores of national leaders in high government posts, five hundred university presidents and professors; and an equal number of playwrights, poets, newspaper editors, and book writers; also hundreds of star actors, singers, dancers, and showmen.

Their names are too many to enumerate, and their contributions of talent, prestige, and energy are also too many for listing. But I cannot pass by the names of my friends Kurt Weill and Arthur Szyk. Weill wrote all the music for all our pageants and rallies. Szyk, one of the best artists of his day, drew all the pictures, scrolls, and ornamentations for our printed propaganda.

The notables on our roster were sufficient seemingly to sweep any cause to victory. That they didn't was due to two factors—our notables were not all of them on our side all the time. They came and went, like volunteer firemen. And the Jewish respectables outnumbered us. However many senators, congressmen, governors, rabbis, priests, college presidents, and puissant dignitaries of every stratum we could muster, the Jewish respectables could come up with five times as many. And not volunteer firemen, but full-time affiliates.

This difference is due to the fact that protest is always a part-time activity; and respectability is a life-time job. There was also another factor against us. Most of our high-powered cohorts and endorsers were Gentiles. Out of the five thousand Important Names we were able to pipe to our side, hardly a handful were Important Jewish Names.

Thus our Gentile Captains of a Thousand, after winning a battle, felt it their duty to step aside modestly and permit the Jewish leaders of the land to finish the victory. We could convince our Gentiles of our cause, but we could seldom convince them that nearly all the fine American Jews whom they admired were the enemies of our cause.

There was no such confusion among these fine American Jews. They knew on what side they were, and they stayed there, battling away vigorously and ceaselessly on two fronts. One was the front of Silence. Directives for this front came from Ben-Gurion, Weizmann, et al. in Palestine. They were the custodians of the Jewish future. They knew what was going on. And American Jewry (like the doomed ones of Europe) translated their cowardly policies of expediency and parochial politics into the noblest of Jewish objectives.

The second Front of American Jewry's respectables was to convince the world that we who were shouting the news of the slaughter were liars, publicity seekers, race racketeers and, at best, misinformed cases of hysteria. We were, they said, the Wrong People.

It is always a losing battle, this trying to outshout authority. Those who have been in one are left with the conviction that it is easier to waken the dead than the living. But what a hopeless world it would be without this record of lost battles.

In addition to the pageants and oratorical marathons staged by our "outlawed" group, the Bergson-Merlin Committees also kept a barrage of full-page newspaper ads going at the Silence. I wrote most of these ads.

The ads in their large type were like the black flags of holocaust. They advertised graphically the slaughter of Europe's Jews, and called for the residents of the White House and Downing Street to cry *halt* to the Germans in their murder. Graphic though they were, and truthful, they failed in their mission.

I offer one tragic example and one (of many) explanations of this failure.

During a midnight walk on Fifth Avenue, my friend Kurt Weill paused under a street light and read me a Swiss newspaper clipping. It was the story of an offer made by the Rumanian Government to the American and British Governments to allow seventy thousand Trans-Dniestria Jews to leave Rumania, at the cost of fifty dollars each for transport to the border. The story stressed that the offer would be voided as soon as the Germans entered Rumania. They were due any week.

Bergson and Merlin, through underground sources, verified the Swiss story immediately. Such an offer had been made through diplomatic channels. The American State Department had received and pigeonholed it. The British had done the same, naturally.

I wrote a full page ad in the New York papers that announced in heavy type:

FOR SALE
70,000 JEWS
AT
$50 APIECE
GUARANTEED HUMAN BEINGS

The ad explained briefly that three and a half million dollars would rescue the seventy thousand Rumanian Jews from murder by the Germans.

On the appearance of this news advertising copy, Rabbi Stephen Wise,[155] Zionist chieftain in New York and guiding light for the city's Jewish respectables, issued the following statement. The date was February 23, 1943:

"The American Jewish Congress, dealing with the matter in conjunction with recognized Jewish organizations, wishes to state that no confirmation has been received regarding this alleged offer of the Rumanian Government to allow seventy thousand Jews to leave Rumania. Therefore no collection of funds would seem justified."

The Jewish Agency in London also denied the Rumanian offer. This denial was cabled to American newspapers, and carried by them. And reading it, American Jews felt grateful to the Jewish Agency for removing the ugly Rumanian problem from their consciences.

Peter Bergson telephoned Undersecretary of State Adolph A. Berle, Jr., and asked him to affirm or deny the Rumanian offer. Berle said he would call back with the answer. He did, the next day. The story was true, said Berle. The State Department had received such an offer from the Rumanian government.

Years later, Bartley Crum, expert on Middle Eastern affairs, confirmed the facts of the offer. Bartley Crum stated what we knew in 1943, and what the Zionists and Jewish Agency, with their vastly superior organizations, must also have known in 1943. Lawyer Crum revealed that the seventy thousand Rumanian Jews could have been saved, and transported to Palestine via Turkey—a few days' ride in a truck; but that because of Jewish pressure the State Department had not given out the news.

But in 1943, we, who called out the plight of the Rumanian Jews to the world, were discredited by the Zionist unions, the established Zionist leadership and their associated philanthropies, as scandalmongers. Our attempt to get the Jews out of Rumania before the Germans came was scotched.

. The seventy thousand Jews who might have been saved were herded into barns by the Germanized Rumanians under General Antonescu, hosed with gasoline, ignited, and shot down when they came blazing and screaming out of their cauldrons.

Was it for this the conspirators of Silence had been holding their high-level meetings, fraternizing with presidents and prime ministers and keeping intact Weizmann's pro-English policy of an "exclusive" (more or less Jew-less) Palestine? This Silence, this wretched business of Jewish leaders lying about the slaughter of Europe's Jewry—trying to hide it, soft-pedal it—for what?

These organizations, these philanthropists, these timorous Jewish lodge members in Zion, London and America—these Zionist leaders who, let their six million kinsmen burn, choke, hang, without protest, with indifference, and even with a glint of anti-Semitic cunning in their political plannings—I sum up against them. These factotums, these policy-makers, the custodians of the Jewish future in Palestine who hung on to their jobs, who lorded it over their real estate holdings in Palestine, who obeyed the British demand that no ruckus be raised about Europe's Jews being murdered, and that nothing be done to disturb the British sign hung out over all the ports of Palestine— "No Jews Wanted"—these Zionist men and women—I haul into the prisoner's dock of this book.

What would have happened to the Jews of Europe had these Leaders raised their authoritative voices in their behalf? Who knows what even the British would have done had Saul cried out in Tel Aviv rather than Uriah Heep? Would an unselfish, passionate demand for the lives of the six million (one third of the world's Jews) by the official Jewish Leaders have awakened the hearts of England and the United States?

I do not know. I answer only out of my faith in humans. Just as they can be blinded to all goodness by the villainy of leaders, so can they be stirred to noble enterprise by the honor and strength of their leaders. My faith says that nearly all the six million Jews could have been saved, and the honor of our century saved with them—had the powerful American Jewry alone united in a campaign to save them. And had those Palestine leaders who stayed mum on the slaughter and were garrulous as geese on the needs of Zionism in Palestine—had they cried out— would they have survived as leaders? Would the British have ousted them, and gutted the "dream of Zionism"?

Again, I do not know.[156] I know only that, by my measure, such honorable human behavior would have been of deeper worth to the world than a dozen States of Israel.

A SONG OF SONGS—?

Chaim Cohen took nine days to argue his appeal before the Supreme Court Judges, five in number.

Hark to the Cohen voice sounding in the Supreme Court.

"All this talk about Kastner's collaboration with the Nazis is fairy tales! Fairy tales! Never in human history—neither Jewish nor Gentile—was there such a miscarriage of justice." [157]

In this statement, Israel's Attorney General implies that the sorrowful verdict of an honorable Jewish judge sitting in judgment on German crimes is worse than the judgments of the Spanish Inquisition, the Stalin purge trials, and the German verdicts under Hitler. (This is taking in only the more recent phases of "human history.")

Cohen rants about Halevi:

"Look at the style the judge uses! This judge said (in his verdict), 'Kastner lied.' . . . 'Kastner lied here again.' Look at that style! The way he uses the word, 'lied,' 'lied,' 'lied'!" [158]

"Kastner did nothing more and nothing less than was done by us in rescuing the Jews and bringing them to Palestine," cries Cohen, vindicating everybody at one stroke. [159]

Cohen defines the Jewish Agency philosophy—"You are allowed—in fact it is your duty—to risk losing the many in order to save the few." [160]

Chaim Cohen reads Rabbi Weissmandel's letter from his Slovakian cave—the cry for help which the Zionist leaders had ignored—and hidden from the world. He recites liltingly now its despairs, whose every sentence is an indictment of the guilt of his colleagues—the abandonment of Europe's doomed Jews in return for England's good will, and in favor of the quicker development of Zionist real estate. And Chaim Cohen weeps as he reads the rabbi's passionate words. Sorrow rends his bosom. (Chaim Cohen's)

194

Chaim Cohen weeps for the exterminated ones a bit tardily—ten years tardily. I am sure they are nevertheless not crocodile tears, but honest Jewish ones. Thus might a great general weep for the multitude of soldiers who had to be killed in order for his battle to be won.

When the newspapers reported that in his appeal to the highest court Chaim Cohen wept over the slaughtered Jews of Hungary, who remembered that ten years before the government clique turned their backs on these same dying ones and served the British with their silence on the subject? A few chronic troublemakers remembered. But the great public of Israel sighed appreciatively over Chaim Cohen's good Jewish heart, and the good Jewish hearts of all the Bosses who were also quick with tears, and rhetoric for the six million victims of the Nazis.

This is not because the Jews of Israel are more gullible than the *goyim* of England and the United States. It's merely that being Jews is of no help; they are no brighter than any other public.

Here are a few final samples of Cohen's political philosophy, as offered to the Supreme Court judges:

"If in Kastner's opinion, rightly or wrongly, he believed that one million Jews were hopelessly doomed, he was allowed not to inform them of their fate; and to concentrate on the saving of the few.

"He was entitled to make a deal with the Nazis for the saving of a few hundred and entitled not to warn the millions. In fact, if that's how he saw it, rightly or wrongly, that was his duty."

Said Cohen:

"If you don't like it, if it doesn't coincide with your own philosophy, you may criticize Kastner and say his policy was a mistaken one. But what does all this have to do with collaboration? [161] . . . It has always been our Zionist tradition to select the few out of many in arranging the immigration to Palestine [the Weizmann Blueprint]. Are we therefore to be called traitors?"

Nazis and Communists have written: "I served my country, as do the patriots of the Western democracies whose ideal is 'My country, right or wrong.'"

Such loyalty and faith in a Party Line is Chaim Cohen's basic theme. He argues, impassionedly, that if the Supreme Court

195

should confirm Judge Halevi's verdict, it would mean that they indict the entire system and government of Israel.

And thus I leave Chaim Cohen intoning his statist Song of Songs in Israel's Highest Court.[162]

HERE IS "NEW EVIDENCE"!

Attorney Tamir has won a great legal victory, but he feels no glow of triumph. This is because he was not so much an attorney arguing a libel case before a judge, as a sort of one-man revolution in a black gown trying to tip over an unpalatable government. Despite his victory, Tamir notes that the government still stands, and that Ben-Gurion and all his henchmen are still the mighty of Israel.

And he girds himself to finish the job. History is full of men who wouldn't give up. The lone Tamir is like that.

Tamir's major plan is to bring Rudolph Kastner to trial as a Nazi collaborator.[163]

There is a little difficulty here. In such a trial, the same government group that embraced Dr. Kastner as one of their finest heroes, will have to turn on him and try to get him hanged as the most evil of men. It is a spectacle hard to imagine—Ben-Gurion and his aides standing with heads bowed and moaning "mea culpa." Nevertheless, Tamir embarks on this project.

First he must dig up new evidence of Kastner's guilt as a Nazi life-saver. Such new evidence plus Judge Halevi's verdict of guilty will leave the government no choice. They will have to bring their own Kastner to trial.

Another certainty. Should the Supreme Court uphold the Halevi verdict in full or in a split decision, the trial of Rudolf Kastner must follow as day does night.

During the trial Tamir filed away scores of clues that pointed to further Kastner pro-Nazi doings. The clues lay in the harmony of the Jew-Killer quartette—Becher, Eichmann, Krumey, and Wisliczeny. These four were all Dr. Kastner's chums. During the Hungarian extermination, all treated him as a court favorite.

Thus, if he went to Becher's rescue, why not to Krumey's, Eichmann's, Wisliczeny's?

Tamir knows the finale of two of the Nazis—Becher and Colonel Von Wisliczeny. Wisliczeny is identified on the Jewish Agency War Criminal List, Card 0-685, as Heinrich Himmler's brother-in-law, as supervisor of the extermination of the Jews in Greece; as officiating at the killing of sixty thousand Slovakian Jews; as helping organize the deportation of Hungary's Jews to Auschwitz.

Hearing that "Willie" Von Wisliczeny had been captured by the Slovaks and was going to be tried for all the aforesaid activities, Dr. Kastner had hurried to the rescue. There was only one way to keep this member of the Budapest Quartet from being strung up: this was to get him out of the bloodthirsty hands of the Slovaks into cooler American mitts. Dr. Kastner writes to the American authorities in Nuremberg about von Wisliczeny.

"It is particularly fitting that the U.S.A. conduct such a prosecution because the German satellites are too implicated in the anti-Jewish program. They may, therefore, not be able to conduct such a trial with all its ramifications in an impartial manner." [164]

A bold letter. Its lie yells out of it—that the Slovaks may feel too guilty as anti-Semites to punish anti-Jewish Von Wisliczeny. The truth is that the Slovaks are boiling with rage against this exterminator; so indignant, in fact, that they stick "Willie's" neck in a noose and finish him off before the Americans can get around to acting on the advice of the Jewish Agency Rescue Chief, as they did in the case of the other Quartet member—Kurt Becher.

But nobody notes this black-is-white Kastner appeal for Von Wisliczeny until Tamir looks at it with his huntsman's eye.

The third of the quartet, Adolf Eichman, has vanished, leaving no footprints; and Tamir focuses on the last musketeer—Colonel Hermann Krumey. Among the things Kastner testified to in Jerusalem about this apple-cheeked bad boy of the S.S. was that he had been convicted as a war criminal by the Americans in Nuremberg and was doing time in some prison. Tamir believes Kastner lied, and that he had helped Krumey as he did Becher.

But Tamir's theory hits a rock. He runs down Kastner's testimony at the 1945 preparatory sessions of the International Court. Dr. Kastner stated:

"Colonel Hermann Krumey directed the killing of Jews in Austria, Hungary and Poland." [165]

Nevertheless, Tamir persists. With a plane ticket and ten dollars in his pocket, Tamir hops from London to the Pentagon in Washington. Within its file bulging walls are the records of the Nuremberg trials. Working alone, with all the doors of organized Jewry bolted against him, and with no other status than that of an inquisitive lawyer subsisting on sandwiches, Tamir pulls the truth about Herman Krumey out of American pigeon holes.

First a record of Krumey's testimony as a War Crimes prisoner. Colonel Krumey testified September 23, 1947, in Nuremberg.[166] American prosecutor Herbert Meyer did the questioning. Tamir reads:

Meyer: What position did you have in Budapest?
Krumey: I was in the department of S.S. Commander Adolf Eichmann.

Then Krumey related that when Vienna fell he was assigned by Eichmann to escort a Rudolph Kastner to Switzerland.

Meyer: Who was Kastner?
Krumey: He was a Zionist leader.
Meyer: What was his job?
Krumey: To help and rescue Jews in Budapest. When the Russians occupied Hungary he came to Vienna with me.
Meyer: Was he Jewish?
Krumey: Oh, yes. And I helped him a great deal in his work.
Meyer: Why did he go to Switzerland with you?
Krumey: I don't know exactly. But I think he was afraid of the negroes who came into Vienna with the French. I know he was also afraid of the Russians. He took his wife along to Switzerland.
Meyer: What did you do in Hungary while you were there?
Krumey: I was in charge of the censorship of the Jewish press.

(This is a lie worthy of Kastner himself. There was no Jewish

198

press in Hungary. The Germans had stamped it out, along with all the journalists, editors, critics, and global experts attached to it.)

Meyer: Where is Kastner now?
Krumey: Dr. Kastner is now in Geneva. I have a letter from him.

And Krumey reads into the record the letter from the Jewish Agency Rescue head in Budapest, Dr. Kastner:

Most Honorable Mr. Krumey,
I have sent a report to the Zionist Congress meeting in Basel in which I have officially clarified and identified the work done by those who were of help to the Jews. . . .
I hope that my efforts in your behalf will enable you to regain your freedom, and to start a new life on a new basis. I shall do all I can to help you in this matter.
With heartiest regards,
Dr. Rudolph Kastner [167]

Later, Tamir runs down another document—Kastner's sworn affidavit given to Benno Selcke, assistant to the Chief of American Evidence Division of Nuremberg. The affidavit identifies Krumey as a good Samaritan to the Jews. Here, Kastner deposes under oath, "I wish to point out that Hermann Krumey performed his duties in a laudable spirit of good will, at a time when the life and death of many depended on him." [168]

Following Kastner's letter and affidavit, Krumey, the goodwill ambassador to Lidice and the Death Camps was released.

Item: Today (1961) Colonel Krumey is again a prisoner in Frankfurt. The charges of war crimes against him are heavy. In the German Prosecutor's hands are only two affidavits in Krumey's favor. They are by Becher and Kastner. [169]

How will the Prosecution be able to rationalize or dismiss this new evidence against Kastner? Tamir returns to Tel Aviv convinced now that all the power and publicity Ben-Gurion and his train-bearers can muster against bringing Kastner to judgment will avail nothing. The laws of Israel are lucidly written, and the judges of Israel are one of its finest achievements. And the State of Israel, itself, is a small glass house in which concealment of perfidious deeds is not possible. Everyone can look in; everyone can see.

Thus Tamir, his suitcase full of new dynamite evidence, daydreams of a house-cleaning trial for Israel. A New Deal must come out of such a trial. Such a trial must put an end to the thirty-nine years of bondage of Palestine's Jews to Ben-Gurion, Agency and Party.

With the new Krumey evidence, the story of the Budapest Quartet is complete in Tamir's files. The evidence is that the four S.S. Colonels and Jewish Agency chief Kastner arranged their escape plot during the time of Jew-killing.

Not precisely, as one arranges a bank merger. There were too many unforeseeable plot turns. But arranged it as an over-all *modus operandi*. Three of the Colonels would return to Germany and take their chances on facing arrest and trial as war criminals. Dr. Kastner would then ride to the rescue of these three and plead for them as a rescuer of Jews, as an official high. in the councils of Jewish officialdom; and his pleading would gain freedom for the three exterminators.

All three, and Kastner also, would dump the guilt of the Budapest quartet on the missing member, after helping the scapegoat achieve invisibility.[170] The Quartet member who went into hiding, to become the sole symbol of Nazi evil in Hungary, was Adolf Eichmann.[171]

There is only one worry in Tamir's battle plan. His chief weapon is now Rudolf Kastner. What if something happens to this weapon?

Shortly after Judge Halevi's verdict, Tamir warned publicly that Kastner now walked in danger and insisted that he be guarded day and night. Two guards from the secret police were assigned to watch that no harm befell Kastner.

With the Supreme Court decision due any day, a friend says to Tamir,

"A second Kastner trial will never take place. Too much is involved. Too many people will get hurt. And it is easily avoidable. With either Tamir or Kastner dead—half the headaches of the Israeli Government would be cured."

BEN-GURION'S CROP OF DILEMMAS

In the winter of 1956, troubles pile up for Ben-Gurion and his henchmen. I will say for Israel's chieftain that he has a striking talent for slipping out of headlocks. For one thing, there is no shame in him. You can floor Ben-Gurion with enough exposés to leave a dozen prime ministers whimpering. Not Ben-Gurion. He thrives on exposure and fattens on scandal.[172] Where other statesmen would be pleading for mercy, Ben-Gurion's voice only rings out that he is still God's gift to the Jews.

And who knows but what he is—a gift somewhere between the parting of the Red Sea and the forty-day rainfall around Noah's Canaan.

High on Ben-Gurion's trouble agenda is a new ill wind. Son Amos Ben-Gurion, Assistant Chief of Police of Israel, has also instituted a suit for libel. Son Amos had lost his temper on reading a pamphlet published by a group of students of the Hebrew University. The group was known as the Line of Volunteers. It published the pamphlets, until recently much admired by Ben-Gurion's Mapai Party.

This latest pamphlet, however, forfeited the Ben-Gurion esteem, for it seemed to proclaim that his son Amos Ben-Gurion was involved in police corruption. Backing up Amos Ben-Gurion in his suit for libel against four of the Line of Volunteer students, were the Israeli Chief of Police, Yechezkel Sahar, and the personnel of Israel's Intelligence Service; also Attorney Michael Kaspi.

The trial is to give the government clique almost as big a black eye as the Kastner case had done. The Supreme Court will convict Chief of Police Sahar as a perjurer, and reprimand Amos Ben-Gurion and his lawyer Michael Kaspi [173] for their crooked tactics in the conduct of the trial. The judges censured Amos, his lawyer, and their array of high-government witnesses —for falsely using the pretexts of national security and national defense to keep incriminating material hidden from the court.[174]

The Amos Ben-Burion mess was an exposé not only of the

dishonorable behavior of Amos, but the first of the anti-Intelligence Service scandals to stir the land.

In the winter of 1957, the Amos trial was at its height, and one of the matters especially plaguing to Ben-Gurion was the fact that the lawyer defending the four university students and clobbering the Ben-Gurion name was Tamir. Yes, Shmuel Tamir, the same one.[175]

An equally depressing matter on the Ben-Gurion agenda was the soon due Supreme Court decision on the Kastner business. The general feeling was it would be a split decision—which would be bad for the government clique.[176]

The decision, when it was delivered, was that—a split one.[176] All five Supreme Court Judges upheld Judge Halevi's verdict on the "criminal and perjurious manner" in which Kastner after the war had saved Nazi War criminal Becher—"without justification." [177] Two of the judges further upheld Judge Halevi's finding that Kastner had collaborated with the Nazis during the war.[178] Three did not.

As a result of this judgment of partial reversal, Greenwald was given a suspended sentence of one year and was assessed five hundred pounds (two hundred and fifty dollars) as court costs. This split decision on Kastner being a Nazi collaborator during the war and the unanimous decision that he rescued war criminal Becher after the war in a criminal and perjurious manner made it imperative that the Government put Kastner on trial. It was also generally known that Tamir had a suitcase full of new evidence against Dr. Kastner, and God knew against whom else!

Then there was Kastner, himself. The Prime Minister had few illusions about him. It had been bad enough in the first trial, the way this talkative Hungarian allowed himself to be cornered by Tamir and reduced to gibbering from the witness box.

And now in a second trial, fighting for his life, with the new evidence smacking away at this same Kastner! It was not going to be good. Who knows what the muddle-head from Kluj will blurt out.

Here history intervenes in Ben-Gurion's behalf, or seems to. Israel's fine army embarks on the Sinai Campaign, meets the

202

army of Egypt, and scatters its regiments to the four winds. The victorious Jews overrun their foe's terrain.

All this re-establishes Ben-Gurion in the world's eyes as a man of heroic mold whom it will take more than a dozen Tamirs and Kastners to dishonor. Who cares about any court room didoes when the cry is, "Onward, Jewish arms!"

The Prime Minister dashes to the radio station one November morning in 1956 to proclaim the victory of the Jewish forces to the nation. The Ben-Gurion voice is sharp and metallic. He announces that the Third Jewish Kingdom now reaches from Dan in the north to the southern straits of Shlomo.[179] (The newly won Sinai Peninsula was three times larger than was the whole of Israel before its victory over the Egyptians.) The eloquent Prime Minister also offers some potent quotations from the ancient Greeks, identifying the newly conquered territory as part of the original land of the Hebrews.

There is rejoicing in the land over its gallant army and over the nation's dauntless leader, Ben-Gurion. But the rejoicing and the dauntlessness are not for long. The next evening Ben-Gurion is back on the radio. His voice falters as he unburdens himself. Israel learns that it is not going to be three times bigger than it was; that it is lucky, after its fine victory, to remain the same size.

Says Ben-Gurion, speaking in a sickly voice on this night of dolorous surrender,

"Neither I nor any authorized spokesman ever said that we intend to annex Sinai Peninsula to Israel. We shall willingly withdraw our forces." [180]

Goodbye, the Sinai Peninsula, goodbye the Third Jewish Kingdom from Dan to the Shlomo Straits. And who is it hog-ties Ben-Gurion this time? Certainly not the British, who are hovering over Cairo themselves and dropping bombs on the Egyptians, from the unheard of height of eighteen thousand feet. The bombs missed, but the British were nevertheless in the air as allies of the Jews.

The people of Israel manage to decipher the newspaper reports and learn that this time it is the Americans whom Ben-Gurion obeys. The international situation for the Americans is a complex one, involving Arab friendship—a non-existent matter; and American oil company investments, a more tangible item.

203

There is also the factor that the Americans do not want to lose the good will of the Egyptians, although, as a matter of fact, they haven't got it. Because if they alienate Nasser, Egypt will join the Communist side. An uninformed Israeli might ask, what can Egypt do for the Communists, except to get in their way? The question is beside the point. The point is that the Americans do not want anybody to join the Communists, even on a stretcher.

The people of Israel ponder the American high policies with bafflement. But there is one fact in the complex business that is obvious to all—Ben-Gurion's flair for obedience to anyone resembling an Anglo-Saxon. A man's soul can be permanently conditioned no less than a dog's salivary glands. The Ben-Gurion soul has practiced bowing to English-speaking masters for thirty-five years. And it must bow to Eisenhower's Kansas accent as automatically as to Lord Moyne's Oxford one.

But not all the leaders of Israel share the Prime Minister's collapsible spine. The army heads protest submission to the American whim about an intact Egypt. Even the obedient Senators in the Knesset raise their voices against the Prime Minister's scurrying submission to the United States orders.

But Ben-Gurion defies army and parliament outcries, as well as public demands. A few months after his surrender broadcast, the Prime Minister orders the victorious Jews to withdraw, not only from Sinai, but from the Gaza strip. This withdrawal throws away the last few yards gained by the spectacular Sinai victory. And the fighting Jews withdraw, full of mutterings.

But the important Jews of Israel are not as masochistic as they were. They no longer consider it an honor to be beaten by the right people. They scowl, grumble, protest in print and oratory. Ben-Gurion and his nobles stand up against the Amos Ben-Gurion scandal, against the Gaza retreat fiasco. And now another deviltry threatens—the Supreme Court decision on the Kastner Appeal; and a possible trial of their man—Kastner—for the worst of crimes.

Forty years of running the Jews of Israel, of winning the esteem of the world by hook or crook, of enchanting nearly all its eleven million surviving Jews—and a Tamir (and a Kastner) have to appear and start making a shambles of everything!

EXIT, DR. KASTNER

On the March night of the Ben-Gurion order to the Jewish army to withdraw from the Gaza Strip, Dr. Rudolf Kastner leaves his editorial offices, where he has been working overtime. There is no report of his mood and manner in this vital hour, so I must imagine them.

Dr. Kastner has had conferences with his $50,000 lawyer, Michael Kaspi, and with various important government officials. About the chances of the appeal, and the possibility of a Kastner trial; and this and that. All is in order. The basic situation is unchanged. Lawyer Kaspi will battle for him. Chaim Cohen remains on his side. And the great leaders of Israel will stand behind him in stalwart array.

He has noticed that the leaders are a little cool toward him socially. They frown and talk curtly in his presence. But Kastner, a realist from way back, knows that into each life some rain must fall. Let them frown and snub him as much as they want, the basic situation will stay the same. When the time comes to fight for his honor and, perhaps, even for his life, the mighty of Israel will be beside him and around him. For Kastner and the government of Israel are one. Who touches Kastner, touches Ben-Gurion and all his nobles. Who smears, exposes, and hamstrings Rudolf Kastner, does a similar disservice to all the finest leaders of Jewry.

Chaim Cohen, himself, said just that to the Supreme Court judges. And there is small likelihood of Chaim Cohen's changing his mind or his philosophy. Because it is obvious even to a child that he, Rudolf Kastner, all alone, could not have done all the things of which the judge found him guilty. Yes, Kastner assures himself on this March night—the more evidence Tamir unearths against him, the harder the government forces will have to fight for him. For Kastner has not allowed his colleagues to forget it for a minute; they will be fighting for their own honor and status as much as for his.

So Dr. Kastner is not too disturbed on this March night of the Gaza retreat. His editorial work finished, he straightens his desk, smooths his hair with a pocket comb, and walks into the Tel Aviv night.

A year ago, when the Kluj business and the Kurt Becher business and the parachutist business were first called to the attention of Israel, he might have felt a bit nervous about entering a dark, lonely street. But not on this night. There may be trouble later. Hotheads will start stewing about Kastner again. But this night the hotheads are off on other topics—the Gaza retreat, the Ben-Gurion salaam to the Americans, the business of Amos Ben-Gurion. This is a night of trouble for David Ben-Gurion, not Rudolf Kastner.

There is also another reassuring fact. After Judge Halevi's verdict, the government had assigned secret police to guard Kastner's life, day and night. They had remained on duty, protecting him for a year and a half. Two months ago the secret police had been relieved on their task. This added to Dr. Kastner's sense of safety. Nobody was after him any longer.

An unruffled Dr. Kastner steps into his parked gray automobile and starts for his home.

I imagine him full of memories. Who had ever more violent and exotic things to remember? The hundred hells of Hungary through which he moved like a favored tourist; the world travels; Nazis, doomed Jews, Hanna Senesh, Becher, Krumey, Himmler, Hoess, Eichmann; plots, perils, conferences, accusations, Kenyermeze, Nuremberg, Kluj, Death Marches, sealed trains—he had survived them all. A man who can survive German devils and Hungarian ones, and climb to greatness on a million Jewish corpses; who can wriggle out of constant disaster with his hair perfectly combed, must feel a pride in himself, must smile a little smugly at any more enemies to come.

My imaginings end here. The rest is fact.

At midnight, Dr. Kastner steps out of his car in front of his home, 6 Emmanuel Street, Tel Aviv. The air is balmy. The night glows with starlight and history. Dr. Kastner starts across the pavement for his front door.

A young man steps out of the shadows and asks, "Are you Dr. Kastner?"

Kastner answers politely, "Yes, I am."

The young man pulls a gun out of his pocket. Kastner sees the weapon and runs. The young man fires a bullet into Dr. Kastner.

Kastner yells and keeps running. Two more bullets from the young man's gun hit him in his head and body. He drops and lies groaning in the street.

There is a witness to the event. A high ex-Haganah officer happens to be in the neighborhood. He has been calling on his girl and is just leaving on his motorcycle when the shooting starts. He sees the assassin jump into a waiting jeep and go riding off.

The ex-Haganah officer rushes to Kastner, bends over him, hears him gasp a few words. The ex-officer mounts his motorcycle and speeds after the jeep. But he fails to pick up its trail. The assassin escapes.

An ambulance arrives in Emmanuel Street, and Kastner is taken to the hospital. In the hospital, after he is operated on, the bullet-riddled Kastner starts regaining his health. It begins to look as if the assassin's work was in vain.

But after ten days of continued improvement in the municipal hospital, a sudden change takes place. A bulletin announces that Rudolf Kastner has taken a "sudden turn for the worse." Dr. Kastner corroborates the bulletin. He dies on St. Patrick's Day, 1957.

And with his death, Tamir loses his greatest weapon against Ben-Gurion and his clique. Of all who mourn Dr. Kastner's death, Tamir is among the sincerest. All the new evidence—worthless. All the planned onslaughts on the defenders and colleagues of Kastner—to be filed away as unfought battles.[181]

There is an impressive funeral for the one-time rescuer of Jews. The government clique is well represented. A proper grief is exhibited.

Also, a number of headaches are cured, although not permanently. The dead Kastner will continue to haunt Israeli politics. The government of Israel and its train-bearing press will work constantly to restore Dr. Kastner's good name, and its own. It will cause the facts of the trial to become vague, to vanish, and even to change from bad into good.

But with all this legerdemain, the truth of Kastner will stay alive. And that sad, foolish and tormented penny-Napoleon from Kluj will become the nation's leading ghost.

I have one more paragraph about Kastner. As a journalist working among Hungarians in Kluj, his name was Dr. Rezo Kastner. When he came to Budapest to work among the Germans, he called himself Dr. Rudolf Kastner. Arrived in Israel and embraced by the government clique as one of their own, he became Dr. Israel Kastner.

Vale, Rezo, Rudolf, Israel—

THE HARLEQUIN MURDER

Three men were arrested, tried, and convicted for Dr. Kastner's murder and sentenced to life imprisonment. Two of them were named accessories.[182]

The actual confessed killer was Zeev Eckstein, age twenty-four.[183]

Until a few months before shooting down Kastner, Zeev Eckstein was a paid undercover agent of the Israeli government's Intelligence Service.[184]

THE STORY OF JOEL BRAND

Mr. Wickham Steed, columnist for the *Manchester Guardian* in England, states: "Two Nazi or Hungarian agents called on the Allies with a certain extortion proposal, which the Allies scorned with indignation."

This mysterious item about Joel Brand and his desperate mission was reprinted in Ben-Gurion's newspaper *Davar* on July 28, 1944. This and no more . . . before Joel Brand's Banquo-like appearance in Judge Halevi's court room nine years later.

The mysterious item was on view in the government press

after emissary Joel Brand had been handed over to the British, and after Hungarian Jewry had been dumped into the German ash barrels.

And now I have a confession to make. Taking a leaf from Zionism, I too have suppressed the Joel Brand story in my book for a while. For, chronologically, Joel Brand appeared in the Greenwald trial while Prosecutor Amnon Tell still reigned in the teapot court room, and before the great Chaim Cohen took over.

I put off the Joel Brand story in my narrative until it could be believed (if ever). But there is a difference between my suppression of the Joel Brand story, and the Zionist scuttling of it, as well as the hiding and scuttling of Joel Brand himself:

A million lives were not at stake in my juggling.

Ben-Gurion's *Davar* reportage quoting the illusive "Wickham Steed" did not even mention the B.B.C. broadcast, made in London on June 20, 1944, on which the item was based. Communist dictators, too, consider it correct procedure to keep their constituencies uninformed about what the wretched world outside is saying. This outside world is usually saying things of a derogatory nature. But what is there derogatory about the B.B.C. broadcast? Why is it cut down to unintelligibility by Ben-Gurion's paper? Here is the broadcast:

"Two emissaries of the Hungarian Government arrived in Turkey to present the Allied representatives with the following offer from the Hungarian Government—all the Jews remaining alive in Hungary will receive exit permits in return for a certain quantity of medical supplies and transport trucks from England and America. The promise was also made that these materials would not be used on the Western Front.

"At this time, the names of the emissaries cannot be revealed.

"Authoritative British circles consider this offer as a crude attempt to weaken the Allies, whose sympathy for the Hungarian Jews is well known; also to create dissension among the Allies.

"There is not the slightest possibility that the British and American governments will agree to enter into any negotiations of this short, although they would like to help the Hungarian Jews."

This was not entirely bad reporting. The emissaries were from the Germans, not the Hungarians. And there was only one emissary, sent out to the world's Jews, not to the Allies. The objective cited, "a crude attempt to weaken the Allies," was one of the possible reasons involved. And the British, speaking for the Allies, do not quite "scorn with indignation" as *Davar* states. Instead they make a cool and cautious statement that cannot be nailed as a lie. They "would like to help the Hungarian Jews."

Who wouldn't "like to help" a million human beings about to be tortured and murdered? The myriad of men, women, and children entering the death houses in Auschwitz don't know about this Christian wish "to help" them, but it is there, spoken with true British restraint by the B.B.C. announcer.

The princes of Israel are so efficient in their silence technique that Tamir, in Judge Halevi's court room, has never even heard of the Joel Brand story.

But the Joel Brand Story comes now to Tamir.

It comes as the whisper of a nightmare. A friend brings him word that there is a certain man in Tel Aviv who has a story to tell about the slaughter of the Hungarian Jews and the connivance of Israel's leaders in it—a story that might fit into the trial.

Tamir would like to discount the story. He has already wasted many nights on "eye witnesses" who, in the end, proved to be liars.

Nevertheless, at night, after court sessions, he holds secret meetings with the new "witness," on the seashore, in hideouts, in his parents' home. He hears a horror story that rings with truth, and he ushers it into the Trial.

I write it now as a climax.

A GHOST IS SUMMONED

Prince Escalus, speaking over the corpses of Romeo and Juliet in Shakespeare's envoi to the tragedy, asks for silence on their story.

"Seal up the mouth of outrage," he pleads.

Can it be done? For a time, yes. But outrage finds its spokesmen. The violated dead do not stay silent. Someone speaks out for them. Someone uncovers and reports it. Not that the report will do any good, or lessen by a single corpse the history of human brutishness. There's no clipping the claws of humanity. Tigers and lions can be tamed and made to sit on circus tubs like tabby cats. But not we, who have heard God speak and developed His gift of reason. (And how loathsomely we wallow in it.)

The Joel Brand story hits Israel cruelly. No longer a stowaway item about some British "Mr. Wickham Steed," who opines something or other in London that nobody can understand about "two agents" with certain "extortion proposals"—which the Allies naturally will "scorn with indignation."

But Joel Brand himself, all over the front pages—not two men, but one—and this one man not at all "scorned" as an agent of an enemy government, but embraced as a fellow Jew—and then betrayed by Jews. This one man takes the witness stand and relates one of the most painful and wretched stories ever to enter the chronicle of the Jews—and the mouth of outrage is unsealed!

But, first, a technicality that belongs to court room melodrama. Tamir, having decided that Brand's is an honest report, must slide the man with the story into the trial. Brand has nothing to do with defendant Greenwald, and his relation to Kastner may be difficult to establish, legally.

Prosecutor Amnon Tell solves the technical problem for Tamir. The Prosecutor summons a government big-wig to offer the court a prettier picture of the Jewish Agency rescue activities in 1944 than Tamir has hung up for Israel's eyes. Menachem Bader, manager of the Israeli Development Ministry, is up there to testify for the government. He will enlighten Judge Halevi on how ardently the far-flung Jewish Agency had worked to rescue Jews from the German inferno.

Menachem Bader is a man of high repute in Israel. In answer to Prosecutor Tell, the slow-speaking, dignified Bader recalls the activities of the Jewish Agency rescue officials in Istanbul in the spring of 1944.

Thus Bader and Tell have opened the door for the man with the story. Joel Brand, too, was in Istanbul in the spring of 1944. Bader's rescue work in that place must include knowledge of and

211

contact with Joel Brand. Tamir's cross-examination ushers Joel Brand's nightmare tale into history.

I omit Tamir's· questions and write only the answers Bader speaks in the Jerusalem court room.

"On May 19th, 1944," Bader testifies before Judge Halevi, "a cable arrived from Vienna informing us that Joel Brand, a member of the Budapest Rescue Committee, was on his way to Turkey. Brand arrived on the appointed day and presented us with his credentials. He gave us a detailed picture of the hell that raged in Nazi Europe.

"After he had told us the facts, Brand laid before us the 'deal' that Adolf Eichmann had proposed.

"Eichmann had offered Brand a deal he called 'Blood for Cargo and Cargo for Blood.' Eichmann had told Brand he would spare a million Jews and send them out of Hungary alive and unhurt in exchange for one thousand tons of tea, one thousand tons of coffee, and ten thousand trucks.

"We sat there horror-stricken and did not believe our senses. Our first reaction was to consider the 'offer' a swindle—a diabolic and malicious scheme.

"But Brand told us that Eichmann had agreed to postpone his killing schedule of twelve thousand Jews a day for two weeks. This was to enable Brand to start negotiations. Brand explained to us that his return to Hungary in two weeks was of utmost importance, as it would show Eichmann that the offer was being seriously considered. Upon his return to Budapest, one hundred thousand Jews were to be released by Eichmann in advance payment and as a sign of his willingness to go on with the trade.

"I remember that first hour with Joel Brand as though it happened yesterday. None of us could speak a word. We sat staring at each other and all our hearts thumped so you could hear them.

"We were all full of suspicion, but we kept silent. We had neither the right nor the moral strength to talk of German traps or German deceit. Our job was to use the straw that fate was offering to our doomed brethren.

"However slim the chances of rescue were, we could not confront Brand with a refusal. The responsibility weighed too grimly on us. If we didn't do everything we could, we would be haunted for the rest of our lives. We saw the doomed million Jews of Hungary in our minds. We had two weeks in which to save the lives of a million Jews.

"Brand's return to Budapest was delayed beyond the two weeks, however, pending instructions from the Jewish Agency in Jerusalem, which was studying a full report of his mission.

"This delay brought letters pouring from the Jews of Hungary. The letters pleaded for Brand's immediate return. They warned us that the extermination of the Jews would start up at a swifter rate if Brand failed to reappear in Budapest. At the same time, British representatives in Turkey, who were in constant touch with us, kept insisting that Brand be deported from Turkey.

"While we were waiting to hear from our leaders in Jerusalem, the British authorities told us that they wouldn't stand in Brand's way if he wished to go to Palestine to report personally and furnish a living account to the Jewish Agency.

"Brand was nervous about the further delay, and also about stepping onto British soil. Our opinions were also divided. Some of us considered the proposal a British trap. Others thought it a genuine proposition. The fact of the matter was that, on arriving at the Syrian border, Brand was arrested and confined by the British.

"After Brand's arrest, Moshe Sharett [at that time head of the political department of the Jewish Agency] made haste to arrive at the Syrian border, and after having waited a day or two, was enabled to meet Brand and talk to him in the presence of a British Intelligence officer." [185]

Bader continues. He tells of how Brand's arrest in Aleppo by the British led to the collapse of his mission. Brand was detained by the British for four and a half months. The Eichmann offer fell through, and the Hungarian Jews were turned into ashes.

Tamir's cross-examination now brings an admission from Bader that, shortly after Brand's arrival in Constantinople (Istanbul), the British had been informed of his presence and his mission—by a Jewish Agency official.

Tamir: Who was this man of the Jewish Agency?
Bader: (quietly) It was Ehud Avriel who informed the British of Brand's arrival.

213

Tamir: Who accompanied Brand to the Syrian border where he was arrested?
Bader: A certain Jew.
Tamir: What Jew?
Bader: (slowly) A certain Turkish Jew.
Tamir: When did the news of his arrest reach the Jewish Agency in Jerusalem?
Bader: Both we and the people at home heard of the matter simultaneously, immediately after the arrest.
Tamir: And when, according to you, did Sharett contact Brand?
Bader: Some twenty-four hours later.

Israel had never heard the story of Joel Brand and his wild mission. Its tragic details had been pigeonholed by the Weizmann, Ben-Gurion regime. Not a word more than the Wickham Steed paragraph had been printed in Palestine, not an official statement made about the Eichmann offer, or the message delivered by Joel Brand to the head Jews of the world.

And Menachem Bader, making his slow, weighty answers, has no worry about anyone contradicting these answers, since nobody knows the story of Joel Brand. But somebody does know. A tense, harsh-voiced Tamir fires it point blank at startled witness Bader.

Tamir: I put it to you that your entire story is a malicious distortion of the truth! I put it to you that Brand's betrayal and arrest was planned and effected by all of you! I put it to you that in compliance with orders from the British, Sharett, together with you, knowingly and purposely trapped Brand and induced him to set out for the Syrian border. Sharett knew all along of the impending arrest, and was waiting for Brand at the border in a nearby British Military camp, *before* the train pulled in.
Bader: (his eyes shifting nervously) You're wrong. You know you're wrong.[186]
Tamir: Did or did not Sharett wait at the border before Brand's arrival?
Bader: I don't know.

214

Tamir: I put it to you, Mr. Bader, that it was Avriel, in person, who accompanied Brand to the Syrian border. The Turkish Jew was non-existent.

Bader: Correct. Ehud Avriel did accompany him, but there also was some sort of Turkish Jew.

Tamir: I put it to you that Avriel witnessed Brand's arrest.

Bader: I do not deny it.

Tamir: But Avriel was not arrested?

Bader: Correct.

Tamir: I put it to you that Avriel was in the service of the British Intelligence.

Bader: I don't think so.

Tamir: You no doubt will agree with me that at least some of you thought that the British were planning to trap Brand and had allowed him to travel to Syria with that aim in mind.

Bader: That is true.

Tamir: And did you inform Brand that his journey to Syria was possibly a British trap directed at arresting him and thus causing disaster?

Bader: We did not inform him.

Tamir: Why didn't you inform him?

Bader: Out of awe and respect for the emissary of the doomed.[187]

As lawyer Tamir continues his hammering at the Bader testimony, one thing becomes certain—Joel Brand's own story must be the climax of this dark drama unfolding in the District Court of Jerusalem.

Israel storms with speculation. Why has the government hidden the Eichmann-Brand story? These government leaders so full of lamentations today for the slaughtered Jews of Hungary, what did they do to try to save those Jews while they were still breathing—and when Brand was sent out to bargain for their lives? What would this long-hidden emissary from the doomed Jews of Hungary say on the witness stand?

Had the Leaders of Israel actively betrayed the Hungarian Jews and handed Brand over to the British—to be rid of him and his blood bargaining? Or was this the ex-"terrorist" Tamir

215

avenging himself against old political enemies by a wanton smearing of the government?

The Tel Aviv headlines shout, "Where is Brand?" "Will Brand Testify?"

The government clique becomes aware of the disaster that threatens them out of this trial. Prosecutor Tell is directed by Prime Minister Sharett through Attorney General Chaim Cohen to end the trial as quickly as he can, and the devil take the Kastner case. It should never have been started. And, hereafter, it will be a wise thing for the government to keep out of the courts, and solve its problems in a less troublesome way.

Prosecutor Tell makes the following startling pronouncement —I quote the court record:

> Tell: The State is desirous of resting its case. I doubt if any more witnesses will be called by us. Perhaps Mr. Ehud Avriel will be summoned to close our list of witnesses. Otherwise I shall rest the State's case tomorrow.
>
> Tamir: In the event that Avriel is not summoned tomorrow, the Defense asks permission to start its case immediately —tomorrow morning. Our first witness is Joel Brand.[188]

This announcement ushers in a series of desperation measures by the Prosecution—an attempt to have the case put off for a whole month—until "after the Passover Holidays," denunciations of the "smear that has been the case for the Defense"; and finally, a demand by the Prosecution that Brand be recognized as their own witness—whom they had fully intended to produce all along.

The Court Protocol at the point where the Prosecution begins to fight for a delay, follows. Tamir argues:

> Tamir: I must inform the Court that Joel Brand is in constant peril. He is being shadowed. Moral and economic pressures have been brought to bear upon him in the attempt to prevent his testimony. It is my duty to demand that the Court Protocol record our warning. Various elements are doing their utmost to suppress this man's evidence. He is, to the best of my belief, in physical danger. Moreover, various documents of the highest importance

have been lately stolen from him. Your Honor, Brand must be summoned immediately.

Tell: This is a scandalous and filthy smear! We intend to take necessary measures to prevent the repetition of such outrageous statements!

Tamir: (coolly) 'I fear neither you nor your regime.

Tell: (blasting) What! Let's hear that clearly for the sake of a precise recording in the Protocol!

Tamir: I reassert my words and join Mr. Tell in requesting that they be set forth in the Court Protocol. For the sake of greater clarity, I hereby state that the government of Israel is the regime referred to. Neither the government nor those who direct and instruct Mr. Tell shall prevent me from carrying out my duty to the end.

Tell: Mark your words! You'll have to answer for them!

Tamir: Is that a hint that an attempt to silence me will be made? I am not intimidated. Your Honor, I request once again that Joel Brand be summoned immediately as first witness for the Defense. For the past five years, this man has not managed to find employment and has wandered about, destitute, devoid of the least chance of earning a living. But last week he was offered a job which involved his boarding one of Shoham's steamers and leaving the country.[189]

On the following morning, a bristling Tell announces that Joel Brand is his next witness. He demands of His Honor that Tamir be kept from leaving the court room, lest he meet the new government witness and sneak in a few words with him.

Tamir, safe in the knowledge that he has "stolen the horse," allows the lock to be put on the barn door. And the journalists alert their editors. The biggest story of the trial is about to break.

"THE MOUTH OF OUTRAGE"

Joel Brand, a blonde, stocky man with a round face, enters the court room. He is sworn in on the witness stand.

On behalf of the Government of Israel, Prosecutor Tell questions the man who had faced Adolf Eichmann and gone forth on one of the saddest missions in history.

> Tell: Were you a member of the Budapest Rescue Committee, Mr. Brand?
> Brand: I was.
> Tell: How old are you?
> Brand: I am 48 years old.
> Tell: No more questions. The witness is dismissed.[190]

So much interest and no more has the government of Israel in the tale Brand has to relate. It is the government's idea of fancy strategy. Produce the troublesome Brand, ask him only two questions, and hand him over to Tamir for cross-examination, with no scrap of information for Defense Counsel to work over. Thus Specter Brand will materialize and dematerialize without damage to the government clique. A little damage, perhaps. Some people might imagine the government of Israel was frightened of what Joel Brand had to reveal. Very well—let them imagine. How long can people keep imagining that the noblest Jewish Leaders are afraid of anything, or guilty of anything?

The only thing wrong with this government strategy is Tamir. He is on his feet, announcing:

"In order to avoid misunderstanding, I hereby inform the court that Joel Brand and I have met some seven or eight times during the past fortnight.

"At our very first meeting I asked him, in the presence of a third person, as to whether he had been summoned to testify by the Prosecution. I specifically stressed that if such were the case, I had no right to contact him. Brand told me, however, that he had not been summoned by the Prosecution and had not been approached. Hence, I considered myself free to discuss the matter with him and obtain the information which he could provide. At my request, Mr. Brand consented to show me various documents, a number of which he placed at my disposal. These are in my keeping till today and I am willing to return them to the witness at any time.

"My talks with Mr. Brand were conducted clandestinely, as I did not wish Dr. Kastner or other government figures to know of our meetings. This was due, in the first place, to my anxiety for Brand's safety. The man carries within him one of the greatest secrets of Jewish history. I wanted to make sure that no harm would befall him, at least until he took the stand. For that reason, I urged him not to reveal our meetings to anyone and to regard them as highly secret." [191]

Tamir cross-examines Brand for three days; and the people of Israel, gaping as at a nightmare, learn specifically of how the leaders of the world's Jewry had turned their backs on the doomed million Jews of Hungary. And more—how these Jewish Leaders, knowing all the details of the extermination, had kept their mouths shut and published not a word of the Hungarian catastrophe while it was going on.

It was a story not to be disbelieved, for its torment and truth were in the man who spoke it. No government question could alter it in the court room,[192] nor could later government threats against Brand outside the court room alter his story. Joel Brand speaks as follows from the witness stand in the Jerusalem court: [193]

"It was mid-April, almost a month before my trip to Turkey (1944). One of the German agents in Budapest instructed me to wait at an appointed street corner and said that I would be brought before Eichmann.

"A half hour later, I was taken to the luxurious hotel where Eichmann had his Headquarters. I was ushered immediately to his room.

"The words which then passed between us have imprinted themselves on my memory till I die."

Brand spoke in German. He now articulates in the dog-bark of a Nazi S.S. officer. The court hears Eichmann's menacing yips out of Brand's mouth:

" 'Do you know who I am?' he asked me. 'I am the man who carried out all the actions [the Jewish extermination] in Germany, Austria, Poland and Slovakia. My next task is Hungary. I have checked up as to whether you and the Joint Distribution Committee are capable of getting things done, and I want to make a deal with you. Blood for Cargo and Cargo for Blood. Now tell me, what is it that you want to salvage—women who can bear children? Men in their prime? The aged? The young? Speak up!'

"I was sitting. A civilian was standing beside us. No other Jew was present. A young woman sat behind the desk, pencil in hand. I presumed that she was taking down our talk in shorthand.

"The meaning of his words dawned on me. I sat there thunderstruck. I never was a politician nor statesman and blurted out the first words that came to my mind:

" 'I am not empowered to decide as to whom you are to murder!' I said. 'I would like to save everybody. I don't understand this deal. Where are we to get the cargo? You have confiscated everything.' Then I became full of hope and went on— 'The local Jews and our friends abroad may perhaps muster sums of money, if lives are to be saved.'

"Eichmann answered, 'Go on then. Go ahead. To Switzerland, to Turkey, to Spain, wherever you please; so long as you can produce the cargo!'

" 'What sort of cargo do you want?' I asked.

" 'Anything at all,' Eichmann said. 'For example—trucks. Ten thousand trucks are worth a million Jews to me.' He paused a moment and added: 'Tea and coffee, too, and soap. One thousand tons of tea and coffee. All these I am in need of.'

"To this I replied, 'I haven't the vaguest idea where all these cargoes are to be obtained. Who on earth will treat this offer seriously? Which official body will believe that delivery of the trucks will in fact induce you to spare a million Jews?'

"Eichmann answered that he was willing to offer one hundred thousand Jews in advance, and on receiving the proportionate payment, he would release another ten per cent. 'Pick them anywhere you want,' he said, 'Hungary, Auschwitz, Slovakia—anywhere you want and anyone you want.'

"On leaving the building, I felt like a stark madman. All the members of our Budapest Committee were waiting for me. Word had been passed to them that Eichmann had summoned me. This was the first time that one of the Committee had faced Eichmann in person.

"We racked our brains. What were we to do with this monster's offer? We talked and talked. Every faction of the Jewish community had sent its representative to sit in the council to decide the matter of Blood and Cargo.

"I had gotten to know the Germans and their cruel lies exceedingly well. But the thought of 100,000 Jews 'in advance' tortured my mind and gave me no respite. I had no right to think of anything but this advance payment.

"Eichmann had also promised to cease the deportations and extermination while negotiations on the deal itself were being carried out. I knew that negotiations of this sort would have to last a number of weeks at least.

"No death and no deportation for a number of weeks! No! We had nothing to lose if this one hundred thousand were given in advance and deportations ended in the meantime.

"Eichmann received me on the 15th, for the last time, and told me, 'You are to set out now. Today we begin to deport twelve thousand per day, but these shall not be exterminated during negotiations. But you, Brand, have to return in a week or two. I can't put your Jews on ice and preserve them forever. If it turns out that the negotiations demand some more time, we'll be considerate. You, however, have to return. Quickly. Your return, coupled with the verbal acceptance of my offer, will inspire me to cease the gassing, and lay down the advance payment of one hundred thousand immediately.'

"On May 18th, I left Budapest and reached Constantinople on the following day. I was flown there in a German diplomatic plane."

At this point, the first day of Brand's cross-examination ends.

On the next day, Brand resumes the witness stand and, in answer to Tamir's questions, states that the inevitable result of his failure to return to Hungary had been Eichmann's renewed extermination of Hungary's Jews. Brand testifies:

"Some time before my departure, we, in Budapest, informed the representatives of the Jewish Agency in Turkey of my coming visit. We received an answer that read, 'Let Joel come. Chaim shall await him.'

"We regarded the above as an answer to our request that a high member of the Jewish Agency come to Constantinople in order to discuss matters with me and make the final decision. Chaim, we took for granted, was Chaim Weizmann, who would attend to the matter personally. This was the greatest hope for the rescue of Hungary's doomed Jews that had ever come to our hearts.

"Every single party and faction of the Hungarian Jewish Community—from the Revisionists to the Hashomer Hatzair, and even the religious groups, were agreed that I set out for Turkey and empowered me to act on their behalf in the matter.

"On landing at the airport in Constantinople, we discovered to our amazement that nobody was waiting to meet us. Moreover, our Turkish entry visa was not arranged and we did not have the right to disembark. We were mortified and astonished at this state of affairs. The Jewish Agency cable from Turkey had explicitly stated that we would be met and taken care of.

"The man who accompanied me from Budapest managed to patch matters up, however, and after a little delay, we made our way to the city."

"The first member of the Palestine Rescue Committee whom I met in Constantinople was Venia Pomeranietz.

"The Committee's address was known to me—Hotel Pira Palace, Constantinople. On leaving the airport, I headed for the hotel ˎnd managed to obtain a room. Venia came into the room immediately after my arrival.

"This was the first time, since the German massacre of Jews had begun, that I ever talked to a Jew in a free country. He asked me whether it was true that Jews were being slaughtered on the other side.

"To a man like myself, who had just arrived from hell, it was bitter to hear that a Jewish Agency official could still have doubts on the subject. We had informed them constantly about what was going on. We knew our letters had reached them. Everything was known to them, as a more or less regular correspondence had been going on between us for some time.

"Shortly after my arrival in Constantinople, a meeting of the entire committee was called to sit with me. I reported to them at great length and told of everything that was known to me. I stressed the fact that my return to Hungary during the next fortnight was imperative. I asked to go back with the next diplomatic plane, which was to leave Constantinople on the following week.

"At this meeting it was decided that one of the important members of the Jewish Agency Executive be summoned to Constantinople. Either Sharett, Greenbaum, or anybody else of equal standing. It was also decided not to inform the British of my arrival. On these matters the decision was unanimous, and everything was clear. I demanded that the British should not be informed. One of the decisions was that Venia Pomeranietz set out immediately for Palestine and see to it that Sharett should come to Constantinople, if possible.

"At one of our meetings we decided that Barlas (a member of the Jewish Agency Rescue Committee in Constantinople) and myself should approach Steinhardt, the American Ambassador in Ankara. Back in Budapest we thought that Steinhardt, being a Jew, had the heart of a Jew, and would certainly be the best man to contact on the Allied side, if any approach to the Allies was to be made at all by me.

"Barlas and I were in the same hotel. On arriving at the station to go to Ankara, I was unable to board the train for lack of necessary travel papers. Barlas had arranged all his papers, but none was given me. I had not even been told that a special permit was required for a trip of this sort.

"I was conducted to a building and confined in a large lobby, which apparently served as the police department dealing with foreigners. Some twenty or thirty officials rushed in and out all day long. I believe that Bader, or perhaps some other member of the Committee, visited me. I can't be sure on that point. I was permitted to spend the night at the hotel and told to come back the following morning. The confinement lasted for two or three days.

"Following my release, I was free to move as I pleased for a week or so. Nobody followed me. I was a free man. Thus, I waited for Sharett, but he did not arrive.

"In the meantime, the Agency rescue officials drafted a tenta-

223

tive agreement to Eichmann's 'offer,' which implied that we were agreed, in principle, on all the basic points. I kept a copy of the draft to deliver to Eichmann in order to induce him to believe that in principle his 'offer' had been agreed to. This draft was to be used if Sharett did not arrive in the next few days and help us decide what to do.

"Finally, it became apparent that Moshe Sharett would not come because of the Turks' refusal to issue him a visa. So I was told by members of the Jewish Agency and Joint Distribution Committees. I was also told that the British were actively preventing his arrival.

"It was then that I was urged to set out for the Turko-Syrian Border in order to meet him. I was assured that within a few days I would be back in Constantinople.

"I told Barlas that the trip was not to my liking. I said that I would rather go to the German Embassy and arrange for my immediate return to Budapest. I was afraid to step on English soil in Aleppo.

"We had a sharp argument on the subject and one of the reasons I offered for returning was the draft agreement which we had drawn up in response to Eichmann's offer.

"Barlas told me not to worry. He repeatedly asserted that I would be back in Constantinople in a day or two, and could return to Budapest immediately afterwards.

"The representatives of the Halutzim (Pioneers) movement, Bader and Avriel, were, in my eyes, people of the highest authority and integrity. This applied to Barlas, too, who, being a man sent from Palestine and representing the Jewish Agency, was regarded by me as authorized to decide on matters.

"I complied with their wishes and agreed to set out for the Syrian Border.

"They gave me my German passport, stamped with a British visa to British Aleppo, and an immigration visa to Palestine. It was clearly understood that all this was in order to enable me to cross the border at Aleppo and there meet Sharett.

"Avriel and myself set out. We slept in the same compartment while aboard the train. To the best of my knowledge, there were no police keeping watch over us. The trip lasted a few days and we ate and sat in this compartment. I practically never left it. No one traveled with us in this compartment."

Tamir asked, "Was there an important Turkish Jew accompanying you in another compartment?"

"I don't have the faintest notion of any Turkish Jew, important or not important. I don't know who traveled in the other compartments. As I said, Avriel left the compartment a few times. I stayed there practically all the time. Avriel did not tell me that an important Turkish Jew was accompanying us. When the train passed Ankara, I was warned by two men who boarded it not to proceed with the trip. They were agents in Turkey of the Revisionist (Jabotinsky) Party in Palestine and the Agudath-Israel Orthodox religious party. They warned me that British Agents were waiting in Aleppo to arrest me.

"I was terrified on hearing this. It meant the failure of my mission and the extermination of my family and a million other Jews in Hungary.

"But I calmed myself with the thought that these two representatives of the small Revisionist and religious parties were nobodies alongside the men of our own Hahalutz movement.

"I told Avriel what I had heard. He brushed the warning aside and told me again not to worry. Everything was going to go smoothly.

"Reassured by Avriel, I agreed to go on to Aleppo as planned, and meet Moshe Sharett at the border.

"Avriel told me he had iron-clad guarantees from the British that nothing wrong would happen to me.

"On leaving Ankara, we traveled for more than a day before reaching the border at Aleppo. About an hour or so before Aleppo, Avriel suddenly turned to me and said, 'Should anything happen to you, Joel, should we be separated and you get arrested, don't speak with the British unless somebody from the Jewish Agency, one of us, be present.'

"An hour or so later we arrived in Aleppo. Avriel left the compartment to arrange something, he said. Just as he left, the British came in and arrested me. I presume that the men who took me were British Intelligence Agents, but I couldn't be sure, as none of them was known to me personally. At any rate, I was compelled to leave the train and I was taken to an English barracks.

"A few hours later, I was brought before an English officer who wanted to interrogate me. Complying with Avriel's instructions, I said that, being a Jewish emissary, I would not utter a word unless a representative of the Jewish Agency was present.

"Some time later this officer faced me again and said, 'We agree to your demand. The interrogations shall take place in the presence of a man from the Jewish Agency.'" [194]

"SET YOU DOWN THIS. . . . THAT IN ALEPPO ONCE—"

How was it that such a story as Brand tells Judge Halevi was never heard before? Did Joel Brand keep it secret during the ten years in Israel? No, Brand talked. He told the story often, to politicians, to journalists—the wrong ones. He told it also to acquaintances in homes, in cafés. But these Jews in the new State of Israel listened to Brand's tale, sighed, and turned away. There were too many Jews in Palestine babbling a little madly about what had happened in Europe. About Germans. The long killing. The incinerator smoke that hung in the sky all day and night. Better to forget those things. Better, also, not to think wrong things about Palestine's great Jews. What other Jews were there for the world to admire?

But now it was no longer a story to be evaded. Every word of it was entering a court record. Joel Brand, the outcast, had finally found the ear of history for his tale. In the record for all time there would stand the account of this overt crime done by the great men of the Jewish Agency: Brand's virtual kidnapping to Aleppo, his arrest and detention there for a long enough time (during which time the Hungarian Jews were slaughtered), and then the hiding of their crime by these same leaders from the Jews of Palestine and of the world, and finally their mourning the murdered ones, and proving their innocence by a show of grief.

Brand returns for a third session of testifying. He goes on with his story:

"The next morning, I was taken by two officers to an elegant Arab villa which served as the residence of high-ranking British officers stationed in the area. There I first met Moshe Sharett. Sharett told me he had been waiting for me for a day or two.

"I had a long talk with Moshe Sharett, but not alone. There were a few British officers present and a young woman who took notes in shorthand. All in all, there were some six or seven people present. We spoke English and German. Our talk lasted a whole day. Sharett knew exactly how things stood. Venia Pomeranietz had seen him in Jerusalem and told him everything.

"Before leaving, Sharett informed me that to his great regret, I would not be able to return to the north and would have to go south. I was taken aback and complained bitterly, but he said there was no other alternative. Thus we parted. I was taken to Cairo, via Palestine.

"In Cairo I was confined in a villa that served as a sort of private prison and had guards posted everywhere. I was interrogated and now talked freely, as everything had already been said in Aleppo. They questioned me every day for ten and twelve hours at a stretch. Many of them. Questions were hurled at me from every side, sometimes simultaneously by more than one officer. All in all, they were quite polite, but persisted in learning every detail of what I knew.

"Day followed day and I could stand it no longer. On the tenth day I went on a hunger strike. I insisted that I be released and allowed to go to Hungary, where men and women were being murdered.

"While on the hunger strike, I kept on talking to them and answering their questions. All throughout the seventeen days of my hunger strike (I drank a little water now and then) I spoke to them.

"On the seventeenth day, one of my captors handed me a note from Ehud Avriel. It urged me not to make difficulties and to testify freely, and stated that everything was being done to ensure the success of my mission.

"One of the gentlemen present during my interrogations was Lord Moyne. He answered my appeal with regard to Eichmann's 'offer' by saying, 'What can I do with this million Jews? Where can I put them?'

(His Lordship had already tried the bottom of the Mediterranean for the Jews on the refugee ships—the Struma, Patria, etc.) [195]

"I wrote a letter to the Jewish Agency Executive as follows: 'It is apparent to me now that an enemy of our people is holding me and does not intend to release me in the near future. I have decided to go on a hunger strike again and will do my utmost to break through the bayonets guarding me.' I added that the above was being written despite my knowing that the military censor would see the letter.

"While being confined in the villa, I was enabled to meet a few of the Jewish Agency Leaders. On these occasions I was driven by the British to the Esplanade or Metropol Hotel and left alone with the Agency gentlemen. My British escort would inform me that I would be picked up a few hours later. This happened about ten times." [196]

Finally, after four and one half months, the British released him. From Cairo, Brand was compelled to go to Palestine. He was not allowed to return to Hungary.

Brand recites the last dismal chapter of his tale. Coming to Tel Aviv, the Holy Land of his youthful dreams, he tried to reach the ear of the moral leader of World Jewry, Dr. Chaim Weizmann.

With the Jewish slaughter in Europe at its bloody height, Brand tells how he wrote desperately to President Weizmann (of the Agency, not yet Israel) imploring him to help the Jews still unslain in Hungary. He enclosed the full Eichmann offer. He pointed out how it could still be accepted, and the last of Hungary's Jews bought out of the German death camps.[197]

Tamir puts in evidence the reply to Brand made by the late President of Israel. Government Attorney Tell stands by "reverently" as this callous letter from Chaim Weizmann is read into the protocol.

Rehovoth, 29 Dec. 1944

Mr. Joel Brand
Tel Aviv
Dear Mr. Brand:

I beg you to forgive me for having delayed in answering your letter. As you may have seen from the Press, I have been traveling a good deal and generally did not have a free moment since my arrival here. I have read both your letter and your memorandum and shall be happy to see you sometime the week after next—about the tenth of January.

Miss Itin—my secretary—will get in touch with you to fix up the appointment.

With kind regards,

Yours very sincerely,
Ch. Weizmann [198]

Brand points out in the court room that while this letter was being written, Jews of the Budapest ghetto were being butchered daily.

The last lines of Brand's testimony, as they appear of page 676 of the Protocol, read:

"Rightly or wrongly, for better or for worse, I have cursed Jewry's official leaders ever since. All these things shall haunt me until my dying day. It is much more than a man can bear." [199]

PERFIDY IN ISRAEL

It is known now (1961) that Eichmann's offer of a million Jewish lives for a few thousand trucks was not an Eichmann whim. It was a plan hatched by Hitler, Himmler, Goebbels, Becher,[200] Goering, and all the leading German thinkers of 1944. The execution of the plan was assigned to Colonel Eichmann.

The very fact that Brand was chosen, and not Kastner, may be proof of their hope to be taken seriously. An honest Jew was needed to bring the offer to the Jewry of the world—a Jew with no known taint of German-love in him. Brand was such a man, the Germans decided. And he was.[201]

But why? When such an inspired Jew-killer as Eichmann, and all the inspired Nazis, decide to offer to stop their Jew-killing, there must be a reason. I find in the evidence several obvious reasons. In 1944, the chief hope Germany's leaders had of escaping disaster was a divorce between Communist Russia and the Western Allies. It was a hope based on much logic. Hitler and his co-students of history must have gone to their deaths still bewildered at the "illogic" of the Western Allies who preferred Red Russia to the Nazi Reich as a friend.

Thus the first answer is that the Eichmann offer of Jewish Blood for Trucks was a separate peace overture toward the West. The trucks, said the Germans, would not be used against the Western Allies. They would be used only against the Russians.

A second reason for the offer was its whitewash possibility. Sparing the lives of the last million Jews might brighten the world's opinion of the fallen Third Reich, and win for it and its leaders a kindlier postwar judgment.

There is a touch of fantasy in this second reason, to wit—why should the Germans imagine that the Allies were concerned about saving Jews? Have the Allies ever bombed the furnace houses in the death camps? Or the bridges leading to Auschwitz? Or allowed the Jews to find refuge in what had been given them as their own land—Palestine?

But a little fantasy in so bedevilled a pack of intellects as the Germans in 1944 is to be expected.

Reason three is the most obvious, and the most German. Should it turn out that the Allies do not give a hoot about saving a million Jews, and that they regard the offer with contempt and derision—that, in itself, will be a psychological victory for the Germans. The Allies will then be on record as having had no wish to save Jews when they could. How, then, will they be able to denounce Germans for killing them? Let Emissary Joel Brand come back to Budapest empty-handed, without ransom for a single Jewish child, and Germany will have proved its case against the Jews—nobody likes them. Or, more practically, will have established the fact that Germany's deliberate torture and murder of six million defenseless and unmenacing humans

(Jews) did not make it an outcast from Western civilization. Germany's case?—"You not only made no protest against the slaughter, you refused to negotiate for the saving of the last million unslaughtered."

And so I restate the story of Joel Brand as I see it in the court of my mind, but it is not old Malchiel Greenwald who will stand trial in my court—but the princes of Jerusalem—the forty-year-long governing clique that has continued to flourish in the world's eyes as leaders of the Jews. I cannot serve warrants on Ben-Gurion, Sharett, or call upon them officially to defend themselves. I can only attempt to take upon me "the mystery of things"—and imagine . . . what I can.

I begin with Joel Brand's return from Colonel Eichmann's headquarters in Budapest with news of the offer. The Budapest Jewish Council meets in full strength. They meet, debate, pray, burst into tears. For a sun suddenly blazes in Jewish darkness. Hope almost drives these Hungarian Jews mad. They were all going to be reduced to ashes at the rate of twelve thousand a day! Now Eichmann, the Furnace-Tender, wants to sell them to the Free World, the wonderful world outside of German hands, where nobody kills Jews!

And he is willing to pay one hundred thousand Jews in advance for the first thousand trucks, and the first hundred tons of coffee and tea!

There is no dissenting voice in the Jewish Budapest Council. Joel Brand must hurry to market to make the sale.

How can he fail, they ask each other? Joel will make the offer to the world's Jewish leaders who hold in their hands the millions of dollars collected in charity drives wherever there are Jews—for the saving of stricken Jews.

Synagogues, cafés, meeting halls, and kitchens all buzz alike with hope. Such a miracle as this has not been heard of since Moses opened the Red Sea for the menaced Jews.

Of course, they will not be allowed to take anything along, so there is no need to pack. But who cares about possessions? They will be allowed to take fathers and mothers and children along. These are possessions enough.

Hungary's Jews lie awake at night, murmuring the word "Palestine."

231

The major matter in my mind is the arrival of the news of the offer in Palestine. When does this happen? The story is known to the safe and free—the Elite of Palestine—almost that same day. And after Brand's arrival by German plane in Constantinople, the Jewish-Agency-Zionist leaders stare at their unhappy problem. For who can doubt what the British would' do if the Agency starts welcoming a million Jews to Palestine! There's no question of it—the Jewish Agency and Zionist leaders will lose their standing as Jewish saviors—if they proceed to save the Jews in disobedience of the British. Such is the Jewish situation in Tel Aviv.

While Hungary's Jews lie sleepless with the name Palestine lighting up their hearts, the leaders of Palestine vote on their course. Nothing will be done for Hungary's Jews without British permission—never granted. And yet the situation must be met face to face. A Jew has to be talked to—by the leaders of Jewry.

The deliberations of the Jewish Leaders on this topic are full of painful undercurrents. Jews like Avriel, Weizmann, Sharett, *et al.* are not creatures divorced from human mood. Sympathy for Jews to be fed into German furnaces is strong in their Jewish hearts.

They suffer at the thought of the doomed million in Hungary looking to them for rescue. They see, not only the faces of their brothers, but the old prayer shawls, the *tvillin,* they know by heart the Hebrew prayers these doomed ones are uttering.

And they wince (in Tel Aviv) at the thought that such rescue might be possible if they act quickly and boldly.

How wonderful to see the lighted faces of Eichmann's First Payment—the first one hundred thousand Jews! To hear the cries of gratitude from mothers and children, plucked at the last hour out of German furnaces! How sweet to hear the tearful thank-yous of learned old men, of gentle rabbis and their sturdy young students!

With pale faces, the Jewish Leaders stare at the problem of Joel Brand, the salesman from Budapest.

Nevertheless—pale, wincing or suffering—the Jewish leaders decide on their course of obeying the White Paper. They decide on the criminal deed that must wreck all hope of saving the million men, women, and children from German slaughter. They will betray Joel Brand to the British.

But first, before betraying him, they are compelled by their high estate to play host to this spectral Banquo from Budapest. There is no escaping it. There are certain things that the Jewish Agency, historic champion of Jewry, must do. It must recognize a cry for help coming from its doomed Hungarian "chapter."

I have mentioned often "the Jewish Agency" as being responsible for this and that action in Palestine. Having come now to May 1944 and to its conduct in the Brand business, I think it well to identify the Jewish Agency of that time—what it was, and what it was not. (Today there is a Jewish Agency, Inc. in the U.S.A. It is a new organization and did not participate in the Palestinian events of the forties.)

To nearly all American Jews and to most of the American press, the Jewish Agency loomed unequivocally in the thirties and forties as an institution devoted to the solving of Europe's "Jewish problem." In the twenties this problem was a minor political matter having to do with the creation of some sort of a homeland for the Jews in Palestine. The problem grew more dramatic in the late thirties. It then had to do with saving the Jewish millions of Europe from being murdered by the Germans.

American Jews who offered their money and participation to the Jewish Agency in Palestine were emotionally certain that such rescue of Europe's Jewry was the primary objective of the "powerful Jewish Agency" headquartered in Tel Aviv and with puissant branches in most of the capitals of Europe.

The American notions of the Jewish Agency were compounded of daydream and lack of information. There was a third content—the emotional belief that a Jewish organization could not ignore the plight of Europe's Jews, could not substitute politics for humanitarianism. Despite all that has happened, most American Jews still hang on to this concept of the Jewish Agency.

The significance of the Jewish Agency begins with its establishment in 1923. It was established by the British to facilitate the execution of the mandate given them by the League of Nations and the U.S.A.—"to prepare a homeland for Jews in Palestine."

The British government asked the leaders of Zionism to submit for British approval a coterie of Jews who would be acceptable as chiefs of the new Jewish Agency. The coterie was submitted and blessed with British sanction. Thereafter the Jewish Agency became the Jewish face for the British rule of Palestine—a sort of caricature of authority to which Jews could give their loyalty.

The Jewish Agency continued to function as a Jewish collaborator and a Jewish front for British policy in Palestine. It was not an elected body, but an appointed one. And just as it had been established by British approval it could be dissolved by British disapproval.

The Jewish Agency, led by Ben-Gurion, Sharett *et al.*, kept its Jewish look through the years of the extermination of Europe's Jews. But it remained unwavering in its loyalty to British policy. When British policy required silence and inaction toward the extermination of Hungary's Jews, the Jewish Agency and its now world famous factotums upheld this policy. Not once did the Jewish Agency inform the world and the Jews of Palestine of the mass murder of a final million Jews being done in Hungary and Auschwitz. Neither the headlines of Ben Gurion's press nor his innumerable orations during this time made reference to the matter of the murder of Jews.

The leaders of the Jewish Agency and of Zionism in 1944 cried out openly against the minority of Jews who fought to open the ports of Palestine to the still unslaughtered Jews of Europe.

I have repeated these facts about the Jewish Agency and its leaders to clarify the incredible adventures that befell Joel Brand on his arrival in Istanbul.

Albert Camus wrote, "To serve falsehood and despotism is the patriotism of the coward." I add—"also of the uninformed."

Thus the Rescue Leaders in Constantinople gather around Brand like a troop of enfevered Samaritans. They listen to his tale with paled faces, with pain-filled eyes. And Brand talks on eagerly to Avriel, Barlas, Pomeranietz. His heart bursts with hope. What a deed to be doing—rescuing a million Jews!

234

Joel Brand has no suspicions. Suspicions of whom? Of these fine Jews of the Jewish Agency?

But the betrayal takes place. The time is not specified in the evidence by Bader or Brand.

Perhaps I behave too politely in my court room. There is nothing doubtful or vague about the whole business. Joel Brand was betrayed by the Jewish Agency to the British for a dozen reasons, all of them unspeakable from any human point of view.

Is the deed done from Tel Aviv or Istanbul or London? Was Weizmann really traveling "a good deal" and incommunicado? Was Ben-Gurion busy with other news? Government official Bader himself testifies that his fellow government official, Ehud Avriel, revealed Brand to the British right away.

Bader is noted for being an honest fellow, but his statement is a foolish one. Does he wish to make the point that Ehud Avriel played informer on his own? True, Avriel is a British Agent. But he is an agent on loan from the inner circle of the Jewish Agency. Whatever are his duties for the British, Avriel is a disciplined member of the Jewish politicalized society.

I pronounce in my own court room that Ehud Avriel was given his "betray Brand" orders by the Jewish Agency leaders in Tel Aviv.

I wonder what Chaim Weizmann said in the "top level" discussion that resulted in the dirty deal of betrayal. I wonder what that righteous "Greek scholar" and Man of the People, Ben-Gurion, said. And what said the clever Moshe Sharett—the one who would have to face Joel Brand in Cairo?

If I had to put such a scene in a play I would not know how to write it. Any more than I would know how to write a scene about three cultured Germans sitting in a room and discussing the most economical way to murder six million Jewish men, women, and children. I would be inclined to overwrite something in both scenes—the tug of conscience, the hidden human pain under the inhuman language.

This scene in London and Tel Aviv that I find hard to imagine takes place. Whatever the grimaces and sighs, these moral leaders of world Jewry come to a decision.

But how do they rationalize such a decision and bring its language within the bounds of decent human speech? I shall let an Israeli journalist of today, a pro-government journalist, naturally, make the kind of statement I am unable to imagine. He is Zeev Laqueur, writing in 1955 in *The Jerusalem Post*. M'sieur Laqueur writes:

"The whole approach of the court in finding fault with Kastner for having failed to make policy from 'a position of strength' is monstrous."

There you have the kind of reasoning that explains the High Command deliberating in Tel Aviv in 1944. The decision to scuttle Brand's mission is not only honorable *per se*—simply because it is *their* decision—but any criticism of their policies is "monstrous."

For in the eyes of the regime, all Jews who deal with the enemy from "a position of strength"—the Irgun, the Lehi—*they* are the betrayers. They who dared everything—death in battle, the gallows—they are the "criminals," the "scum," the "gangsters."

This hocus-pocus reasoning that attaches shame to the brave —this unimaginable rationalizing—is not a Hebraic trait only.

The judges of Joan of Arc were Frenchmen afraid of the English who sat in power over them. Having, out of this fear of their masters, decided on the heresy of Joan, her judges too found her continued defiance of their cowardice wicked—probably "monstrous."

Thus, with the help of journalist Laqueur, and a little history to assist me, I am able to walk the crooked mile to the Joel Brand decision. The conference is probably a short, cool spoken scene. Quickly the debaters agree that it is folly to make policy from a position of strength, and it is wiser to continue "making policy" from a kneeling position.

But now the Jewish Leaders realize that a little cunning is needed if Brand is to be handed on a platter to the British. For Joel Brand is nervous about the British. He knows that if they detain him, his own family and a million others will pack the German incinerators.

Zion has a man for the job—Ehud Avriel. And Jewish Leader Avriel does the job well. He soothes the fearful Emissary. How? By smiling on him as a fellow Jew. By chanting the lullaby names of Weizmann, Ben-Gurion, Sharett, to him.

Surrounded and "aided" by the people he most venerates in

the world, Emissary Brand darts around Istanbul. He is arrested by the Turks. He is released—all too quickly for the Jewish Agency timetable.

And now he wants to go to call on the United States Ambassador in Ankara, a Jew named Steinhardt. Maybe Steinhardt, having a Jewish heart, can help. Maybe he can induce Steinhardt's country, the glorious United States, to help. But there's a snag. Brand can't get to Ankara. The Jewish Leaders somehow can't manage to get the right travel papers for Joel Brand. They will later manage to get the most difficult of papers for the emissary, papers allowing him to leave Turkey and enter British territory. But this simple police pass that would allow Brand to hop a train to Ankara is too much for them.

Thus, the Jewish Leaders prevent Emissary Brand from calling on the important Jew—Ambassador Steinhardt.

Had Brand made his visit, possibly all that would have happened is that Ambassador Steinhardt would have gotten into a peck of trouble and been recalled by President Roosevelt for harassing the British in their war effort. Emissary Brand, however, cannot reach the Ambassador, and continues to dart around Constantinople—and to meet only with his Jewish rescuers.

But Joel Brand is a man of honest enterprise and a little cunning. He fears he is being delayed by small talk of "important officials due any day" and important officials "going over the Basic Situation."

Suddenly he gets an idea. If the Jewish Leaders in Istanbul will draw up a document agreeing to the big swap of Cargo for Blood, he will be able to fly back with it to Eichmann, and a hundred thousand Jews will be saved, automatically.

The Leaders draw up the document for Eichmann. Emissary Brand trembles with joy. His mission is a triumph. All he has to do is deliver the document to Eichmann! And there will be no massacre! A hundred thousand men, women, and children will be released from the queue outside the death furnaces!

But Joel Brand does not get back to Budapest with his priceless document. The Jewish Leaders talk him out of it. How can he think of returning to Budapest without first meeting face to face their great leader Moshe Sharett? Sharett is Weizmann's

237

right hand man. Sharett will put the whole matter on a top political level and make it all official.

Brand wavers. Is Sharett coming to Istanbul? Certainly, the officials answer him. A day or two and he will be sitting right in this Turkish chair.

And Brand waits. He does not fly off with hallelujahs to Budapest. He sits on a hot stove—on a great furnace whose fires are kindling—and he waits for the famous Moshe Sharett.

Oddly, the Turks won't let Moshe Sharett come to Istanbul. Avriel can come there, Bader, Pomeranietz, Barlas and innumerable other Agency-Zionist officials. The riff-raff of Europe can come to Istanbul. But not Moshe Sharett.

The record shows that Moshe Sharett was in Istanbul a few months before Brand's ill-fated arrival there. The bright-spoken Sharett came and went with nobody throwing up any road blocks.

I wonder why Joel Brand does not see the crudity of all the lies. Why he does not put together all the plot turns against him?—nobody to meet him at the airfield, no papers to allow him to get to Steinhardt in Ankara, the insistence against his returning to Budapest with his "governor's pardon" for a hundred thousand Jews. And now the inability of the much-traveled Moshe Sharett to travel to Istanbul. I wonder how Brand can fail to spot the duplicity and betrayal in which he now walks.

But I am not a bewildered man with a million lives at stake if I make a wrong move. Nor am I a man infatuated since childhood with the nobility of Jewry's Leaders.

Joel Brand is. He listens desperately, nervously, and suspects nothing. His faith is in Weizmann, Ben-Gurion, Sharett and the other respectables. His soul is full of homage toward them.

Now the time has come to hand Joel Brand over to the British. It is a ticklish hour for the Jewish Agency. The Leaders tell Brand he will have to meet Moshe Sharett in Aleppo. Aleppo is on English soil.

The prospect frightens Brand. He argues. What if the British arrest him? Too much time has already passed. He promised Eichmann to be back in two weeks. Eichmann may start burning Jews any minute. Twelve thousand a day.

It is hard to believe that these fellow-Jews in Istanbul will not suddenly cry out to Joel—"Go back to Budapest. Quickly! We are fooling you, hoodwinking you, betraying you."

No such sentimental collapse happens. Instead, the unhappy Joel Brand is urged on in another direction. If the great Moshe Sharett is willing to come to Aleppo to meet him, how can Joel refuse? And how can he worry about anything wrong happening when the highest officials of Palestine have all sent assurances that there is no danger?

And during all these days of Joel Brand's desperate talking, pleading, darting about Istanbul—in jail, out of jail; meeting more Jewish Leaders from Palestine and listening to more and more reassurances—it has all been arranged.

It was all settled shortly after the emissary from Hungary's doomed arrived in Istanbul. He is to be kept from telling his story to the world, he is to be kept from returning to Budapest with his precious document. He is to be lured to Aleppo. In Aleppo the British will arrest him.

TRAIN TO PONTIUS PILATE'S VILLA

Aleppo-bound Joel Brand sits in his train compartment with his friend Avriel, who smiles and chats like a parent calming a troubled child.

The train stops at Ankara and Fate comes aboard. A young Jabotinsky disciple from Palestine, Joseph Klarman, finds Brand in his compartment and speaks to him. He warns Brand. The British are waiting to arrest him in Aleppo. He begs Brand not to go on.

Jewish Leader Avriel sneers on hearing of the intruder. He knows him—one of the toughs from Tel Aviv, a Jabotinsky hothead.

Unknowing, the million Hungarian Jews, still alive, wait for the outcome of this talk on the train at Ankara. If Joel Brand will believe what this "troublemaker" from Palestine tells him, the million may escape the German ash barrels. What a moment this is, a moment that could change history.

But it changes nothing. Joel Brand does not believe the "troublemaker." Brand is a Jew trained to believe only in Respectability, such as rides with him in the compartment. Truth can scream itself hoarse at him in a compartment. But his allegiance must go to the patrician Vandyke beard of Weizmann, to the diplomatic frock coat of Sharett. Besides, does not his friend Avriel remind him constantly by his presence and purring cheeriness that all is well?

Emissary Brand shakes off the truth-teller. He rides on to Aleppo. His ride is a death march for a multitude. But there is Leader Avriel to purr cheery words to him. Nothing can possibly go wrong, dear Joel. Remember that the highest Jewish officials have told you this again and again—

Suddenly, an hour out of Aleppo, All-is-Well Avriel whispers to companion Brand that something may happen. He, Brand, may be arrested by the British, and separated from his good guide, Avriel. If this happens, Joel must promise not to answer any British questions unless an official of the Jewish Agency is present.

Brand stares at his sly companion as the train roars on. He may be arrested? But he was assured when he started for Aleppo! He asks desperately for more assurance.

But now Jewish Leader Avriel is silent as in a nightmare.

In Aleppo the British take over. They will hold Joel Brand captive for four and a half months.

One of the cruelest moments in Brand's story is in Avriel's farewell sentence—before he ducks out of the compartment— the speech bidding Brand not to answer British questions unless a member of the Jewish Agency is present.

At the last moment the betrayer demands a pledge from his victim—in the name of Jewish loyalty. Most certainly the British will do all in their power to keep the secret. Still, Avriel feels, it won't harm to get Brand to be his own policeman.

And Brand, still trusting, promises. He will speak only in the presence of his Jewish Leaders. The rest of the time—silence.

When he is arrested and marched to British headquarters, Brand's feverish dream seems to be coming true. He meets one of the great Jewish Leaders. Not quite Chaim Weizmann, but almost. Moshe Sharett is there to hear his wild tale of Eichmann's Blood for Cargo offer.

Israel's leading diplomat Moshe Sharett, Reuven Shiloach, Zvi Yehieli, and other Jewish Leaders are present. Here are the rescuers of whom the doomed Jews of Europe dreamed, and in whose support the Jews of the United States are united today (1961).

But something has gone wrong. In a nightmare our loved ones suddenly appear with unfamiliar faces and look at us with queer expressions. We shudder and move deeper into the bad dream. Brand feels this terror.

Brand talks to Sharett for eighteen hours, without stop. He has a tale to pour out, an Iliad of murder and hope. The English take shorthand notes. Sharett listens solemnly and clucks with compassion.

When his wild sales talk for the doomed Jews is finally done, Brand hears the Leader of the Jews, Moshe Sharett, speak the decision. Says Leader Sharett,

"I'm very sorry, Mr. Brand. I have been given to understand that you will have to travel southwards (to British Cairo) and not go back at this time to Budapest."

And now a hoarsened, bewildered Brand is put in an army car and driven by British guards through Haifa, through Tel Aviv, through the new land of the Jews, past the offices of the Leaders of the Jews—to a British jail. As the car moves on, a wild hope keeps Brand staring at the crowded streets. The Jews will rescue him! They will stop the car, take him from the two English soldiers in the car, and bring him in triumph to the high quarters of Dr. Weizmann and Ben-Gurion.

But no Jews rescue Joel Brand. He arrives at his British prison. Sharett, Weizmann, Ben-Gurion have kept Brand, his mission, and his imprisonment, a secret. During all this time the Hungarian Jews have been burning—12,000 a day. Soon there will be no further danger of Jews disturbing the White Paper by trying to pry their way into Palestine.

After Sharett leaves, Brand recalls an odd thing. Moshe Sharett said he had been a guest at the British villa for a day or two before Brand's arrival. Then everybody must have known the

British were going to arrest him. All the Jewish officials who had talked to him day after day in Istanbul. And wept over his story. And drawn up the paper for Eichmann. They all must have known, and hid their knowledge.

In the British jail Joel Brand's innocence leaves him. His faith in the honesty of Jewish hearts no longer blinds his soul.

The British asking him polite questions are no different from the German bargainers! He has told them about the furnaces Eichmann has lighted now. It is a month since he left Budapest on his salesman errand. It is going on now—the killing of twelve thousand a day!

Brand pleads for the burning ones. He screams. He goes on a hunger strike.

The British officers evidently complain to the Jewish Agency officials in Tel Aviv about Brand's unmannerly behavior. And the Agency rebukes Brand. Leader Avriel himself instructs him to cooperate with the British. It seems he is somehow misbehaving toward his captors.

During the four and a half months, a number of Jewish officials visit Brand, and other big shots keep dropping in on him for chats. No reason for this is given by Brand. I wonder at their boldness. I would not like to hear his wild, honest heart begging for the burning Jews of Hungary.

As each Day of the Twelve Thousand passes, Brand sees more and more clearly what his soul refused at first to imagine. He sees, detail by detail, the trickery that wrecked his mission. The sly arguments. The lies, the ruses, hypocrisies. Remembering them all in their true light now, Joel Brand wants only to die.

For seventeen days Brand takes no food. His hunger strike is more than a wish for death. It is his judgment on the world. He cannot break bread with human beings. He has seen all the faces conspiring in massacre.

Everywhere he looks with his awakened mind he sees the humanless face of man. Everyone—Great Britain, the United States, and the leaders of world Jewry—traitors all! Murderers. How can the kindly, human-loving world turn its back on the wild destruction of six million guiltless people?

Answer—it can.

After four and a half months, Joel Brand is released. Here,

(I am not sarcastic) is curious evidence of Anglo-Saxon "humanity."

It would have been shrewder for the British to see that no Joel Brand survived with his horror tale to tell. He could well have died "as a result of his hunger strike." The Jewish Leaders of Palestine would have raised no outcry over such a bulletin.

But Brand is allowed to stay alive. Like the Americans, the British are humane as individuals. Political murder is one thing. Murdering innocent captives is another.

So the British let him go. Nobody feels too happy about the Joel Brand business. On the other hand, nobody feels too unhappy. Political objectives exonerate leaders from feeling guilt. They regard their actions, however cruel and vicious their results, as impersonal deeds dictated by national demands.

Thus it comes to pass that though there are six million Jews murdered, there is no guilt. Neither German, Briton, American, nor Jew feels guilty.

EVERY MAN HAS TWO TONGUES

The Hungarian Jews are nearly over and done with. Joel Brand, released from prison, arrives in Palestine. The Jewish Leaders are as humane as the British. They also allow Brand to stay alive. And Joel Brand walks the streets of the new Zion.

He walks these streets, still intent on his mission. He visits the headquarters of Mapai, of Histadrut, of the Jewish Agency. Wherever there is a Headquarters for important Jews, there Joel Brand enters, talks, pleads. And he sends out scores of letters to all the Jewish Bosses of Palestine. There are still Jews to be saved in Hungary, he pleads. He pleads also that the Jewish Bosses allow him to return to Budapest, and share the fate of the Jews he was unable to save.

But his pleas and letters arouse only indifference or irritation. A last hope flickers in this nuisance of an Emissary. He has written to Sharett, Ben-Gurion, Bader, Avriel, Barlas. These are all big Jewish leaders. But there is one above them, Dr. Chaim

Weizmann. Sometimes the truth is kept from a King by those close to him.

Joel Brand puts aside his bitterness, his disillusion. The butchery of Jews is still going on in Budapest. There is still a small deal to be made with Eichmann; a deal for those not yet killed.

In his room in Tel Aviv, Joel Brand summons back into his soul the memory of his faith in Jewish leaders. And he writes his last appeal to the Leader of Leaders—the man who is to be the first president of Israel when its freedom is won by its outlawed fighters.

Brand writes it all out politely for Dr. Weizmann to read, his mission that began in Budapest, that was spiked in Istanbul; his arrest in Aleppo, the hideous slaughter of the Jews in Hungary and Poland; all the details, all the facts—including his discovery that the Jews of Europe are being betrayed by the Jews of Palestine, who work with the British.

Chaim Weizmann answers Joel Brand's letter. Weizmann's words to the Emissary from Budapest are the only Israeli government statement to enter the court record in Jerusalem.

Some pages back I called Weizmann's letter callous. But I have more to say of it now.

I study the letter again:

Rehovoth, 29th Dec. 1944

Mr. Joel Brand
Tel Aviv

Dear Mr. Brand,

I beg you to forgive me for having delayed answering your letter. As you may have seen from the Press I have been traveling a good deal and generally did not have a free moment since my arrival here. I have read both your letter and your memorandum and shall be happy to see you sometime the week after next—about the 10th of January.

Miss Itin—my secretary—will get in touch with you to fix up the appointment.

With kindest regards,

Yours very sincerely,
Ch. Weizmann

Chaim's letter fascinates me. It is one of the great human

documents of our century. I have read it a number of times and each time it makes a new confession.

At first reading I thought it only the callous letter of a leader whose sense of importance had blinded him to all human values. I noted that Dr. Chaim Weizmann, "the greatest Jewish statesman," has no word of sympathy to offer Joel Brand on the extermination of Hungary's Jews.

Instead, with mock humility the great man requests, "I beg you to forgive me for having delayed, etc."

In this pose of punctiliousness, Dr. Weizmann politely sidesteps the genocide in Hungary as if it were a faux-pas not for discussion.

"Manners before morals, Lord Windermere."

Manners before murder, Chaim Weizmann.

But a re-reading of the opening line startles me. This opening line addressed to Joel Brand, the betrayed emissary of the Jews, begins, "I beg you to forgive me—"

These six words are a social cliché out of the "Ever-Ready Letter Writer" in all languages. They are also written by a Jew who conspired to turn a Jewish emissary from the pogrom over to the British.

After first reading this callous and vacuous letter from Weizmann, I wondered why he had written it. Why send so evasive a letter to a man whose soul is in an inferno? Surely Joel Brand is as easy to ignore as Eichmann's offer to spare the lives of a million Jews!

A re-reading brought a deeper meaning to its words. Masking its utterance in glibness, Chaim Weizmann's unhappy soul spoke its atonement to Joel Brand—and felt a certain relief—"I beg you to forgive me—"

Weizmann's second sentence reads,

"As you may have seen from the Press I have been traveling a good deal and generally did not have a free moment since my arrival here."

This sentence, on the surface, seems to say a number of foolish things. In it Chaim boasts of his fame a little whimsically. The Press reports all his movements in large and constant headlines. You say kittenishly "as you may have seen" about something enormously visible.

245

And, of course, one's mail isn't forwarded while one is busy on such important travels. His widely reported travels explained, Dr. Weizmann continues to point out that even when standing still he has "not had a free moment." A phrase that pleads modestly with Joel to imagine the multifarious duties of Jewish leadership.

But why all this apology about a little tardiness as a correspondent? Particularly with a man he is never going to see and whose subsequent letters he is never going to answer.

Obviously (to me) Chaim Weizmann is not apologizing for any tardy letter-answering. I submit that a man as busy with the chores of statesmanship as Weizmann would feel no need to apologize in such persuasive detail for not having answered some "nobody's" letter. It is another and deeper guilt in Chaim that pleads for forgiveness and that tries to explain itself to its victim.

His travels were constantly reported in the press and, after returning to Palestine, Dr. Chaim Weizmann "generally did not have a free moment."

The word "free" has a glib social meaning like the word "forgive." But Chaim Weizmann is not a whiskey-sipping fox hunter in a red coat, awf'lly busy with hounds and horses. Weizmann is a Jewish leader caught up in the climax of a two thousand year Jewish dream of freedom. The word "free" must come out of Chaim Weizmann's deepest vocabulary.

When he writes with seeming casualness that he has had no free moment, he is pleading that he is not a free man. His duties as Jewish politician, his loyalties to Zionist aims in Palestine— these matters imprison him.

Laden with honors, admired by the world (especially the British part of it) Chaim Weizmann blurts out the truth—he is not free for a moment. On the move or standing still, Chaim's letter whispers, all eyes are on him; he is not free to behave as a Jew might, as a human being might. Only as a politician must.

After these two first sentences of atonement, Chaim Weizmann's deep need for writing the letter is appeased. He can write sentence three without collaboration from his conscience. Sentence three offers a full-length portrait of a Jewish Leader in action. Its brazenness, duplicity, and mock courtesy, bow the troublesome Joel Brand into limbo.

Dr. Weizmann has read Brand's letter (great and busy man though he is). And he has found a word for Joel Brand's story of the million burning Jews. He calls it a "memorandum." Thus, to Dr. Weizmann, it (the genocide) is a memorandum to be put on file for further consideration when he can find "a free moment."

Having made this concession, a nervousness overcomes writer Chaim. Dr. Weizmann must extricate himself from the danger into which his guilt toward Brand has led him. This is the danger of any further contact with the accusing finger of Joel Brand. Chaim's soul bowed secretly to this figure. Now Dr. Weizmann's frock coat brushes him off.

Dr. Weizmann writes he will be happy to see Brand. When? "Sometime the week after next—about the 10th."

Then, fearful that even this is a bit too definite, Dr. Weizmann makes sentence number four a new paragraph—Miss Itin, his secretary, will get in touch.

In vaudeville, the old joke line was "Don't call us, we'll call you."

Did Miss Itin, the secretary, call? A "zoch und vey!" as my Tanta Chasa used to say—not knowing the phrase "in a pig's eye!"

Thus, having eased a buried uneasiness about the betrayal of Joel Brand and the extermination of Hungary's Jews, Dr. Chaim Weizmann sends his foolish-seeming letter to the man he is never going to see.

I have a feeling, however, that in the few years of life that remained to him, Chaim Weizmann thought often of the stranger from Budapest.

247

"GIVE THEM THE FOILS, YOUNG OSRIC"

Moshe Sharett and the sorrowing government wish to make a mournful answer about the dead Jews of Hungary.[202] Sharett sends word to Judge Halevi's court that he is eager to make a statement—but not if he is to be cross-examined by Tamir. Tamir counter-proposes that he will question Moshe Sharett only in his softest tones. But this is not enough. The Prime Minister wishes full immunity from Tamir on his funeral oration, or he will not appear in court. He doesn't.[203]

Instead, Prime Minister Sharett will deliver his statement to the masses of Israel. Ehud Avriel, who did not do so well as a witness in the court room—he had aroused roars of laughter until he had to cry out, "I am not here to make people laugh!"— is given the *aliya* of assembling the masses.

Lullaby Avriel organizes a memorial mass meeting in honor of the parachutist Peretz Goldstein. This was the young Jewish hero who was in the Hanna Senesh rescue unit. He was handed over to the Nazis in Budapest by Kastner and exterminated. This was Judge Halevi's verdict. And Kastner's clique are eager to mourn him and give Sharett a chance to make a speech without cross-examination. This event takes place at Kibbutz Magaan.

All the government princes and their sword bearers are on hand. The new parachute officers of the army attend. In a place of honor stand the survivors of the sixteen original parachutists. Present also is Catherina Senesh, mother of Hanna.

Avriel has done his work well. A great crowd is present in the Kibbutz, with its Jewish heart on its sleeve.

Prime Minister Sharett walks proudly to the microphone. At the same moment an airplane swoops down out of the cloudless heavens. The government diplomats have arranged a symbolic touch. The plane is to drop the Prime Minister's Statement from on High.

But this brazen circusing of the government's "answer" fails

248

in a dire way. The plane that is to drop the speech goes out of control and crashes into the crowd.

Seventeen people are killed, four of them heroes of the original rescue parachutists. Two of these four had survived Nazi death camps. Scores of men and women are injured.[204]

But Sharett is not deterred. Seven days later, he delivers his statement as part of the mourning service for the seventeen dead. It is carried over the radio. In his statement, Sharett speaks of "Eichmann's satanic offer," made through Joel Brand. Sharett, an excellent speaker, always polished, always grammatical, declaims:

"It had no chance to succeed. But we did our best. I rushed to discuss it with the British in London."

Sharett "rushed" to London on June 27, 1944, after Brand had been handed over to the British, after the Germans had done to death most of Hungary's Jews. And, in London, did impetuous Jew-rescuer Sharett pour out the desperate Joel Brand story to any of the hundreds of newspapermen from all over the world covering London at the time?

To nary a one. Twenty-five per cent of the Jews of Hungary are still left for burning. But Zionist Sharett keeps his mouth shut. He will not embarrass his English hosts—Eden and Churchill—by bringing up this unpleasant subject publicly.

To digress a moment—but still on the subject of Sharett's London mission: Following Sharett's rush to London, in July, 1944, Prime Minister Winston Churchill wrote a letter to Anthony Eden:

Understandably, the persecution of the Jews in Hungary is the greatest and most horrible crime ever committed in the history of the world. And this was done with the aid of scientific devices and by a so-called civilized people. It is clear beyond doubt that everybody involved in this crime who may fall into our hands, including those who only obeyed orders in committing these butcheries, must be killed.

The grin of caricature in Churchill's eloquent outburst—to Anthony Eden—lies in the date of the letter, July 11, 1944. All the Jews were dead. You could denounce their murderers with

249

tardy eloquence—on July 11, 1944—and not disturb the White Paper policy that had assisted in the murder.[205]

The upshot of Prime Minister Sharett's rush to London? A well-kept secret. No word of Joel Brand's attempt to help Hungary's Jews has reached anybody who might help them.

In the mourning speech for the seventeen dead in 1953, Sharett quoted pleadings he had made (*in camera*) in behalf of the Hungarian Jews in 1944.

The seventeen dead at Kibbutz Magaan, and the radio broadcast by Sharett in 1954, are the government's riposte to the Joel Brand story.

ENVOI

I began to write this book in 1955. A year later, when it was half finished, I put the manuscript in a drawer.

Why go on, I thought. Such a new place, Israel. So small its boundaries. So many its enemies—why attack it? Why should I be the one to rake up its "past"?

I had worked for the creation of a Hebrew State in Palestine. I still believed in the charm and necessity of such a State. No such gaiety had come to the Jews in two thousand years as the new Israel offered. Better to forget, I thought.

But after six years I fished my half-finished manuscript out of the drawer and went to work on it. Not because of Adolf Eichmann re-appearing in the news of the world, and focusing a nervous attention on Israel. Eichmann had not yet been caught.

I started writing because I had been looking on the world. I had watched it fall sick.

All was serene in my domain. Love, hope, gratitude abounded in my home. We who lived in it were as unwarlike as so many summer fire flies. I imagine most homes are the same.

And yet the world continued to arm itself, to scream at itself, to brag of its new God-like powers of destruction.

In this contrast between my home and the fi-fo-fumming of

statesmen lay the measure of the sickness which has smitten the mind of man.

A world readying itself for atomic war. A shivering world. I saw it as a figure with glaring eyes that stood on a window ledge high above a street, jabbering at the sky and threatening to jump off.

A fine place for the descendant of Moses, Christ, Socrates, Shakespeare, Michelangelo, Beethoven, and George Washington to be standing. Ah, this sad figure of a world—hair rumpled on its high ledge, burbling to the wind all the reasons it has for committing suicide. A writer should not turn his back on it. He should speak to it, however vain his words.

It had come to me that the story I had begun to tell was not of Israel, alone, but of a disaster on which the human mind has been spiked—its dedication to the winning of arguments at any cost. Confronted by the almost certain prospects of exterminating mankind if it keeps on arguing on what are the right ideals for living, this mind of ours is unable to quit the debater's arena.

I used Joel Brand as a climax in my report of the trial because he seemed to me a lone, sad human whose adventures revealed the dismal truth of our civilization. After three thousand years of various refinements; of millions of poems, philosophies and prayers—we are back to our pre-Biblical origins—keen on annihilation.

Brand is not only the story of a Jew betrayed by other Jews. Joel Brand is the modern drama of human hope and kindly intentions finding no ear in our time.

Brand is our century's Everyman. Good of heart, noble of purpose, he must go on his savior mission. He must operate out of the ancient Jewish belief that God's spirit is in man, and that life is therefore sacred. In a world tearing itself apart, he must go in quest of goodness.

And he must be crushed by a politicalized society—not only the government of the Jews, half-hatched in Palestine, but the governments of all the Allied nations.

There are thousands of Joel Brands loose in my own country today. They don't plead for the lives of far-off Jews, but for the lives of one hundred and eighty million American neighbors.

These missionaries plead for the figure not to jump from

the window ledge. For, as in some involuted dream, the figure is one of themselves. The figure is we.

The government of the Jews could not save the Jews. The "situation was too complex." No more can the governments of the United States and Russia save their own people. Their "ideals" are too important. Intoning implacably its ideals, government must ride its course to the Apocalypse. It cannot pause in its heroic dash for oblivion to look where it's going.

At least, so it seems as I write these last pages. I hear no voices challenging the death's-head ideals of the United States. I hear only the ideal speaking, its tongue speaking as always of love. The love of country, the love of freedom, the love of a better way of life.

What a dire word *love* has been in history. It has launched more carnage than any war cry of the species. For it is never love that an ideal has to offer, but love and death. It is always, "Love me, or I'll kill you."

Even Jesus Christ who said, "Do unto others as you would have them do unto you," cried out also, " Woe unto you, Chorezian! Woe unto you, Bethsaida! Thou which are exalted shall be brought down to Hell for denying me!"

And how more potent is love when it has an atom bomb to further its courtship.

No voices rise to challenge Authority in my country. But there were many such voices in Israel. The voices of . . . the cigar-stub chewing Don Quixote, Malchiel Greenwald; of the black-gowned stalwart Shmuel Tamir, stirring up a tempest of truth in a teapot of a courtroom, of the wise and formal-minded Judge Benjamin Halevi doing his honest job; of the sad-faced hawker from Budapest, Joel Brand; and of the scores of unknown men and women who appeared before Judge Halevi as the simple witnesses of truth. . . .

And before that, the voices of the young Hebrew heroes that spoke their noble words from the gallows—Avsholom Haviv, Meier Nakar, Eliyahu Beit-Tzuri, Dov Gruner . . . And of Abrasha Stavksy, the hero "I saw slain," killed by Ben-Gurion's soldiers; of his Jew-smuggling companion, Joseph Katznelson; of the unafraid poetess, Hanna Senesh; of the commander of hundreds and router of thousands, Gideon, of the old historian prophet Klausner, of my colleagues Peter Bergson, Samuel Merlin and Mike Ben-Ami, coming to win legions in the United States . . . Of these voices, and many others. And most of all—the voice of the Byronic Vladimir Jabotinsky, and of the one-armed desert D'Artagnan of Tel Hai—Joseph Trumpeldor.

It was because these voices had been raised before mine that I feel the need to tell this story of Perfidy.

Betrayal of Everyman is the business of the day in all the world's nations. An evil of silence toward its betrayers has come into the world.

The outcry that rose up in Judge Halevi's court room against the false face of Israel's anointed and celebrated leadership is one of the few hopeful sounds I have heard in our time. I feel a hope for tomorrow in reporting it.

Jerusalem has been long famous for its export of miracles. . . .

REFERENCE NOTES

ABBREVIATIONS:
C.C. 124/53 in the D.C. Jerusalem: Criminal Case 124/53 in the District Court of Jerusalem.

"Eichmann Confessions" published in *Life*, November 28 and December 5, 1960: as dictated by him to Danish Nazi officer William Sassen, the summary of which appeared in *Life* magazine.

1. Ratified by the League of Nations on July 24, 1922.
2. British White Paper Cmd. 6079 of 1939: PALESTINE: Statement of Policy.
3. Debate in the British House of Commons, May 24, 1939.
4. *The New Judea* (official organ of the Zionist Organization of England) XIII (April, 1937).

As distinct from this attitude of Weizmann stood the alarm of Max Nordau and Vladimir Jabotinsky.

In the Zionist Congress of 1911, *22 years* before Hitler came to power, and three years before World War I, Nordau said, "How dare the smooth talkers, the clever official blabbers, open their mouths and boast of progress. . . . Here they hold jubilant peace conferences in which they talk against war. . . . But the same righteous Governments, who are so nobly, industriously active to establish the eternal peace, are preparing, by their own confession, *complete annihilation for six million people,* and there is nobody, except the doomed themselves, to raise his voice in protest although this is a worse crime than any war . . ."

Vladimir Jabotinsky, in 1936, declared: "It is not our task to establish in Palestine a home for *selected people,* not even a state for a small portion of our people. The aim of our efforts is to organize a systematic *massive Jewish evacuation* from all the countries in which they live . . ."

And in April, 1940, he declared in New York, "The transfer of millions of Jews to their homeland will *save the European Jewry from extermination,*" and again, "*evacuation of the masses is the only cure for the Jewish catastrophe.*"

5. Article by S. N. Behrman in Weisgal, Meyer, editor. *Chaim Weizmann —The Builder of Zion, The Statesman, The Scientist.* Jerusalem: Hebrew University.
6. The State of Israel was proclaimed and established on May 14, 1948. Weizmann was appointed president of Israel by the Provisional Government in June, 1948 (*Who's Who in Israel, 1952*). He was sworn in as President nine months later on February 17, 1949. Weizmann

hung on to his status as a citizen of Great Britain until a week after taking office as Israel's president. No longer able to continue as a British citizen, he then adopted citizenship as an Israeli.

7. The following letter was written by Henry Montor, Executive Vice-Chairman of the United Jewish Appeal. It states the official attitude of the Jewish leaders of Palestine toward the rescue of the six million European Jews whose extermination was well under way.

February 1, 1940

Rabbi Baruch E. Rabinowitz
Congregation B'nai Abraham
Hagerstown, Maryland
Dear Rabbi Rabinowitz:

... I am enclosing herewith two items which may be helpful in revising your judgment on several aspects of the situation relating to the refugees on the Danube. ...

The United Palestine Appeal is a fund-raising instrument of the Jewish Agency for Palestine, as well as the Jewish National Fund. Whatever may be the attitude of the Jewish Agency toward unregistered migration [the refugees from Nazi persecution] to Palestine, it cannot, as a legally constituted body, publicly emphasize any interest in or sympathy with such immigration as it may and does have. ... As you know, provisions of the White Paper provide for an annual immigration schedule of 10,000 a year. ... Public emphasis on unregistered immigration and acknowledgment by such a body as the Jewish Agency that it not only endorses, but finances, such unregistered immigration can only strike a disastrous blow at the possibility of facilitating the entry of legal, properly qualified immigrants into Palestine. ...

... "Selectivity" is an inescapable factor in dealing with the problem of immigration to Palestine. By "selectivity" is meant the choice of young men and women who are trained in Europe for productive purposes either in agriculture or industry and who are in other ways trained for life in Palestine, which involves difficulties and hardships for which they must be prepared physically and psychologically. Sentimental considerations are, of course, vital and everyone would wish to save every single Jew who could be rescued out of the cauldron of Europe.

But when one is dwelling with so delicate a program as unregistered immigration, it is, obviously, essential that those people sent to Palestine shall be able to endure harsh conditions under which they must live for weeks and months on the Mediterranean and the difficulties which await them when they land on the shores of Palestine.

... There could be no more deadly ammunition provided to the enemies of Zionism, whether they be in the ranks of the British Government or the Arabs, or even in the ranks of the Jewish people, if Palestine were to be flooded with very old people or with *undesirables* who would make impossible the conditions of life in Palestine and destroy the prospect of creating such economic circumstances as would insure a continuity of immigration. ...

Until the resources of Palestine are adequately developed, immigration of from 30,000 to 60,000 a year may be possible. ... Under these circumstances, therefore, is it not essential for responsible leaders to concern themselves with the necessity of selecting immigration, particularly under the arduous conditions that surround unregistered immigration at the present time . . . ?

Cordially yours,
Henry Montor
Executive Vice-Chairman

8. In his article *The National Sport*, Jabotinsky stated:

"The National Sport which I heartily recommend to the Jewish youth is free immigration [into Palestine]. It helps to acquire a homeland for homeless masses and turn them into a nation. . . ."

In a public rally in Warsaw in 1939 (before the Declaration of War) Jabotinsky declared:

"I state with shame that the people behave now as if they were already doomed. I have not found anything like it, neither in history nor in novels. Never did I read of such acquiescence with fate.

"It is as if twelve million educated people were put in a carriage and the carriage was being pushed towards an abyss. How do such people behave? One is crying, one is smoking a cigarette, some are reading newspapers, someone is singing—but in vain will you look for one who will stand up, take the reins into his hands and move the carriage somewhere else. This is the mood. As if some big enemy came and chloroformed their minds. I come to you now to make an experiment. The last experiment. I cry to you: 'Put an end to this situation! Try to stop the carriage, try to jump out of it, try to put some obstacle in its way, don't go like sheep to the wolf'."

9. In 1933 one of the Mapai leaders, Chaim Arlosorov, was assassinated on the beach of Tel Aviv. Months later two Arabs confessed that they were the actual killers. However, a few hours after the assassination David Ben-Gurion, then Chairman of the Jewish Agency, declared in far-off Warsaw that he was convinced that Arlosorov was assassinated by Jewish Revisionists (*Davar* daily, June 29, 1933).

Following Ben-Gurion's notion, the Jewish Agency and Mapai Party collaborated with the British Police in concocting murder charges against three revisionists: Abrasha Stavsky, Zvi Rosenblatt, and Aba Achimur, a noted philosopher and historian and one of the leaders of the Revisionists. After a lengthy trial, which agitated Palestine for years, the three were found innocent by a British Court and acquitted. But in the meantime, Ben-Gurion and his disciples had exploited their empty murder charges to get a strong grip over the Zionist Organization.

10. *Haaretz*, the leading Israeli daily of February 27, 1942, quoting an official communiqué from the British Legation in Ankara which has reported a message of Andolio, the semi-official Turkish news agency.

11. *Hamerad* (*The Revolt*) by Menachem Begin, Chief Commander of the Irgun Zvai Leumi, quoting the official "Declaration of War" by the Irgun against Great Britain.

12. Official address to the Histadrut Convention in Tel Aviv as quoted in *Davar* (Israeli daily and the official organ of the Histadrut) on November 23, 1944.

13. Evidence testifying to this torture technique was given during the

Civil Case of Paul Kollek v. *Herut* (Civil Case No. 503/49 in the District Court of Tel Aviv).

14. "War among brothers—never!" Official declaration of the Irgun, published in the Irgun underground organ, *Herut*, on December 3, 1944: "This may be an undiplomatic declaration. But let the people know: under *no conditions* shall we raise our weapons against rival Jews."

15. Official testimony of David Ben-Gurion, Chairman of the Jewish Agency for Palestine, before the Anglo-American Committee of Enquiry in Jerusalem, as quoted in *The Jewish Case Before the Anglo-American Committee of Enquiry on Palestine as presented by the Jewish Agency for Palestine*. Jerusalem: Publishing Department of the Jewish Agency, 1947.

16. Nedava, Joseph. *Olei Hagardom (Those Who Mounted the Gallows)*. Tel Aviv, 1952.

17. Invalids (Pension and Rehabilitation) Law, 1949.

18. A letter dated May 7, 1958 by David Ben-Gurion addressed to Judge Joseph Lamm of the Tel Aviv District Court, Vice President of the B'nai Brith in Israel, in reply to an official demand by B'nai Brith in favor of the repatriation of the remains of Jabotinsky to Israel: "Israel does not need dead Jews, but living Jews, and I see no blessing in multiplying graves in Israel."

19. This decision is echoed in an official statement of Moshe Sharett (Shertok), head of the Political Department of the Jewish Agency, at the United Nations at Lake Success on November 13, 1947, declaring that the Jewish Agency agrees to the exclusion of the whole municipal area of Jaffa from the boundaries of the future Jewish State.

20. From an address by David Ben-Gurion on July 23, 1948 in a meeting of his party, Mapai, as quoted by the official daily of Mapai, *Hador*.

21. In an interview published in the Israel weekly *Yaad* on August 17, 1960, Itzchak Greenbaum, member of the first Israeli Government, stated: "The attitude of the Israeli Government [during the war of Independence] was not to take Jerusalem from the Arabs in order not to hurt the Christian and the Moslem World."

22. Begin, Menachem. *Hamerad (The Revolt)*. Hebrew Edition. Israel, 1950.

23. Official statement in the Provisional State Council (Parliament) of Israel as quoted in *Hamashkif*, Israeli daily, on June 24, 1948.

24. On the day of the British withdrawal from Palestine, the British Colonial and Foreign Office published a Termination of the Mandate explaining the withdrawal: "Eighty-four thousand troops . . . had proved insufficient to maintain law and order in the face of a campaign of terrorism waged by highly organized Jewish forces equipped with all the weapons of the modern infantryman. Since the war 338 British subjects had been killed in Palestine, while the military forces there had cost the British taxpayer one hundred million sterling. . . .
    . . . The declared intentions of Jewish extremists showed that the loss of further British lives was inevitable. . . .
    In these circumstances His Majesty's Government decided to bring to an end their mandate and to prepare for the earliest possible with-

drawal from Palestine of all British forces. They accordingly announced . . . that the Mandate would end on the 15ʰh May, 1948, from which date the sole task of the British forces in Palestine would be to complete their withdrawal by the 1st August, 1948." (The New York Times, May 14, 1948).

On February 1, 1947, the former Colonial Secretary, Mr. Oliver Stanley, spoke on behalf of Churchill and said: "The Government had conceded exactly what the terrorists demanded . . . Rather than this country should suffer further humiliations of this character we would prefer that we clear out of Palestine and tell the people of the world that we were unable to carry out our Mandate there."

Churchill's speech in the House of Commons on March 3, 1947, as quoted by *The Palestine Post* on March 4, 1947: "Shouting angrily and thumping a dispatch box in front of him, Churchill demanded to know how long this state of squalid warfare in Palestine, with all its bloodshed, would go on before some decision was reached. Churchill said it was costing thirty or forty million sterling a year and keeping 100,000 Englishmen away with the military forces. How long is this to go on? Are we just to drift month after month with these horrible outrages and countermeasures, which are necessary, but none the less objectionable?"

25. Official charge sheet of the Attorney General v. Malchiel Greenwald in Criminal Case 124/53 in the District Court, Jerusalem.

26. Ben-Gurion said in an interview with the reporter of *Haaretz*, Israeli daily, on October 2, 1959, "The Germany of today is not the Germany of yesterday. We have to win over the friendship of the people of West Germany; we have to treat West Germany as any other nation."

27. "On the Holocaust and on the Reaction," statement by Itzhak Greenbaum, Chief of the Rescue Committee of the Jewish Agency, addressed to the Zionist Executive Council on February 18, 1943 and published in his book, *Beeyemei Khurban Veshoah* (*In days of Holocaust and Destruction*), 1946.

28. Halevi, a graduate of the Universities of Freiburg, Göttingen, and Berlin, left for Palestine in 1933 and spent one year in an agricultural settlement. He later was one of the three judges who tried Eichmann in Jerusalem.

29. The number later increased to 1,680.

30. Kastner's testimony in the trial from the protocol of The Attorney General v. Malchiel Greenwald in Criminal Case 124/53 in the District Court, Jerusalem, later referred to as Protocol of C.C. 124/53 in the D.C. Jerusalem.

31. Interrogations of Kurt Becher in Nuremberg by American interrogators Captain Richard A. Gutman, Mr. S. Jaari, and Mr. Richard Sonnenfeldt on March 27, 1946, as quoted in the official protocol kept by the American National Archives and Record Service.

32. Kastner's testimony in C.C. 124/53 in the D.C. Jerusalem.

33. Wisliczeny's testimony in Nuremberg.

34. Final verdict by the International Military Tribunal in Nuremberg.

35. Becher's own written statement to his interrogators in Nuremberg.

36. Eichmann statement to the Israeli police, regarding Becher: "Becher told me of an assignment which he had received from Reichsfuhrer S.S. Himmler and pressed me from then on for the immediate commencement of the evacuation of Jews (to Auschwitz) because otherwise he wouldn't be able to carry out his Reichsfuhrer's order. Becher referred regularly to the Reichsfuhrer order which he would be able to carry out only if the evacuation were driven forward with utmost pressure."

37. During the trial a special committee to help the defense of Greenwald was formed and was headed by the Israeli historian and writer, Professor Joseph Klausner. Its chief members were Meir Rubin, Vice-Mayor of Jerusalem, Professor Joseph Rivlin of the Hebrew University, and Dr. Joseph Schechtman of New York. Also helping the defense, mainly with information, was Itzchak Sternbuch of Montreux, Switzerland, who was active during World War II in special rescue efforts on behalf of the orthodox organizations. Active with them was also Dr. Rudy Hecht of Swiss origin, who was a special representative of the Hebrew Committee for National Liberation in Europe and later was a witness for the defense in the trial of Malchiel Greenwald.

38. Exhibit 22, C.C. 124/53 in the D.C. Jerusalem.

39. Protocol, C.C. 124/53 in the D.C. Jerusalem.

40. Amendment of Evidence Rules (Privileged Evidence) Law, 1958 (Proposed law No. 342, March 16, 1958.)

41. Affidavit before Mr. Benno H. Selcke, Jr., of the American Evidence Division of the International Military Tribunal in Nuremberg on August 4, 1947.

42. Protocol, C.C. 124/53 in the D.C. Jerusalem.

43. Official wanted list of German war criminals issued by the Legal Department of the American Occupying Forces.

44. Affidavit by Walter H. Rapp, head of the Evidence Division of the Chief of Counsel of War Crimes at Nuremberg, Germany, and Deputy Chief of Counsel to Brigadier General Telford Taylor, Chief of Counsel. Affidavit given in Tel Aviv on February 6, 1957.

45. Protocol, C.C. 124/53 in the D.C. Jerusalem.
In his report to the Jewish Agency Kastner quoted a statement made by Becher to him about Himmler:
"Do you know that Himmler never cursed Jews? He was forced to; he is not a mass murderer. He has a tender heart. Even now you cannot imagine how difficult it is for him to hurt a Jew!"

46. Nazi and Nazi Collaborators (Punishment) Law, 1951.

47. His largest holdings, the "Koelner Aussenhandelsgesellschaft" of Koeln, Bremen, and Frankfurt.

48. Becher's assets were recently estimated by reliable German newspapers to be $30,000,000.

49. Testimony of Mr. Rafael Ben-Susan, economic editor of *Haaretz*, Israeli daily, at C.C. 124/53 in the D.C. Jerusalem.
See also *Yaad*, Israeli weekly dated February 1, 1961 and June 7, 1961.

50. Adolph Hitler's speech, April 19, 1942, in Levai, Eugene. *Black Book*

of the Martyrdom of Hungarian Jewry. Zurich: Central European Times Publishing Co., Ltd., 1948.

51. *Davar,* official daily of the Histadrut in Palestine, June 2, 1943.
52. Lavai, Eugene. *Black Book of the Martyrdom of Hungarian Jewry.*
53. Testimony of Professor Benjamin Aktzin, Dean of the Faculty of Law, Hebrew University, Jerusalem, at C.C. 124/53 in the D.C. Jerusalem.
54. *Davar,* official daily of the Histadrut in Palestine on January 12, 1945, reporting on the conference of World Jewish Congress.
55. *Commandant of Auschwitz: the Autobiography of Rudolph Hoess.* Cleveland and New York: World Publishing Co., 1959.
56. Kastner's report to the Zionist Congress in Basel, Switzerland, 1946; "Eichmann Confessions" published in *Life* magazine, November 28 and December 5, 1960.
57. In his trial, Eichmann admitted that the extermination of the Jews was conducted as strategic warfare, and that an important psychological element was deluding the Jews about the real intention of the Germans.
58. Testimony of Moshe Krauss, Chief Secretary of the Palestinian Bureau in Budapest in C.C. 124/53 in the D.C. Jerusalem; also Kastner's cross examination in C.C. 124/53 in the D.C. Jerusalem.
59. "Eichmann Confessions," published in *Life* magazine, November 28 and December 5, 1960.
60. Kastner's testimony in C.C. 124/53 in the D.C. Jerusalem.
61. Lavai, Eugene. *Black Book of the Martyrdom of Hungarian Jewry.*
62. In his "Confessions" in *Life* magazine, Eichmann writes, "I had already given orders to collect these Jewish officials in advance. Because I planned to work with them I wanted to be sure they would not be harmed by any right-wing hysteria."
63. Kastner's cross-examination in C.C. 124/53 in the D.C. Jerusalem.
64. Kastner's testimony in C.C. 124/53 in the D.C. Jerusalem.
65. Kastner's report to Zionist Congress in Basel, 1946.
66. "Eichmann Confessions," published in *Life* magazine, November 28 and December 5, 1960: "In Hungary my basic orders were to ship all the Jews out of Hungary in as short a time as possible. Now, after years of working behind a desk, I had come out into the raw reality of the field. As Muller put it, they had sent me, the "master" himself, to make sure the Jews did not revolt as they had in the Warsaw Ghetto. I use the word "master" in quotation marks because people used it to describe me. . . . Since they had sent the "master," however, I wanted to act like a master. I resolved to show how well a job could be done when the commander stands 100% behind it. By shipping the Jews off in a lightning operation, I wanted to set an example for future campaigns elsewhere. . . . In obedience to Himmler's directive I now concentrated on negotiations with the Jewish political officials in Budapest . . . Among them Dr. Rudolph Kastner, authorized representative of the Zionist Movement. This Dr. Kastner was a young man about my age, an ice-cold lawyer and a fanatical Zionist. He agreed to help

keep the Jews from resisting deportation—and even keep order in the collection camps—if I would close my eyes and let a few hundred or a few thousand young Jews emigrate illegally to Palestine. It was a good bargain. For keeping order in the camps, the price . . . was not too high for me.

". . . We trusted each other perfectly. When he was with me, Kastner smoked cigarets as though he were in a coffeehouse. While we talked he would smoke one aromatic cigaret after another, taking them from a silver case and lighting them with a silver lighter. With his great polish and reserve he would have made an ideal Gestapo officer himself.

"Dr. Kastner's main concern was to make it possible for a select group of Hungarian Jews to emigrate to Israel. . . .

"As a matter of fact, there was a very strong similarity between our attitudes in the S.S. and the viewpoint of these immensely idealistic Zionist leaders. . . . I believe that Kastner would have sacrificed a thousand or a hundred thousand of his blood to achieve his political goal. . . . 'You can have the others,' he would say, 'but let me have this group here.' And because Kastner rendered us a great service by helping keep the deportation camps peaceful, I would let his groups escape. After all, I was not concerned with small groups of a thousand or so Jews. . . . That was the 'gentleman's agreement' I had with Kastner."

67. Testimony of Yechiel Schmueli of Kluj in C.C. 124/53 in the D.C. Jerusalem.

68. Later in the trial the witness, Joel Brand, testified that S.S. Colonel Von Wisliczeny told him:

"Our system is to exterminate the Jews through the Jews. We concentrate the Jews in the ghettos—through Jews; we deport the Jews—by the Jews; and we gas the Jews—by the Jews."

Dr. Rudolf Verba, a Doctor of Science now serving at the British Medical Research Council, was one of the few escapees from Auschwitz. In his memoirs published in February, 1961, in the *London Daily Herald* he wrote:

"I am a Jew. In spite of that—indeed because of that—I accuse certain Jewish leaders of one of the most ghastly deeds of the war.

"This small group of quislings knew what was happening to their brethren in Hitler's gas chambers and bought their own lives with the price of silence. Among them was Dr. Kastner, leader of the council which spoke for all Jews in Hungary. . . .

"While I was prisoner number 44070 at Auschwitz—the number is still on my arm—I compiled careful statistics of the exterminations . . . I took these terrible statistics with me when I escaped in 1944 and I was able to give Hungarian Zionist leaders three weeks notice that Eichmann planned to send a million of their Jews to his gas chambers. . . . Kastner went to Eichmann and told him, 'I know of your plans; spare some Jews of my choice and I shall keep quiet.'

"Eichmann not only agreed, but dressed Kastner up in S.S. uniform and took him to Belsen to trace some of his friends. Nor did the sordid bargaining end there.

"Kastner paid Eichmann several thousand dollars. With this little

261

fortune, Eichmann was able to buy his way to freedom when Germany collapsed, to set himself up in the current Argentine. . . ."

69. An unexpected example of Kastner's behavior in misleading the Jews popped up during the current Eichmann trial (1961).

Witness for the Prosecution Dr. Joseph Melkman, a Dutch Jew, testified how he, together with other Jews, were being taken on a train for deportation. "It was in the railway station at Bergen-Belsen. I stood there near the entrance of the train. . . . Suddenly a car came and two persons got out of it. One of them was in the uniform of the S.S., a Colonel. . . . This officer talked to me . . . and asked me what our conditions were. He was accompanied by a man wearing civilian clothes. When the officer finished talking, the man in civilian clothes told me his name was Kastner. . . . Kastner said: 'I promise you that you will be sent to a good place' . . . in fact the trains were meant to be sent to the East (for deportation) but because of unexpected war situations we could not proceed directly and we had to turn about until finally we were liberated."

70. Protocol, C.C. 124/53 in the D.C. Jerusalem.

71. Exhibit of the Defense No. 158 in C.C. 124/53 in the D.C. Jerusalem.

72. Cross-examination of Hillel Danzig in C.C. 124/53 in the D.C. Jerusalem.

73. Testimony of Yechiel Schmueli in C.C. 124/53 in the D.C. Jerusalem.

74. Testimony of Mr. Joseph Katz of the town of Nodvarod in C.C. 124/53 in the D.C. Jerusalem.

75. Testimony of Mr. David Rosner of Kluj in C.C. 124/53 in the D.C. Jerusalem.

76. Testimony of Mr. Levy Blum of Kluj in C.C. 124/53 in the D.C. Jerusalem.

77. Cross-examination of Kastner in C.C. 124/53 in the D.C. Jerusalem. In his trial Adolph Eichmann answered the Court:

Q. You have mentioned camouflage orders which came from Himmler. These activities facilitated . . . the mobilization of Jews to the service of annihilating themselves by misleading the victims.

A. Yes.

Q. How did the Warsaw Ghetto revolt effect the following operations?

A. I think that the conclusion of the Nazi leaders was that they expected a revolt in Holland and Hungary. . . . It was therefore decided to accelerate the deportation of Jews. . . . They were afraid of Jewish resistance. . . . It was all organized like a Military Campaign, including psychological warfare."

78. Ibid.

79. Bar-Adon, Dorothy and Pessach. *Seven Who Fell.* Palestine: "Sefer" Press, 1947.

80. Ibid.

81. Ibid.

82. "The Return of Hanna Senesh," *Pioneer Woman*, XXV, No. 5. May, 1950.

83. Bar-Adon, Dorothy and Pessach. *Seven Who Fell.*

84. *Ibid.*
85. Palgi, Joel. *Ruakh G'dala Ba'ah* (*The Great Wind*), Israel: Hakibutz Hameuchad, 1948.
86. Palgi's testimony in C.C. 124/53 in the D.C. Jerusalem.
87. Bar-Adon, Dorothy and Pessach. *Seven Who Fell.*
88. *Ibid.*
89. *Ibid.*
90. Kastner's cross-examination in C.C. 124/53 in the D.C. Jerusalem.
91. Hanna arrived in Budapest in July. Kastner admitted knowledge of her arrest in August.
92. Testimony of Mrs. Catherina Senesh in C.C. 124/53 in the D.C. Jerusalem.
93. Protocol C.C. 124/53 in the D.C. Jerusalem.
94. Levai, Eugene. *Black Book of the Martyrdom of Hungarian Jewry.*
95. *Ibid.*
96. *Ibid.*
97. *Ibid.*
98. Cross-examination of Bader in C.C. 124/53 in the D.C. Jerusalem.
99. Rabbi Weissmandel refers here to the Auschwitz protocol, a detailed report drafted by Dr. Rudolf Verba and a colleague. Both escaped from Auschwitz a few weeks before the deportations started and sent warning to the Jewish leaders in Slovakia and Hungary. This information was not published by the Jewish Agency. Moshe Krauss sent the full details of Auschwitz to the Jewish Agency representative in Geneva, Mr. Chaim Pozner, who also failed to publish it. Two Hungarian Jews, George Mantello and Joseph Mandl, managed to reveal the facts to the world in the month of July through news agencies.
     See also note 68.
     Dr. Verba had detailed knowledge about the atrocities and the activities of Eichmann. Because of the importance of the Auschwitz statements, which indicated the exact figures on the Auschwitz victims, Judge Moshe Landau, in the Eichmann trial, asked the Attorney General why he did not call this escapee from Auschwitz as a witness. The attorney general, Mr. Gideon Hausner, answered that the government couldn't cover the travel expenses of its witnesses.
100. In a Polish town, all the Jews assembled in the Synagogue before their extermination and cursed the Jews of the free world, who did nothing, while they were being taken to their death. (*Magen Bessetter*, official documentary publication of the Jewish Agency for Palestine, 1948).
101. In the preface to his book, *Pathway to a Promised Land*, Ira Hirschman of the American Refugee Board writes:
     "Americans are kindly and humane. Their failure to act before the establishment of the War Refugee Board was due, in my opinion, chiefly to the fact that they were not then, and are not even today, fully aware of the horror and extent of the stupendous tragedy prepared for a guiltless people. . . .
     "History will tell that our government achieved marked success through the War Refugee Board in rescuing the remnants of persecuted minorities and in checking their slaughter. Had we acted as

vigorously and decisively at an earlier date, we undoubtedly could have saved many times the number of people that we did."

102. In the Kastner trial, the following testimony was given by witness Joseph Katz from Nodvarod, who was deported to Auschwitz and worked there in a tailor shop:

Tamir: Was Auschwitz bombed from the air by the Allies while you were there?

Katz: Yes. The industrial plants were bombed. Also the military targets were accurately bombed.

Tamir: Were the gas chamber buildings bombed?

Katz: No.

Tamir: Were they visible from the air?

Katz: Very much so.

Tamir: Were the crematoria bombed?

Katz: No.

103. During his last years in Mount Kisco, N.Y., Rabbi Weissmandel related in his book, *Min Hametzar* that when one of his messages fell into German hands, the Germans were much pleased by his plea for the bombing of the bridges on the Auschwitz run. The German attitude, wrote the Rabbi, proved their understanding of how the Allies felt about the extermination of the Jews. Writes Rabbi Weissmandel, the Germans were convinced that telling the Allies which bridges should be blown up to save Jews made those bridges safe from all attack; and they could be used thereafter by the Germans for troop transportation.

The plea to bomb the Auschwitz Crematoria and the bridges leading towards it was finally addressed to the British authorities.

The British Government delayed answering until September, 1944, (by then most of the Hungarian Jews were annihilated). In an exhibit filed in the Eichmann trial it was revealed that on September 1, 1944, Mr. Richard Law, of the British Foreign Office, referred to the proposals of the bombing and stated: "The matter received the most careful consideration of the Air Staff, but I am sorry to have to tell you that, in view of the very technical difficulties involved, we have no option but to refrain from pursuing the proposal in present circumstances. . . ."

The British Government never explained what were "the very great technical difficulties" involved in sending one or two bombers to bomb the very visible Auschwitz crematoria or the easy targets of the bridges leading towards it.

In an interview with the correspondent for the Israeli *Maariv* on the 1st of June 1961, Air Marshall Sir Arthur Harris, who served as the Chief Air Officer of the British Bomber Command from 1942 until 1945 stated: "I can't recall that I ever heard of such a plea [to bomb Auschwitz] . . . To the best of my recollection I never knew of the existence of German extermination camps until we liberated Bergen-Belsen [at the close of the war]."

British Colonel Leonard Cheshire admitted to the *Daily Telegraph* on June 2, 1961, that "the bombing of Auschwitz in 1944, although difficult, was feasible. Had we known that the Jews requested to bomb the place there would have been no difficulty at all in mobilizing an air group to carry out this task."

104. Exhibit of the Defense No. 36, C.C. 124/53 in the D.C. Jerusalem.
105. The first Palestinian underground organization, led by Aaron and Sarah Aaronson, which helped the British to fight the Turks in the first World War, aimed at establishing in Palestine a free Jewish State.
106. The first organized armed Jewish guards in Palestine.
107. Tamir presented the Court with volumes of the Palestinian *Davar* daily, covering the four relevant years of the war. They were accepted as official exhibits.
108. Joel Brand.
109. The famous Palestinian Detention Camp formed by the British for political detainees.
110. Marx, Karl. *A World Without Jews*, ed. Dagobert D. Runes. New York: Philosophical Library, 1959.
111. Kastner's cross-examination in C.C. 124/53 in the D.C. Jerusalem.
112. Kastner's cross-examination in C.C. 124/53 in the D.C. Jerusalem.
113. *Eichmann in Hungary,* documents edited by Jeno Levai, Panonia Press, Budapest 1961.
114. Testimony of Moshe Krauss in C.C. 124/53 in the D.C. Jerusalem. Krauss has also filed a court case against the Jewish Agency in Palestine for not paying his salary and for throwing him out of his job without even compensation.
115. Exhibit No. 1 in C.C. 124/53 in the D.C. Jerusalem.
116. Kastner's cross-examination in C.C. 124/53 in the D.C. Jerusalem.
117. Protocol, C.C. 124/53 in the D.C. Jerusalem.
118. Kastner's last cross-examination and testimony in C.C. 124/53 in the D.C. Jerusalem.
119. *The Jerusalem Post,* Israeli English daily, September 20, 1954.
120. "Eichmann Confessions," published in *Life* magazine, November 28 and December 5, 1960.
121. Protocol, C.C. 124/53 in the D.C. Jerusalem.
122. When the trial started.
123. The German reparations to the State of Israel and World Jewish institutions.
124. At the beginning of the trial, immediately after Tamir took up the Defense, he asked for a postponement in order to prepare the Defense. The request was contested by the Prosecution. Judge Halevi imposed a payment of £20 on the accused—costs for "negligence in the preparation of the Defense." A few months later, the Prosecution requested a postponement of the trial in order to prepare itself more fully. Judge Halevi granted this postponement and then restored the £20 to Greenwald.
125. One of the central figures of the Israeli foreign office.
126. Attorney General Chaim Cohen said in his summation, "Either Kastner should be sentenced to death, if the allegations are true, or—if they are not—Greenwald should die by the hand of God."
127. Testimony was brought in the trial of an official complaint filed against

Kastner at the Zionist Congress of Basel in 1946. After a few hours hearing, the inquiry, which was conducted by members of the Mapai party, was stopped in the middle and an official communiqué declared Kastner exonerated.

128. During the same session of the Zionist Congress, Kastner was interrogated secretly by a special Haganah court, but no verdict was reached, publicly.

129. The special representative of the American Refugee Board, who was stationed in Berne, Switzerland.

130. Protocol, C.C. 124/53 in the D.C. Jerusalem.

After the war, S.S. General Walter Schellenberg, Chief of Himmler's Intelligence, stated in a special document, now in the custody of Mr. Hillel Storch of the World Jewish Congress in Stockholm, that Kastner had served throughout the war as an agent of the German S.S. among the Jews in Hungary.

131. In his final plea to Judge Halevi, Tamir challenged the Court:
"The Defense invites the Court to release itself from the environment surrounding it, to uproot itself from its very midst, to raise itself to a higher level, and to be willing and able to pass a verdict on a whole community, on a whole leadership within which the Court lives and whom the Court trusts. This is a gigantic psychological obstacle. But the Defense trusts the Israeli Court of Justice. And although the burden is almost too heavy for a single human being to carry, we challenge the Court to pass judgement in view of facts only, facts so clear that nothing can withstand them."

132. S.S. General Jutner, Chief of the Waffen S.S. on the Eastern Front, who accompanied Hoess on the visit to Budapest; who had always been met by Kastner according to the latter's testimony.

133. During the trial a member of the Jewish Agency Executive, Eliyahu Dobkin, testified that he never authorized Kastner to give an affidavit and a recommendation in favor of Becher on behalf of the Jewish Agency or anyone else. However, although Becher was released from detention as a direct result of Kastner's intervention in the name of the Jewish Agency, and although this affidavit serves as a clean bill of health for Becher up to this very date, the Jewish Agency refused to inform the allies or German authorities that the affidavit was given in its name without its knowledge or approval.

134. Statement by Richard H. Gutman, January 1, 1961:
"From the summer of 1945 to the summer of 1946 I was stationed as an intelligence and interrogation officer of the U.S. Army in Oberursel, Germany. . . . One of the men I interrogated was Standartenführer (S.S. Colonel) Kurt Becher. . . . At the time of the attack against Poland he was under the leadership of Fegelein, a member of the Reiter S.S. which committed the worst excesses in occupied Warsaw. I remember that during the interrogation it came out that Becher had contracted a venereal disease during the Polish campaign. . . . Undoubtedly Becher knew much more than he was willing to tell and was directly involved in many different aspects of the "final solution" to the Jewish problem as envisaged by Hitler, Himmler, Eichmann, etc., than he would ever be willing to admit. But his constant refer-

ence to the fact that he was a "friend" of the Jews and that he knew they would vouch for him was too much for me to take. I put him in solitary confinement for which he loudly thanked me because, as he put it, 'it gave me a chance to reflect on all the terrible things that had happened.' I finally escorted him by jeep to Nuremberg where I delivered him to the prison authorities.

"Shortly after I had delivered Kurt Becher, war criminal and leading S.S. officer on Himmler's staff, I found that due to the intercession of Mr. Rudolf Kastner, Becher was enjoying a comfortable existence in the witness wing of the Nuremberg prison. . . . I was shocked and couldn't believe it and went to see Kastner. . . . When I said to Kastner that I didn't understand his loyalty and concern for a man like Becher he answered me, with a sentimental and far-away look in his eye, that when he once went into an S.S. office, he saw their belts hanging on the clothes rack. And on the belt buckles was inscribed the motto, *'Meine Ehre ist True'*—My Honor is Loyalty."

135. From the judgement of Judge Dr. Benjamin Halevi, President of the Jerusalem District Court, given June 22, 1955, Protocol, C.C. 124/53 in the D.C. Jerusalem.

136. Dr. Moshe Keren in an article in *Haaretz*, Israeli daily, dated July 14, 1955.

137. Dr. Moshe Keren in an article in *Haaretz*, Israeli daily, dated July 8, 1955.

138. *Herut*, Israeli daily, June 23, 1955.

139. *Hatzofe*, Israeli daily, June 23, 1955.

140. *Lamerchav*, Israeli daily, June 23, 1955.

141. *Haboker*, Israeli daily, June 23, 1955.

142. *Maariv*, Israeli evening paper, June 23, 1955.

143. *Yediot Acharonot*, Israeli evening paper, an article by the editor, Dr. Herzl Rosenbloom, June 23, 1955.

144. *Davar*, Israeli daily, June 23, 1955.

145. *Kol Haam*, Israeli daily, June 23, 1955.

146. *The Jerusalem Post*, Israeli daily, June 23, 1955.

147. *Yediot Acharonot*, Israeli evening paper, June 26, 1955.

148. However, the judgment was never forgiven Halevi. When the Eichmann trial came up, the government, through Minister of Justice Pinhas Rosen and the new Attorney General, Gideon Hausner, acted in an unprecedented manner by introducing and passing through Parliament a special law which was intended to deprive Halevi of the right to preside over the Eichmann trial. The same Minister of Justice, Rosen, launched in Parliament a special pressure campaign on Halevi to disqualify himself from sitting in the Eichmann trial.

149. *Davar*, Israeli daily, June 27, 1955.

150. Official statement to the "Voice of Israel," the Governmental Israeli broadcasting service on June 23, 1955.

151. Item: While Halevi was reading his judgment, Kastner hurried to Prime Minister Sharett, who immediately contacted Minister of Justice Rosen. As Judge Halevi finished reading the judgment, the minister of justice

(in the absence of Chaim Cohen, who was abroad) called on the acting attorney general and instructed him to announce the following morning that an Appeal was to be filed.

152. Dr. Azriel Carlebach in *Maariv*, Israeli evening paper, on June 24, 1955.

153. Amendment of Evidence (Examination of Witnesses) Law—1956. (Proposed law No. 257, 1956).

154. Amendment of Procedure (Examination of Witnesses) Law, 1957.

155. When the Emergency Committee to Save the Jewish People of Europe called upon the American Government to establish a War Refugee Board, Rabbi Stephen Wise, testifying before a special committee of the American Congress, objected to this proposal.

156. The line of the Irgun, as proclaimed in all its publications, was that the fight for the rescue of the masses of Jews in Europe coincided with the real aim of Zionism—the establishment of a true viable State of Israel.

157. Chaim Cohen in the Appeal before the Israeli Supreme Court, January 20, 1957.

158. Chaim Cohen himself said in that very Appeal that Kastner "behaved as a fool" and that he lied in court more than once.

159. Chaim Cohen also said, "The man Kastner does not stand here as a private individual. He was a recognized representative, official or non-official, of the Jewish National Institutes in Palestine and of the Zionist Executive; and I come here in this court to defend the representative of our national institutions."

160. Chaim Cohen admitted, "that Eichmann, the chief exterminator, knew that the Jews would be peaceful and not resist if he allowed the prominents to be saved, that the, 'train of the prominents' was organized on Eichmann's orders to facilitate the extermination of the whole people." However, he added that "there was no room for any resistance to the Germans in Hungary and that Kastner was allowed to draw the conclusion that if all the Jews of Hungary are to be sent to their death he is entitled to organize a rescue train for 600 people. He is not only entitled to it but is also bound to act accordingly." He continued explaining that this attitude toward extermination had always been the system of the national Jewish institutions, who gave emigration certificates to Palestine only to a few of the masses who wanted to emigrate—emigration based on selectivity.

161. Chaim Cohen attacked Judge Halevi bitterly, stating that he had no right to make a decision now as to the duties of Kastner ten years ago. To this Judge Goitein, of the Supreme Court, said, "You took upon yourself the risk of filing this trial ten years after the events took place. It is you who took it."

162. In his Supreme Court reply Tamir said:
"I shall defend before you not only an historical judgment, not only the truth, but also the hundreds of thousands of slaughtered people against whom the most horrible defamation was made here—that they were like sheep to be taken to slaughter. I shall prove that one cannot purify and exonerate Kastner without exonerating Becher and Himmler and without concurring with what Hitler said of the hundreds of thousands of Jews—'garbage of the earth'. . . . There is no human being

268

who is authorized to deprive 800,000 Jews of the clear knowledge as to what awaits them; who is allowed to deprive them of their right to try and escape, to jump from the train or even commit suicide with honor; to deprive a mother of her right to tear away the eyes of the beast before it assails her child; to deprive them of their right to choose between life and death."

Referring to the patronage given to Kastner by the S.S. high command during the last year of the war, Tamir said in his summation, "Thus the circle is closed. The same Krumey who exterminated the Jews has sent Kastner into the Kluj ghetto; the same Krumey brings him a few days before the end of the war safely, in a special car, to the Swiss border.

. . . "I know that this Kastner is a victim and is a very miserable, ruined human being. But tolerance toward his crimes may mean an unheard of cruelty toward the exterminated Jewish people. . . . This is not a trial of Greenwald or even of Kastner alone. The question is whether the same fate would have befallen all the Jews of Hungary had they known the whole truth. I challenge this court not to issue a moral death penalty on these Jews after their death. Because it is this the learned Attorney General is calling upon you to do.

"The whole nation is now facing an immense moral test, through you. I pray that we shall stand the test."

163. In Israel, the complaint of a single citizen against a suspect of Nazi collaboration was enough to detain him and start a police inquiry. In the case of Kastner, despite the finding of the president of the District Court—which came after a trial lasting continuously for a full nine months with dozens of witnesses and hundreds of documents—neither the police nor the attorney general's office was willing even to start an interrogation of Kastner. An official complaint filed by Tamir on behalf of Greenwald after Judge Halevi's verdict also remained without response.

164. Exhibit No. 33, C.C. 124/53 in the D.C. Jerusalem.

165. During the Greenwald trial, as well, Kastner stated on oath that "Krumey was one of the chief exterminators" and as such "he deserved no help," and that in fact he, Kastner, never did anything for him.

166. Interrogation of Hermann Krumey on September 23, 1947, by American interrogator Herbert H. Meyer, file No. 2010 as quoted in an official protocol kept by the American National Archives and Record Service.

167. Letter dated February 5, 1947, sent from Geneva and attached to Interrogation of Hermann Krumey on September 23, 1947, by American interrogator Herbert H. Meyer, file No. 2010, as quoted in an official protocol kept by the American National Archives and Record Service.

168. Affidavit by Rudolf Kastner given on May 5, 1948, in Nuremberg, Germany to Benno H. Selcke, Jr. of the American Evidence Division of the International Military Tribunal in Nuremberg.

169. Becher starts his affidavit in favor of Krumey by identifying himself as the man who cooperated with the Jewish Agency. Krumey, in turn, was one of the witnesses for Eichmann in the Jerusalem trial. Servatius,

the Attorney for Eichmann, submitted his affidavit as part of the defense.

170. When Eichmann was caught, however, a partial rift developed between him and Becher, each of them throwing part of the responsibility on the other in order to try and exonerate himself.

171. For years after the war, the Israeli authorities neither asked for the extradition of the German war criminals from Germany nor searched for Eichmann's hideaway. It was only after the Kastner trial developments that the subject was revived in the country and the search started.

172. The last three scandals involving Ben-Gurion:
   A. The Lavon affair where the majority of his own government practically determined that Ben-Gurion's own group was responsible for the frame-up against Pinchas Lavon, former minister of defense, in connection with a grave security matter.
   B. The Israel Beer affair—a shady Israeli military historian who was groomed by Ben-Gurion as the official military historian. After attributing almost every Israeli victory to Ben-Gurion's brilliance, Beer was handed his post by Ben-Gurion. This post gave him access to the most secret military files. In spite of the warning of the Intelligence Service, Ben-Gurion refused to fire Beer until he was finally caught and exposed as a Russian spy.
   C. Ben-Gurion's declaration that every Jew living outside Israel is Godless.

173. Final judgment in the case of Yechezkel Sahar v. the Attorney General, Criminal Appeal No. 20/61 in the Supreme Court, Jerusalem.

174. Final judgment in the case of Eliakim Haetzni and others v. Amos Ben-Gurion, Civil Appeal 256/57 in the Supreme Court, Jerusalem. This judgment, unanimously upheld by the Supreme Court, was delivered by Judge Moshe Landau, later presiding judge in the Eichmann trial.

175. During this trial, the Ben-Gurion group, aided by the Israeli Intelligence Service, published a special weekly called *Rimon*. Its main theme was a violent smear campaign against Tamir, who was described as, "the enemy of the people." The management of the weekly posted special notices on the walls of Tel Aviv for weeks with a picture of Tamir and derogatory captions. The weekly was financed by secret funds.

176.
   A. *Supreme Court Judge Shlomo Chesin:* excerpts from his Kastner Appeal verdict:
   "I make a further step and say that even if Kastner knew the whole bitter truth when he came to Kluj on May 3, 1944, and even if he concealed it from the people of Kluj, leaders and rank and file alike—still this doesn't serve as a proof that he did so because of seeming "obligation" towards the Germans and because of his wish to help the Germans in their extermination. He didn't warn Hungarian Jewry of the danger facing it because he didn't think it would be useful, and because he thought that any deeds resulting from information given them would damage more than help. . . . What point was there in telling the

270

people boarding the trains in Kluj, people struck by fate and persecuted, as to what awaits them at the end of their journey. . . . Kastner spoke in detail of the situation, saying, 'The Hungarian Jew was a branch which long ago dried up on the tree.' This vivid description coincides with the testimony of another witness about the Hungarian Jews, 'This was a big Jewish community in Hungary, without any ideological Jewish backbone.' (Moshe Shweiger, a Kastner aide in Budapest, protocol 465)

"I fully agree with my friend, Judge Agranat, when he states that, 'The Jews of Hungary, including those in the countryside, were not capable, neither physically nor mentally, to carry out resistance operations with force against the deportation scheme.' . . . From this point of view no rescue achievement could have resulted by disclosing the Auschwitz news to the Jewish leaders there, and this . . . is a consideration which one can properly conclude that Kastner had in front of his eyes.

". . . And I take one more step. I am certain that the silence of Kastner when he arrived in Kluj was premeditated and calculated and did not result from his great despair because of the helplessness of the Jewish community. Even then, I say, this is still not considered willful collaboration and assistance in the extermination, because all the signs indicate that Kastner's efforts were aimed at rescue and rescue on a big scale . . . And towards the end I take one last step. In doing so I go very far and say that even if Kastner ordered himself to keep silent knowingly, in submission to the strong will of the Nazis, in order to save a few Jews from Hell—this is still no proof that he stained his hands by collaborating with the enemies of his people and carrying out their plan to exterminate most of the Jewish community in Hungary.

"Even if, through these activities of his—or rather, his omissions—the extermination became easier. And as to the moral issue, the question is not whether a man is allowed to kill many in order to save a few, or vice-versa. The question is altogether in another sphere and should be defined as follows: a man is aware that a whole community is awaiting its doom. He is allowed to make efforts to save a few, although part of his efforts involve concealment of truth from the many; or should he disclose the truth to many though it is his best opinion that this way everybody will perish. I think that the answer is clear. What good will the blood of the few bring if everybody is to perish? . . . As I said, I am not arguing with the basic factual findings of the learned President of the Jewish District Court [Judge Halevi] but it seems to me, with all due respect, that his findings do not, as of necessity, demand the conclusion he has arrived at. That is to say, collaboration on the part of Kastner in the extermination of the Jews. And that they better coincide with bad leadership both from a moral and public point of view. . . .

"Counsel for Greenwald stated excitedly that if the deeds of Kastner shall be approved of, the people of Israel have no future because every leader will act like him in an hour of tragedy. He also says, in discussing the arguments why Kastner didn't call for revolt, that lack of arms should not have been a reason for non-resistance. The meaning of which is that the Jews of the ghetto side of Hungary had to fight and die for the honor of the nation and for the name of God. In this context he indicates that the rebels in the Warsaw ghetto fell and with their death brought glory to the name of God. This is also a philosophy. And the history of the Jewish people, full of blood, tells us a lot of such moral heroes. But there is also another philosophy, different from this and contrary to it, and this different philosophy has roots in the pages of history. Jeremiah the prophet, for example, preached surrender to the enemy and a peace treaty with them and Rabbi Yochanan Ben Zakai preferred to save that which it was possible to save in an hour of tragedy. Still no one has accused them of selling their souls to the devil. . . . There is no law, either national or international, which lays down the duties of a leader in an hour of emergency toward those who rely on leadership and are under his instructions. There is also no law attaching responsibility to a leader who does not act with reasonable responsibility of leadership.

"In my opinion, one can say outright that if you find out that Kastner collaborated with the enemy because he did not disclose to the people who boarded the trains in Kluj that they were being led to extermination, one has to put on trial today Danzig, Herman, Hanzi Brand, Revis and Marton, and many more leaders and half-leaders who gagged themselves in an hour of crisis and did not inform others of what was known to them and did not warn and did not cry out of the coming danger. . . .

"Because of all this I cannot confirm the conclusion of the District Court with regard to the accusation that Greenwald has thrown on Kastner of collaboration with the Nazis in exterminating the Jewish people in Hungary during the last war."

B. *Supreme Court Judge Moshe Silberg*: excerpts from his verdict in the Government's Appeal of Judge Halevi's verdict:

"The aim of the Nazis was an easy and peaceful extermination without special efforts, without casualties to themselves. This aim had been achieved in full, or almost in full. Except for two places, the exterminators did not meet with any resistance on the part of their victims nor even any refusal whatsoever to board the trains. This shocking success of the Nazis was, as was clearly proven, a direct result of the concealment of the horrifying truth from the victims. And the main question is did Kastner participate in the concealment of this truth? . . . How did Kastner behave while in Kluj, and did he inform while there, any of the leaders of the facts known to him? We have seen earlier that the inmates of this ghetto did not know, boarding the trains, that their last stop was Auschwitz; and therefore one of the two answers is a *must*. Either Kastner did not disclose to the local leaders the secret of Auschwitz or the leaders did not inform the masses the secret known to them from Kastner. A third possibility is non-existent. . . .

"One thing is, in my opinion, proven beyond any doubt. The meaning of the testimony of Danzig is that Kastner did not disclose to him any of the facts (about Auschwitz) known to him. . . . And then Kastner comes and not only doesn't he uproot from our hearts the suspicion against him, but he further indirectly confirms the truth of the words of Danzig and Hermann about this point. . . . It was proven to us that when Kastner was in Kluj on the third of May that he did not disclose to the local leaders what was known to him. And if he did not tell these things by word of mouth while he was there, he definitely did not disclose it in the ten telephone conversations from Budapest which he had with his father-in-law, Dr. Fisher, after the third of May. . . .

"And how did he behave towards the other countryside towns? Did he inform them of the Auschwitz news? Definitely not. Nobody even claims it. . . . The gist of the question facing us in this trial is: this agreement to save the prominents—was that part of a general plan or was it consideration for a general non-rescue? And therefore it is very important for us to know not only what was the external communicative connection of Kastner with the Jews of the countryside, but also what was his internal mental connection with them. And here is how this attitude is revealed in his testimony: 'I had a connection with Kluj. What connection the other members of the committee had, *I don't know*. *I don't remember* that the committee had a telephone connection with the towns of the countryside. . . . I know the town of Nodvarod. There were more than 20,000 Jews there. . . . *I don't remember* if we had a connection with this town. *I also don't remember* whether through a sub-committee, which had a telephone connection, we had a connection with this town. *I cannot answer* the question whether we could reveal to this town underground information. . . . I do not remember if any of the members of the committee visited any of the towns in the countryside.'

"Explanations are superfluous! Such *forgetfulness* would not come upon him even ten years later, had the general rescue of the Hungarian Jews, three-fourths of whom lived in the countryside, been the main aim for which he toiled all the months of that summer. For *he* was the head of the committee, the central personality and the driving spirit in it. How can he 'not remember' whether a personal or telephone contact of any kind was made with the masses of Jews, the rescue of whom was seemingly his main consideration?

"The conclusion is, therefore, that that which he did not remember in the spring of 1954 in Jerusalem did not concern him in the summer of 1944 in Budapest.

"I do not say that he was the only man who possessed information among the leaders. It is quite possible that somebody else as well does not have a clear conscience with regards to this concealment. But we are dealing here with the guilt of Kastner and we do not have to make judgments on the guilt of others. . . .

"The declaration of the learned Attorney General therefore shrinks into an opinion. . . . 'Kastner was convinced and believed that there was no ray of hope for the Jews of Hungary, almost for none of them, and as he, as a result of his personal despair, did not disclose the secret of the extermination in order not to endanger or frustrate the rescue of the few—therefore he acted in good faith and should not be accused of collaborating with the Nazis in expediting the extermination of the Jews, even though, in fact, he brought about its result.'

"I am compelled to state that it is very difficult for me to conceive such an intention. Is this good faith? Can a single man, even in co-

273

operation with some of his friends, yield to despair on behalf and without the knowledge of 800,000 other people? This is, in my opinion, the decisive consideration in the problem facing us. The charge emanating from the testimony of the witnesses against Kastner is that had they known of the Auschwitz secret, then thousands or tens of thousands would have been able to save their lives by local, partial, specific or indirect rescue operations like local revolts, resistance, escapes, hidings, concealment of children with Gentiles, forging of documents, ransom money, bribery, etc.—and when this is the case and when one deals with many hundreds of thousands, how does a human being, a mortal, reject with complete certainty and with an extreme 'no' the efficiency of all the many and varied rescue ways? How can he examine the tens of thousands of possibilities? Does he decide instead of God? Indeed, he who can act with such a usurpation of the last hope of hundreds of thousands is not entitled to claim good faith as his defense. The penetrating question *quo warrento* is a good enough answer to a claim of such good faith. . . .

"If the superintendent of a big hospital lets thousands of sick people die so that he may devote himself to the sure rescue of one soul, he will come out guilty, at least morally, even if it is proven that he as an individual erroneously thought that there was no hope of saving the other patients. He is a collaborator with the angel of death.

"Either a complete atrophy of the soul or a blind involvement with complete loss of senses and proportion in his small but personal rescue operation could bring a man to such a gigantic, hazardous play.

"And if all this is not enough to annul the claim of good faith which was put before us on behalf of Kastner by the Attorney General, then Kastner himself comes and annuls it altogether. Not only did he never make this claim, but his own words prove the contrary. He writes in his report to the Jewish Agency that the Committee sent emissaries to many ghettos in the countryside and pleaded with them to organize escapes and to refuse to board the trains. And though the story of these pleadings is untrue, and the silence of Kastner in Kluj is proven, the very uttering of these statements entirely contradicts the claim that Kastner had concealed the news about the fate of the ghetto inmates in good faith and only as a result of his complete despairing of the chances of escaping or resisting the Germans. You can not claim at the same time helplessness and activity. Anyway, such a claim is not convincing. . . .

"We can sum up with these three facts:

A. That the Nazis didn't want to have a great revolt—'Second Warsaw' —nor small revolts, and their passion was to have the extermination machine working smoothly without resistance. This fact was known to Kastner from the best source—from Eichmann himself. . . . And he had additional proofs of that when he witnessed all the illusionary and misleading tactics which were being taken by the Nazis from the first moment of occupation.

B. That the most efficient means to paralyze the resistance wheel or the escape of a victim is to conceal from him the plot of the coming murder. This fact is known to every man and one does not need any proof or evidence for this.

C. That he, Kastner, in order to carry out the rescue plan for the few prominents, fulfilled knowingly and without good faith the said desire of the Nazis, thus expediting the work of exterminating the masses.

"And also the rescue of Becher by Kastner. . . . He who is capable of rescuing this Becher from hanging proves that the atrocities of this great war criminal were not so horrifying or despicable in his eyes. . . . I couldn't base the main guilt of Kastner on this fact had it been alone, but when it is attached even from afar to the whole scene of events it throws retroactive light on the whole affair and serves as a dozen proofs of our conclusion."

C. *Supreme Court Judge Shimone Agranat:*

"I sum up my final conclusions as to the conduct of Dr. Kastner during the extermination of the people in the country as follows:

A. During this period Kastner was motivated by the sole motive of rescuing all Hungarian Jews, i.e., rescuing the maximum number which, considering the circumstances of time and place as assessed by him, could have been saved.

B. This motivation coincided with the moral duty of rescue by virtue of his task as manager of rescue in Budapest.

C. Influenced by this motive, he exercised a system of financial or economical negotiations with the Nazis.

D. This system can withstand the test of reasonableness.

E. His behavior on the date of his visit to Kluj (May 3) and thereafter —both from the active aspect (the plan of the prominents) as well as the passive aspect (the not informing of the 'Auschwitz news' and not encouraging resistance operations and large scale escapes)—coincides with his loyalty to the same system in which he saw during all relevant times the only chance of rescue.

F. Therefore, one cannot find moral defects in that behavior; one cannot find any causation between it and the expediting of the deportation and the extermination and one can not consider it amounting to the degree of collaboration with the Nazis."

D. *Supreme Court Judge Isaac Olshin* (President):

"Let us not forget that the court is not called here to give Kastner a clean bill of health or a confirmation certificate evaluating his activities from a national point of view. A public Commission of Inquiry— in front of which Kastner could have defended himself as a party and not a witness—was more appropriate to deal with all of this. In this respect I fully agree with Attorney Tamir, Counsel for the Defendant, who has proposed it in one of the early stages of the trial.

"The task of the court was to examine whether the respondent (Greenwald) did prove the truth of the libel, i.e., that Kastner was an indirect killer of hundreds of thousands of Hungarian Jews through his criminal activities and through his collaboration with the Nazis; this and nothing more. The learned President in the District Court answered this question with a big 'Yes.'

"This court too has to examine one question only. That is whether, in light of the conclusions which have to be drawn, from the evidence or

275

from the findings and in view of the onus of proof which lay upon the respondent (Greenwald) due to this cruel libel—was the learned President justified, legally, in his said answer? . . . From this point of view the question here is not whether we like the ways of Kastner or not. From this point of view one has to convict the respondent (Greenwald) if he was not successful in proving the act of betrayal of which he accused Kastner beyond reasonable doubt. Even he who is inclined to the opinion that the respondent (Greenwald) has managed to raise a doubt which is not beyond the reasonable doubt in this matter, has to convict the respondent (Greenwald)."

E. Supreme Court Judge I. D. Goitein:

"Apart from the factual difficulties, we are also faced with an uneasy legal question. As it is impossible to find out today what were the acts or rather what was the motive of the acts of Dr. Kastner in 1944, isn't the way out of the entanglement to ask Dr. Kastner himself and then at least we shall have a statement of the accused, if not a confession, out of which it will be possible to judge one way or another? And, indeed, Dr. Kastner did testify in the lower court and the court didn't trust him. The Attorney General as well, here before us, did not ask us to trust this testimony—described it using almost every word except 'lie'—which was enough to prevent us from putting our trust in it. And if this is the case I think that the respondent (Greenwald) fulfilled his duty because he is not a government prosecutor who is prosecuting Kastner in a criminal case. It is enough that he has managed to convince the lower court, who fulfilled the task of jury and judge alike, that the man whom he accused lied in court and behaved in a way which left the cold impression that his conscience is not clear and that he is afraid and is trying to conceal things that shouldn't be revealed to the sun. We didn't see Dr. Kastner in the box and didn't listen to him.

"However, the facts which were revealed substantiate the findings of the lower court and prevent us as a court of appeal from interfering.

"I should add also that the evidence that was brought and which is not argued against by anybody on the Kastner-Becher relations after the war and the collaboration of Kastner by rescuing Becher from the gallows, do not coincide with viewing Kastner as a National Jewish Zionist personality; and coincide with the findings of the lower court—that the acts committed during the war were acts of collaboration with the Nazis. The conclusion of the learned judge does not contradict the facts which were revealed but emanate reasonably from them."

177. The five Supreme Court Judges were in agreement in upholding Judge Halevi's decision that Kastner, "in a perjurious and criminal way," saved Kurt Becher, a major German war criminal, from the punishment awaiting him in Nuremberg.

Judge Silberg summed up the Supreme Court finding on this point: "Greenwald has proven beyond any reasonable doubt this grave charge. Important are the six following facts:
A. That Becher, chief of the Economic Department of the Waffen S.S. and one of the chief aids of Himmler, was a war criminal and not merely in the technical sense of the word, but in its most real and horrifying aspect. Kastner writes in his report to the Jewish Agency, 'Be-

tween the institutions of the S.S. there was a perfect coordination: the "Jewish Kommando" liquidated—the Economic Department "cashed in." That is to say that he too, with Becher, had a hand in the extermination of the Jews. It was the extermination which made the extortion more effective.

B. That the rescue acts made by Becher, if there were any such, were made for alibi purposes only and not out of love for Jews or out of a feeling of repentance. Kastner himself hinted to that effect in his London affidavit of September 13, 1945, given to the International Tribunal.

C. That his (later) affidavit in Nuremberg in favor of Becher was not a merely dry factual affidavit, but a recommendation most positive and warm on this war criminal, before the Allied and German authorities and towards the day when his case will be brought before them. The same Becher who, during the last days of the Hitlerian Germany, started to fear and not in vain, the facts that Kastner knew about him. (See Kastner testimony)

D. That he signed the affidavit not in his name alone but also in the name of the Jewish Agency and the Jewish World Congress. This was done undoubtedly to add very heavy weight to the recommendation included in the affidavit, for the facts themselves were not known either to the Agency or the Jewish World Congress.

E. That a few months after this affidavit Becher was released from prison.

F. That in his letter to the Minister of Finance, Kaplan, Kastner states that Becher was released by the Allied authorities owing to his personal intervention.

I shall not touch here upon all the many contradictions—endless in number—in which Kastner contradicts himself in connection with this affidavit. It is enough for us that a Jewish man, an ex-Zionist leader, dared to recommend [mercy], almost in the name of the whole Jewish people, for one of the major sharks of the German war criminals before the authorities who detained him, and to cause, alone or together with others, the release and the evasion of punishment of this great criminal."

178. After the five Justices had handed down their judgments, which acquitted Greenwald in the matter of Becher being saved by Kastner and convicted him by a majority of 3 to 2 in accusing Kastner of collaboration, both sides were given the right to plead as to the punishment.

Tamir did not plead for mercy on behalf of his aging client and spoke no word as to the kind and amount of punishment. He thus summed up the trial:

"Honorable Court,

"I address this honorable court and claim that the entire nation must be grateful to Greenwald for having disclosed what Justice Silberg and all of you set down. 'That a fellow Jew, a one-time Zionist public figure, had the gall—on behalf of almost all the Jewish people—to commend one of the major war criminals to the authorities holding him under arrest, and to bring about . . . the release and evasion of punishment for that same major criminal.'

"Greenwald's cry came out of Jewish pain . . . the anguished cry of one who has lost all his family; one of the simple folk who raised his voice in bitter protest, while all the nation, headed by its notables and dignitaries, kept silent.

"The Honorable Justice Cheshin has already pointed out in his judgment—frank and outright to the bitter end—that the State of Israel, which has not brought any single Nazi criminal to trial as yet, has launched its authority and might against a fellow Jew—a brother of the victims—whose heart and soul were full of agony over these horrifying crimes."

179. *Bamachane* (*in the Camp*), the Israel Army weekly, November 8, 1956.
180. Broadcast over "Kol Israel," November 8, 1956.
181. Chronology of the trial:

May 5, 1953—The Attorney General of Israel presents a criminal complaint to the District Court of Jerusalem against Malchiel, son of Menachem Greenwald, for libel against Dr. Israel Kastner.

January 1, 1954—The indictment is read to the accused, Malchiel Greenwald. The accused declares that he is not guilty, asks for a postponement in order to contact a lawyer.

January 17, 1954—The accused appears for the first time in the company of his Defense Counsel, Advocate Shmuel Tamir.

January 18, 1954 through February 23, 1954—The direct examination and testimony of Dr. Rudolf Kastner.

February 24, 1954 through March 4, 1954—The cross-examination of Dr. Kastner by attorney Tamir.

March 8, 1954—Reëxamination of Dr. Kastner by the representative of the prosecution, Amnon Tell.

March 9, 1954—The reëxamination of Kastner by Amnon Tell continues and further cross-examination by Tamir.

March 10, 1954—Dr. Kastner's testimony ends.

April 1, 1954—The testimony of witness number 16 of the Prosecution, Joel Brand, member of the Rescue Committee of Budapest, who went to Istanbul with Eichmann's proposition of exchange of Hungarian Jews against trucks and merchandise.

Cross-examination of Joel Brand by Advocate Tamir.

April 1, 1954 and April 2, 1954—Cross-examination of Joel Brand by Tamir.

June 1, 1954—The trial is renewed after a postponement at the request of the Prosecution. The Attorney General of the Government of Israel, Mr. Chaim Cohen, takes over the conduction of the Prosecution. Reëxamination of Joel Brand.

June 2, 1954—Cross-examination of Ehud Avriel by advocate Tamir.

June 3, 1954—Advocate Tamir requests to recall Dr. Kastner and Joel Palgi to the witness box. The Judge approves the request and decides on his own initiative to recall Joel Brand also.

June 4, 1954—Renewed examination of Joel Brand by the Court. Further cross-examination of Dr. Kastner by Tamir.

June 13, 1954—The accused, Malchiel Greenwald, reads a statement from the box of the accused.

June 14, 1954—Testimony of the fourth witness for the defense, Mrs. Catherina Senesh, mother of the parachutist Hanna Senesh.

September 16, 1954—Further testimony of Dr. Kastner, upon request of the Defense Counsel, S. Tamir.

End of the testimonies in the trial.
September 19, 1954—Summation of the Attorney General, Mr. Chaim Cohen.
September 22, 1954 through October 3, 1954—Summation of the Counsel for the Defense, S. Tamir.
June 21, 1955—The Verdict.
June 23, 1955—Declaration of Appeal by the Ministry of Justice.
August 21, 1955—Appeal by the Attorney General presented.
January 20, 1957 through January 25, 1957—Summation of Appeal by the Attorney General, Mr. Chaim Cohen.
January 27, 1957 through February 5, 1957—Summation of answer by advocate S. Tamir.
February 5, 1957 through February 27, 1957—Summation of the Prosecution in the Appeal.
March 3, 1957—Kastner shot near his house by Zeev Eckstein.
March 15, 1957—The death of Dr. Rudolf Kastner.
January 17, 1958 through January 19, 1958—Judgment by the Supreme Court.
November 28 and December 5, 1960—*Life* magazine publishes Eichmann's confessions in which he tells of Kastner's collaboration with him.

182. The Attorney General v. Joseph Menckes, Zeev Eckstein and Dan Shemer, in the District Court, Tel Aviv.

183. *Ibid.*

184. *Ibid.*

185. Protocol, C.C. 124/53 in the D.C. Jerusalem.

186. In the Eichmann trial a report of Mr. Sharett to the Jewish Agency in London on June 27, 1944 was exhibited. In it he stated that he waited for four days in Aleppo to meet Brand.

187. When Kastner testified how he, according to his version, allowed parachutist Joel Palgi to hand himself over to the Nazis, he added similar words, "He did it out of awe and respect to the emissary of Jewish Palestine."

188. Protocol, C.C. 124/53 in the D.C. Jerusalem.

189. *Ibid.*

190. *Ibid.*

191. *Ibid.*

192. In later statements and in a book which he published, Brand described how he was terrorized by high government officials, including Ben-Gurion and Sharett's direct aides, to falsify his testimony and perjure himself, and how later he was threatened with imprisonment in a lunatic asylum if he persisted in penning his memoirs.

193. The full testimony, which for ten years was unknown to the Israeli public, was later repeated by Brand as a witness for the Prosecution in the Eichmann trial.

194. Protocol, C.C. 124/54 in the D.C. Jerusalem.

195. Lord Moyne was killed in Cairo a few months later by two members of the Lehi (Stern Group) from Palestine (Eliyahu Beit-Tzuri and Eliyahu Chakim). They were later executed by the Egyptians after a

special demand from Winston Churchill to have them hanged, instead of being given a life term in prison. On hearing of the death of Lord Moyne, Chaim Weizmann declared that his death was more painful to him than the death of his own son, who fell in the battle of London.

Following the attack on Lord Moyne, Weizmann rushed to Palestine to help organize the Jewish Agency onslaught on the Irgun Zvai Leumi and Lehi.

After the Kastner trial, Brand wrote a book telling his story (*Advocate for the Dead*). Ehud Avriel demanded that in his book Brand change the name of Lord Moyne and state that the man told him, "Where shall I put a million Jews—what shall I do with them?" was not Lord Moyne but another, unknown, British official. Avriel also made this change in his own written version of Brand's mission.

However, in the Eichmann trial, Brand repeated under oath his testimony that it was Lord Moyne in person who uttered this expression.

196. Protocol, C.C. 124/53 in the D.C. Jerusalem.

197. The original of this document and the original of the subsequent document exhibited by Tamir were mysteriously stolen from Brand a few days before his testimony. However, before they were stolen, Brand gave Tamir photostatic copies of the documents.

During his testimony, Tamir wanted to enter these copies as official exhibits in the protocol. Prosecutor Tell tried to prevent the submission of these documents. He argued that since Mr. Brand was a government witness, Tamir was not allowed to meet him and receive documents from him. And therefore Tamir had committed an offense by filching such a document from the witness.

Tamir replied:

"Your Honor, the Prosecution originally presented this Court with an official witness list. This list named all the witnesses scheduled to appear for the State. Insofar as Joel Brand's name was not listed therein, I was entirely free, both legally and morally, to contact him and obtain documents and information pertaining to this trial. One of the main reasons for the existence of a witness list is to establish the precise framework which is out of bounds for the opposing side."

The court room waited tensely for the Court's decision. Judge Halevi pronounced it:

"I hold this document legal and admissible as evidence. I find no place, even *prima facie*, for the supposition that a criminal act has been perpetrated [in its procurement]."

Both documents were included in the protocol.

198. Protocol, C.C. 124/53 in the D.C. Jerusalem.

199. Protocol, C.C. 124/53 in the D.C. Jerusalem.

200. Brand testified in the Eichmann trial that Becher was standing in civilian clothes behind Eichmann when the latter made the offer to him.

201. See also Eichmann's testimony in his Jerusalem trial.

202. Tamir had challenged Sharett to appear in court to testify and answer Brand's charges.

203. Instead, Avriel had tried to submit to the Court a report by Mr. Sharett to the Jewish Agency Executive in London. Judge Halevi upheld Tamir's contention that the document was not admissible unless it was

vcrified by Mr. Sharett in person so that its veracity could be subject to cross-examination.

In the Eichmann trial, Attorney General Gideon Hausner submitted the document again. Advocate Servatius, Eichmann's lawyer, didn't contest it and the Court accepted it, indicating that it was acceptable in the absence of objection by the Defense. Regarding all this, Homer Bigart, special correspondent of the *New York Times* to the Eichmann trial, writes on June 12, 1961:

"To exonerate Zionist leaders of charges that they had reacted indolently, helplessly in the face of the Hungarian tragedy, Mr. Hausner introduced several documents from the archives of the Weizmann institute. . . ."

The *New York Times* special correspondent added, "The Israeli *Jerusalem Post* reported that Mr. Sharett had said that he had offered to testify on the Hungarian episode, 'but so far had not been called by the Prosecution.'

"This was the first time any newspaper here had mentioned this omission. Attorney General Gideon Hausner had called more than one hundred witnesses against Eichmann, some of them fetched at great expense from the United States and Western Europe. Yet Mr. Sharett, who lived within a mile of the court room, has not been called."

204. *Haaretz* daily. July 3, 1954.

205. During all these months, the British cabinet had refused to bomb Auschwitz or the roads and bridges leading to it or take any other effective step which would help prevent annihilation or delay it.